D0921076

BONHOEFFER, CHRIST AND CULTURE

EDITED BY KEITH L. JOHNSON
AND TIMOTHY LARSEN

IVP Academic
An imprint of InterVarsity Press
Downers Grove, Illinois

InterVarsity Press
P.O. Box 1400, Downers Grove, IL 60515-1426
World Wide Web: www.ivpress.com
Email: email@ivpress.com

*InterVarsity Press® is the book-publishing division of InterVarsity Christian Fellowship/USA®, a movement of
students and faculty active on campus at hundreds of universities, colleges and schools of nursing in the United States
of America, and a member movement of the International Fellowship of Evangelical Students. For information about
local and regional activities, write Public Relations Dept., InterVarsity Christian Fellowship/USA, 6400 Schroeder
Rd., P.O. Box 7895, Madison, WI 53707-7895, or visit the IVCF website at <www.intervarsity.org>.*

Cover design: Cindy Kiple

Interior design: Beth Hagenberg

Images: Dietrich Bonhoeffer: ullstein bild / The Granger Collection, NYC. All rights reserved.

ISBN 978-0-8308-2716-9

Printed in the United States of America ∞

Library of Congress Cataloging-in-Publication Data

A catalog record for this book is available from the Library of Congress.

P	23	22	21	21	20	19	18	17	16	15	14	13	12	11	10	9	8	7	6	5	4	3	2	1
Y	34	33	32	31	30	29	28	27	26	25	24	23	22	21	20	19	18	17	16	15	14	13		

For Jeffrey P. Greenman

CONTENTS

ABBREVIATIONS

DBW   *Dietrich Bonhoeffer Werke*. Edited by Eberhard Bethge et al.
       17 vols. Munich and Gütersloh: Chr. Kaiser-Gütersloher Ver-
       lagshaus, 1986–1999.

DBWE   *Dietrich Bonhoeffer Works*. Edited by Wayne Whitson Floyd
       Jr. et al. 16 vols. Minneapolis: Fortress Press, 1995–2012.

INTRODUCTION

KEITH L. JOHNSON AND TIMOTHY LARSEN

INTEREST IN THE LIFE, MINISTRY, WRITINGS AND THOUGHT of
Dietrich Bonhoeffer (1906–1945) has grown to the point that we now
take his ubiquity for granted. It is therefore worth pausing a moment to
realize just how unlikely this is. He has been dead for nearly seventy
years now. While respected by his peers during his lifetime, they themselves would not have recognized him as one of the most important
thinkers or leaders of their era. Many of the endeavors he spent the most
time and energy upon turned out to be, at best, moderate successes; just
as often, his efforts produced little or nothing worthy of note at the time.
He left a corpus of writings, some of them unfinished, and that often are
difficult to read and contain references and ideas increasingly removed
from the context of contemporary readers. Add to that the fact that we
live in a time when people are less and less likely to read books from the
past or to attend to figures from previous generations, and it seems remarkable that his writings are read at all.

Yet today in the second decade of the twenty-first century Bonhoeffer
is read as much or more than ever—and that is saying something, since
in the years following his death he became one of the most widely read
and respected Christian thinkers of the twentieth century. More remarkable is the fact that he has become one of those rare figures who is
read and cited widely both inside and outside the academy. As to the
latter, despite being some six hundred pages long, Eric Metaxas's *Bon-*

hoeffer: Pastor, Martyr, Prophet, Spy rose to the top spot on a *New York Times* bestseller list. As to the former, the carefully edited sixteen-volume series of the English edition of the Works of Dietrich Bonhoeffer being produced and published at considerable expense by Fortress Press reveals the serious commitment of the scholarly community to continue exploring Bonhoeffer's thought and developing his legacy.

While a prisoner of the Nazis, Bonhoeffer wrote a haunting poem, "Who Am I?" in which he contrasted his own impressions of himself with what others said he was like. He wonders, "Am I then really all that which other men tell of?" Since his death, people from various perspectives have often wondered how others see such a different Bonhoeffer from the one they see. Or, to put it another way, Bonhoeffer's works at times can seem almost a kind of Rorschach test, telling us primarily something about what the people encountering them stand for and believe rather than something about Bonhoeffer himself. This is to frame the matter too subjectively, however, as Bonhoeffer's thought was variegated and complex. To take just one seeming dichotomy, the fact that Bonhoeffer often is claimed as an ally by both pacifists and just-war theorists tells us something not only about the commitments of the person viewing Bonhoeffer's legacy, but also about the nature of that legacy itself. Indeed, one could make the case that any one of the four descriptors in the subtitle of Metaxas's book—pastor, martyr, prophet and spy—could be used to describe *the* defining contribution of Bonhoeffer's life. His involvement in any one of these areas by itself would be enough for a single life, let alone one cut short at the age of 39. Yet even these four diverse identifiers do not include the one that is perhaps most prominent in this collection: Bonhoeffer the *theologian*.

This volume was collected from the papers delivered at the 21st Annual Wheaton Theology Conference held on the Wheaton campus in April 2012. One of the themes of Bonhoeffer's *Letters and Papers from Prison* is the "world come of age," and with the theme "Bonhoeffer, Christ and Culture," the Wheaton Theology Conference came of age. The first conference was organized by Dennis L. Okholm and the late Timothy R. Phillips. Phillips was a gifted teacher of theology. When a former MA student in theology returned to visit in the early 1990s,

Professor Phillips asked him about his perspective on the theology program. Among other things, the student mentioned that he was surprised that Wheaton had not introduced him to the writings of Dietrich Bonhoeffer. Phillips replied with what had been the standard view, that Bonhoeffer was only a minor theologian. So, in the wake of a conference dedicated exclusively to Bonhoeffer's theology held on the Wheaton campus less than two decades later, we return again to the startling fact that Bonhoeffer's reputation continues to grow beyond anyone's expectations.

Evangelicals, of course, have appreciated Bonhoeffer's writings for at least several decades now, but they have primarily appreciated them as *devotional* literature. *The Cost of Discipleship* is undoubtedly evangelicals' favorite Bonhoeffer book, and it is overwhelmingly read by them not primarily for theological information but for spiritual formation. Likewise, *Life Together* is beloved by many evangelicals as an edifying classic of the spiritual life. Increasingly, however, Bonhoeffer also is becoming a more important conversation partner for evangelical *theologians.* Not every contributor to this volume would necessarily self-identify as an evangelical, but many would, and therefore this book can be seen as representing—in part and among other things—a current sampling of a serious evangelical theological engagement with the thought of Dietrich Bonhoeffer.

This engagement produces fruitful results not only because Bonhoeffer shares many characteristics and commitments with evangelicals, but also because, in significant ways, he lived and thought in a world far removed from the evangelical tradition. Philip G. Ziegler's essay explores Bonhoeffer's unique background by assessing the influence of Bonhoeffer's time, place and tradition—particularly represented by the influence of Martin Luther and Karl Barth—on his life and thought. Ziegler's focus on Bonhoeffer's unique background forms a nice pairing with Timothy Larsen's often surprising account of the evangelical reception of Bonhoeffer's theology from the latter half of the twentieth century to the present. Larsen explores how and why some evangelicals embraced Bonhoeffer while others rejected him, and his account of the shifting nature of evangelical thought about Bonhoeffer's theology re-

veals much about changing attitudes within the tradition. Charles Marsh
shows that Bonhoeffer's own views and self-perception changed at a key
moment in his personal and theological development, and his biographical essay helps us understand better how Bonhoeffer the *theologian* relates to Bonhoeffer the *Christian*.

Many of the essays in the volume appropriate Bonhoeffer's theology
constructively in order to engage contemporary questions. Stephen J.
Plant's essay explores the unique political challenges facing Bonhoeffer
and his colleagues in Nazi Germany, and he then applies several of Bonhoeffer's most striking theological and ethical insights to the contemporary political situation and the church's thinking about its relationship
to the state. Daniel J. Treier's essay explores Bonhoeffer's various remarks about technology and puts him into conversation with Jacques
Ellul in order to help the church discern how best to use the technological resources that are so prominent in the contemporary world.
Keith L. Johnson's essay creatively appropriates Bonhoeffer's theological
insights to some of the key questions driving Christian higher education
in order to help the Christian academy figure out how to best integrate
the insights of the Christian faith with academic learning while also
staying firmly connected to the life and ministry of the church.

Reggie L. Williams's groundbreaking essay shows how Bonhoeffer
himself creatively appropriated insights from many of the African
American intellectuals, writers and poets associated with the Harlem
Renaissance during his visit to the United States. His deep engagement
with the realities of the race divide shaped his thinking profoundly, not
least by enabling him to see sooner than most that the racist implications of Nazi policies could not be accommodated by the German
church. Williams's work is a sign that there is still much to discover in
the Bonhoeffer corpus, because new eyes can find things in Bonhoeffer's
writings which have hitherto gone unobserved.

One of our goals for the conference always has been to offer intellectually rigorous and scholarly work that would be of service to the
academy while also being attentive to issues of the spiritual lives of ordinary believers in the wider church. This ecclesial commitment is most
thoroughly expressed in this volume in Lori Brandt Hale's reflections on

questions of Christian vocation in light of Bonhoeffer's remarks on that issue. Her essay offers a poignant account of how our often messy lives can be transformed by God's grace. Joel D. Lawrence takes one of Bonhoeffer's most transformative ideas—the notion that the church is called to exist as a "church for others"—and asks the question of *how* the church can actually move toward this vision. His deeply moving vision for a community that shifts from selfishness to selflessness through ecclesial practices ordered by and around Christ's death provides an excellent example of how the insights of the academy can be applied to the concrete life and ministry of congregations. Finally, Jim Belcher's account of his pilgrimage through some of the key locations in Bonhoeffer's life shows how Bonhoeffer's commitment to spiritual disciplines and a life ordered by worship provided him the resources he needed to confront the challenges he faced at the end of his life. Belcher suggests that the contemporary church has much to learn as it considers its own challenges in a much different time and place.

Taken together, these essays show that not only does this volume refuse to engage in academic theology in a way that is divorced from the life of the church, but it also refuses to handle Bonhoeffer's thought in an antiquarian way that traps it in a time and context that becomes more remote with every passing decade. Far from this, a major contribution of this book is that it deploys insights from Bonhoeffer to address issues in our twenty-first-century world: higher education now, the present state of technology, the vocational realities of today, spiritual disciplines for a new generation and so on. Bonhoeffer was, of course, very much a man of his time in many ways, but because he also was centered on Jesus Christ—the one who is the same yesterday, today and forever—his life and writings continue to speak to believers long after his death.

This volume is possible only because of the rich partnership between the Wheaton Theology Conference and InterVarsity Press. Once again, we are grateful to IVP for their insight, guidance and support. We are also grateful for the leadership of Jeffrey P. Greenman, associate dean of the biblical and theological studies department at Wheaton. Not only was this conference topic originally his idea, but his love for Bonhoeffer, the academy and the church set the vision for this conference and the volume that resulted from it. As this is his last year at Wheaton, we are particularly aware of the enormous contribution he has made and of the gift of his presence and friendship. For leadership, both professional and personal, and his mighty contributions to making the Wheaton Theology Conference what it is today, this volume is dedicated to him.

1

DIETRICH BONHOEFFER

A Theologian of the Word of God

PHILIP G. ZIEGLER

INTRODUCTION

What kind of theologian was Dietrich Bonhoeffer? What motivated his theological questioning? What commanded his attention in matters of Christian doctrine? From whence did his theological thinking and writing proceed? At what did it aim? In what follows, I suggest a way in which we might begin to ask and answer such questions. I do so aware that more than a half century after Bonhoeffer's execution in Flossenbürg in April 1945, women and men by the thousands continue to be fascinated by the story of his life and death, and moved by the integration of clear Christian conviction, civil courage and "moral leadership,"[1] which mark him out as an extraordinary figure in recent church history. This capacity of Bonhoeffer's life story to continue to seize imaginations is remarkable and welcome. And yet among the proliferating portraits of this Protestant saint it is more than possible to lose sight of Bonhoeffer's central vocation as a *theologian*.[2] It can be difficult

---

[1]For an appreciation of Bonhoeffer centered on this last theme, see Geffrey B. Kelly and F. Burton Nelson, *The Cost of Moral Leadership: The Spirituality of Dietrich Bonhoeffer* (Grand Rapids: Eerdmans, 2002).

[2]The phrase alludes to Stephen Haynes's instructive survey of the diverse receptions of Bonhoeffer which populate the history of his influence: *The Bonhoeffer Phenomenon: Portraits of a Protestant Saint* (Minneapolis: Fortress, 2004). It is also notable that *theologian* is conspicuously absent from the subtitle of Eric Metaxas's recent and widely read biography, *Bon-*

for contemporary readers to access and understand the character, substance and import of Bonhoeffer's work as a teacher of Christian doctrine in its historical context despite being very well positioned to do just that, possessed as we are of a complete critical edition of his writings and many recent historiographically sophisticated studies of the landscape of church and theology in early twentieth-century Germany.[3]

There are two decisive contexts for understanding Bonhoeffer's theological identity. The first, and more narrow, is the German church struggle of the 1930s and its wider ecumenical environment in which Bonhoeffer was immersed. The struggle for the integrity of the Protestant churches in Germany under Nazism was a matter of burning concern for Bonhoeffer, and he aligned himself from the very first with its most radical proponents and served its cause up to the time of his imprisonment. Explaining his decision to return to Germany from America in the summer of 1939, Bonhoeffer wrote to his friend Edwin Sutz simply: "I am being pulled irresistibly back toward the Confessing Church."[4] The second and wider context within which to understand his profile as a theologian is that provided by the intellectual ferment of European Protestant thought during the first decades of the twentieth century. Bonhoeffer learned and practiced his theological art amidst the churn of the "high" liberal theology of his Berlin teachers, impulses from the contemporary "Luther renaissance" and the explosive devel-

---

hoeffer: Pastor, Martyr, Prophet, Spy (Nashville: Thomas Nelson, 2010). Clifford Green has very recently observed how commonly Bonhoeffer's theology can be cast as an "epiphenomenon" of his political resistance, as "Bonhoeffer the theologian disappears from view behind the popular image of the martyr and even saint." See his foreword to Michael P. DeJonge, Bonhoeffer's Theological Formation: Berlin, Barth and Protestant Theology (Oxford: Oxford University Press, 2012), p. xi.

[3]Dietrich Bonhoeffer Werke, 17 Bände, ed. E. Bethge et al. (Munich/Gütersloh: Chr. Kaiser/ Gütersloher Verlaghaus, 1986-1999). The English edition is nearly complete: Dietrich Bonhoeffer Works, 16 volumes, ed. Clifford Green et al. (Minneapolis: Fortress, 1995-2012). Recent studies valuable for understanding the theological and ecclesiastical context of Bonhoeffer's work include Victoria Barnett, For the Soul of the People: Protestant Protest Against Hitler (New York: Oxford University Press, 1992); Matthew Hockenos, A Church Divided: German Protestants Confront the Nazi Past (Bloomington: Indiana University Press, 2004); and Gerhard Besier, Kirche in der Dritten Reich, Band 3 Spaltungen und Abwehrkämpfe 1934 bis 1937 (Berlin: Propyläen, 2001). For a condensed and accessible discussion of revisionist trends in scholarship, see Robert Bates, "In Our Own Image," Epworth Review 36/4 (2009): 30-47.

[4]Dietrich Bonhoeffer, Theological Education Underground, 1937-1940, DBWE 15:215.

opment of dialectical or crisis theology, of which Karl Barth was the leading exponent.

In this essay, I want to recommend that we approach Bonhoeffer as a *theologian of the Word of God* in order to illumine something crucial of the form, substance and scope of his theology as a whole in view of these two decisive contexts. The phrase "Word of God" is a compact and polyvalent designation for the center of Bonhoeffer's theology, and provides, I suggest, a key for its interpretation. A theology of the Word of God comprises several motifs. It sets out from acknowledgement of revelation understood as a divine performative address which judges, forgives and commands. It sees this divine activity concentrated definitively in the person of Jesus Christ. Attending to the Bible as a unique creaturely medium of the Word, such a theology affirms the concreteness and contemporaneity of God's promise and claim. It does so because it acknowledges the vital and eloquent presence of Christ to the world. Given that God's Word of redemption determines the very reality of the world in some deep sense, such theology seeks further to discern the contours of the world as it has been remade by grace and to reflect on the shape of a truly human life therein. As Bonhoeffer observed, "Revelation gives itself without precondition and is alone able to place one into reality."[5] Whether treating the doctrine of God, the doctrine of salvation, the doctrine of the church or the matter of Christian life, the vocation of a theologian of the Word of God is always to hold reason in obedience to Jesus Christ, for "the relevant is and begins where God himself is in his Word."[6] The prospect for an authentic and powerful Christian theology exists, Bonhoeffer argued, "as long as only one word, that is to say, the name of Jesus Christ, is not extinguished in us. This name abides as a word, the Word, around which all our words revolve. In this Word alone lies clarity and power."[7]

My concentrated effort here to profile Bonhoeffer as a theologian of the Word of God involves two steps. First, I offer a few remarks con-

---

[5]Dietrich Bonhoeffer, *Act and Being*, DBWE 2:289.
[6]Dietrich Bonhoeffer, *No Rusty Swords: Letters, Lectures and Notes, 1928-1936*, trans. Edwin H. Robertson and John Bowden, ed. Edwin H. Robertson (London: Collins, 1965), p. 311.
[7]Dietrich Bonhoeffer, *Conspiracy and Imprisonment, 1940-1945*, DBWE 16:208.

cerning Bonhoeffer's relationship with the theologies of Martin Luther and Karl Barth—two great and formative practitioners of the theology of the Word. Second, I explore some tracts of Bonhoeffer's corpus which may not be so familiar but which—as the scale of this material in the new critical edition suggests—represent his main theological preoccupations throughout his extended engagement in the German church struggle after the Nazi seizure of power in 1933. Here I focus in particular on his vigorous embrace of the evangelical truths attested in the Barmen Theological Declaration of 1934, the chief text of the church struggle. Reflecting on the intensity and focus of Bonhoeffer's devotion to Barmen as a confession of the church may serve to help illustrate simultaneously the crucial importance of Scripture in Bonhoeffer's theology as well as the unshakable centrality of Jesus Christ, the present and powerful Word of God's own freedom ever addressing himself to the church. While not "evangelical" in the sense this term now carries broadly in English language theology, Bonhoeffer's theology is profoundly *evangelisch* in the historic sense of that term in the European usage: that is, his theology is a sustained effort to learn afresh the substance and significance of Pauline and Lutheran faith and to attain to a better witness to the gospel of God which has been honored, as he once styled it, by "all genuine Christian thinking from Paul, Augustine, Luther, to Kierkegaard and Barth."[8]

BETWEEN MARTIN LUTHER AND KARL BARTH

Bonhoeffer was a highly cultured European intellectual of his era—widely read, musically talented and trained, uncommonly well-traveled, excellent at tennis, fond of smoking. He was a prolific amateur (in the

---

[8]Dietrich Bonhoeffer, "Concerning the Christian Idea of God," *Journal of Religion* 12, no. 2 (1932): 184. For an account which emphasizes the liberal and critical elements in this cast of mind, see Theo Hobson, "Bonhoeffer's Ghost," *Theology* 109, no. 852 (2006): 439-50. On Bonhoeffer's relation to Kierkegaard, see both Matthew Kirkpatrick, *Attacks on Christendom in a World Come of Age: Kierkegaard, Bonhoeffer, and the Question of "Religionless Christianity"* (Eugene, OR: Wipf & Stock, 2012) and Geffrey Kelly, "Kierkegaard as 'Antidote' and as Impact on Dietrich Bonheoffer's Concept of Christian Discipleship," in *Bonhoeffer's Intellectual Formation*, ed. P. Frick (Tübingen: Mohr Siebeck, 2008), pp. 145-66. Barry Harvey treats Bonhoeffer's relation to Augustine's theology in his contribution to the same volume, "Augustine and Thomas Aquinas in the Theology of Dietrich Bonhoeffer," pp. 11-30.

best sense) in the study of languages and literatures, philosophy, history and popular scientific writing. His family home and formal education led to theological studies at the leading German faculties of the day, most importantly in Berlin where he worked under world-leading modern historians of the Christian tradition including Karl Holl, Reinhold Seeberg and Adolf von Harnack. While Bonhoeffer would ever acknowledge his personal debt to his Berlin teachers, he came rather quickly to chafe against them and steadily moved beyond their theological ambit through the influence of two encounters, on the one hand with Martin Luther and on the other with Karl Barth.[9]

Having previously only known Barth from his writings, Bonhoeffer enthused about his first meetings with the older Swiss theologian in Bonn in 1931, saying: "There is really someone from whom one takes away much; yet I sit in the impoverished Berlin and complain because no one is there who can teach theology. . . . When you see Barth you know at once . . . that there is something worthwhile to risk your life for."[10] It is fair to say that Barth was for Bonhoeffer the most significant contemporary theological authority and that he wrote his own theology with Barth always in mind.[11] Right up into the late years of the war, Bonhoeffer understood himself to be one of Barth's few loyal advocates in Germany, and saw to it that he both visited Barth and acquired proof copies of the newest volumes of *Church Dogmatics* on each of his trips into Switzerland.[12] His criticisms of Barth—present forthrightly from the outset though varied in content over the years—were ever fraternal and friendly, looking for ways to do better justice to the promise

---

[9]See H. Martin Runscheidt, "The Significance of Adolf von Harnack and Reinhold Seeberg for Dietrich Bonhoeffer," in *Bonhoeffer's Intellectual Formation*, ed. P. Frick (Tübingen: Mohr Siebeck, 2008), pp. 201-24. See also Bonhoeffer, *Letters and Papers from Prison*, DBWE 8:498-99.

[10]Dietrich Bonhoeffer, *Ecumenical, Academic and Pastoral Work: 1931-1932*, DBWE 11:20-21 and DBW 17:92-93, both in personal correspondence from the latter half of 1931. These translations are taken from Andreas Pangritz, "Dietrich Bonhoeffer: 'Within, Not Outside, the Barthian Movement,'" in *Bonhoeffer's Intellectual Formation*, p. 257.

[11]John D. Godsey, "Barth and Bonhoeffer: The Basic Difference," *Quarterly Review* 7, no. 1 (1987): 17, and Andreas Pangritz, "Dietrich Bonhoeffer," p. 279. This latter essay presents a compressed account of the argument developed in Andreas Pangritz, *Karl Barth in the Theology of Dietrich Bonhoeffer*, trans. B. and H. M. Rumscheidt (Grand Rapids: Eerdmans, 2000).

[12]See Bonhoeffer, *Conspiracy and Imprisonment*, DBWE 16:278.

of the essential theological convictions they shared, chief among them the primacy, particularity and concreteness of God's gracious self-revelation in Jesus Christ as the formal and material principle of any Christian theology.[13] From his early dissertation criticisms of what he considered Barth's abstract view of God's freedom through to his late prison worries about the atrophy of the Confessing Church into a fixation on orthodoxy owed in part at least to a "positivism of revelation" arising from Barth's teaching, Bonhoeffer aimed to take Barth's insights and to drive them further—in these two cases respectively, first, to press beyond a formal notion of divine freedom (freedom *from*) to a substantive one (as freedom *for*) christologically understood; and second, to radicalize even further the theological critique of religion pioneered by Barth in order to win a new and powerful hearing of the claim of the gospel upon the world through a "non-religious interpretation of biblical concepts."[14]

Beginning with *Act and Being*, Bonhoeffer openly aligns himself with Barth's struggle to reaffirm the sheer contingency of divine revelation and, on this basis, to understand theology itself as form of thinking decisively shaped by the utterly gracious and effective reality of revelation in Christ. Though he disagreed with Barth over various particulars—disputing, for example, the place of dialectics in theology as well as certain Reformed elements of Barth's Christology and theology proper—Bonhoeffer always affirmed this central thrust of Barth's theological revolution.[15] Such a view of revelation must, Bonhoeffer contends, "yield an epistemology of its own" in which we know ourselves only as people

---

[13]See Eberhard Bethge, *Dietrich Bonhoeffer: A Biography,* ed. Victoria J. Barnett, rev. ed. (Minneapolis: Fortress, 2000), p. 178. For a recent and penetrating account of these criticisms in Bonhoeffer's early academic work and their confessional basis, see DeJonge, *Bonhoeffer's Theological Formation.* Among earlier accounts, see Pangritz, *Karl Barth in the Theology of Dietrich Bonhoeffer*; Godsey, "Barth and Bonhoeffer," pp. 9-27; and Paul L. Lehmann, "The Concreteness of Theology: Reflections on the Conversation between Barth and Bonhoeffer," in *Footnotes to a Theology: The Karl Barth Colloquium of 1972,* ed. H. M. Rumscheidt (Waterloo, ON: Corporation for the Study of Religion in Canada, 1974), pp. 53-76.

[14]On these see, respectively, Bonhoeffer, *Act and Being,* DBWE 2:84-85, 124-25 and *Letters and Papers,* DBWE 8:429.

[15]These disputes over theological method—the *extra calvinisticum*, the *finitum non capax infinitum* and the formal definition of divine freedom—are considered closely in the literature cited above in n. 10.

who have been "placed-into-the-truth" by God's address, and thus admit that our very existence is "founded by means of and 'in reference to' God's Word," that is, the Word of the person of Christ.[16] Christian theology must be theology of the Word of God because Christian faith itself arises solely from this source, or not at all.

Both Bonhoeffer's alignment to and his arguments with Barth on such matters have their mainsprings in the influence of Martin Luther. Recent scholarship is increasingly alert to the abiding influence of Luther and the theological traditions of classical Lutheranism on Bonhoeffer.[17] Luther remained for him a living dialogue partner and is the most frequently cited theologian in Bonhoeffer's writings. The German Protestant church was, for Bonhoeffer, essentially a Lutheran church, which is to say, a church *of the Reformation.*[18] For this reason, Bonhoeffer's theology self-consciously engages in the protracted debate concerning the reception and interpretation of Luther's legacy for the church in modern Germany. From the time of his two dissertations, Bonhoeffer repudiates Karl Holl's widely influential portrait of Luther as progenitor of the religion of individual conscience. He does so precisely because Holl's view illegitimately "circumvents" Luther's insistence that God has "bound the divine self to the mediating Word."[19] In works like

---

[16]Bonhoeffer, *Act and Being,* DBWE 2:31, 160, 134. Walter Lowe speaks fruitfully of how theology in this way understands reason itself to be "contextualized" by the reality brought about by God's self-revelation. See his "Bonhoeffer and Deconstruction: Toward a Theology of the Crucified Logos," *Union Seminary Quarterly Review* 46, no. 1-4 (1992): 214.

[17]See Wolf Krötke, "Dietrich Bonhoeffer and Martin Luther," in *Bonhoeffer's Intellectual Formation,* pp. 53-82, which presents a comprehensive account of his relation to Luther to demonstrate how "Luther . . . represented an unparalleled theological, intellectual and spiritual impulse and source for his own experience of faith and reality" (p. 57). Also see *Bonhoeffer und Luther: Zentrale Themen ihrer Theologie,* ed. K. Grünwaldt, C. Tietz and U. Hahn (Hannover: VELKD Verlag, 2007) and DeJonge, *Bonhoeffer's Theological Formation,* especially pp. 83-100. Also instructive are Jonathan Sorum, "Bonhoeffer's Early Interpretation of Luther as the Source of His Basic Theological Paradigm," *Fides and Historia* 29, no. 2 (1997): 35-51, and Christian Gremmels, "Bonhoeffer und Luther," in *Bonhoeffer und Luther: Zur Socialgestalt des Luthertums in der Moderne,* ed. C. Gremmels (Münich: Chr. Kaiser Verlag, 1984), pp. 9-15.

[18]The importance of this self-understanding of the German Protestant church as essentially shaped by the Reformation comes out sharply in Bonhoeffer's reflections on his experiences with Christianity in America. See "Protestantism Without Reformation," in *Theological Education Underground, 1937-1940,* DBWE 15:438-62, especially pp. 442-44, 461-62.

[19]Bonhoeffer, *Act and Being,* DBWE 2:141. On the debate with Karl Holl, see DeJonge, *Bonhoeffer's Theological Formation,* p. 118.

Discipleship he openly polemicizes against misunderstanding and abuse of Luther's teachings on radical grace and good works, and indeed throughout the period of the church struggle he refutes as merely *pseudo*-Lutheran the racialist exploitation and distortion of the doctrines of the two regiments and orders of creation. He consistently called on his students to rediscover the authentic teaching of the Reformer; they should, he said, "Just listen to the Bible. Just read what Luther wrote," because in confusing times one must "go back to the very beginning, to our wellsprings, to the true Bible, to the true Luther."[20] This true Luther was himself, in Bonhoeffer's judgment, simply a skilled hearer of the gospel. And what Luther heard in the gospel was the gracious promise of divine righteousness in Jesus Christ. The most decisive thing Bonhoeffer took over from Luther was precisely this insistence on the *solus Christus:* the Christian thinks and speaks of God evangelically only as she thinks and speaks of Jesus Christ, the Word of God come low in humility to save.[21] For this reason, becoming a theologian, Bonheoffer held, involves responsible study and listening to the witness of Scripture in order to become "attentive to the Word of God, which has been revealed right here in this world," for it is a matter of life and death that one hear *this* truth.[22] We do well to note that Bonhoeffer emphasizes that the Word comes to us *right here in this world.* This stress on the concreteness of the worldly site of our encounter with God in Christ is something Bonhoeffer learned from Luther: a theology of the Word of God is concerned precisely for *this* gospel truth in the midst of and for the sake of *this* created and fallen world.

At the conclusion of his 1931-1932 lectures on the recent history of Christian systematic theology, Bonhoeffer laments the disjunction between the work of academic theology and the present situation of the churches. Observing that Luther himself had been perfectly able to

---

[20]Bonhoeffer, *Berlin: 1932-1933*, DBWE 12:443, 435. In the latter lecture, "What Ought a Student of Theology to Do?" he also adjures that "one should learn from the Holy Scriptures *and the confessions of the Reformation* what is the pure and true teaching of the gospel of Jesus Christ" (p. 434, emphasis added).

[21]A point eloquently made and developed by Wolf Krötke, "Dietrich Bonhoeffer and Martin Luther," p. 56.

[22]Bonhoeffer, *Berlin,* DBWE 12:433.

preach powerfully into the church's need in his own time *and* write technical theology of a high order, Bonhoeffer pleads rhetorically: "Who will show us Luther?"[23] We can rightly say that in some sense Bonhoeffer labored to provide an answer to this question in his own subsequent theological work.[24] Central to this effort was his theological leadership in the Confessing Church and his advocacy of the strong reading of the Barmen Theological Declaration advanced by the "Dahlemite" party to which he publicly belonged. Moving now to consider several key aspects of Bonhoeffer's theological work in this vein, we may come to see more sharply the overarching importance of his self-understanding as a theologian of the Word of God.

THE BARMEN THEOLOGICAL DECLARATION AND THE BIBLE

In a circular letter from October 1935, Bonhoeffer describes the establishment of the Preachers' Seminary in Finkenwalde, including its physical appointments and setting. Amidst the "utterly plain" and "functional" furnishings of the rooms which serve as lecture hall, dining hall and chapel together, Bonhoeffer notes that "on the wall hang the two great portraits of the Apostles by Dürer."[25] Bonhoeffer calls them great (*grosse*), presumably not only because of their size—over two meters tall if reproduced to scale—but because of the significance of their subject matter. The paintings, originally done by Dürer as a gift to the city council of Nuremberg in 1526, depict four apostles in two pairs: to the

---

[23]Bonhoeffer, *Ecumenical, Academic, and Pastoral Work: 1931-1932*, DBWE 11:244.

[24]A suggestion made by Gremmels, "Bonhoeffer and Luther," p. 10.

[25]Bonhoeffer, *Ilegale Theologenausbildung: Finkenwalde 1935-1937*, DBW 14:90. Gerhard Vibrans describes going along shopping with Bethge and Bonhoeffer on the occasion when the reproductions were purchased from a second-hand shop: see Dorothea Andersen et al., eds., *So ist es gewesen. Briefe im Kirchenkampf 1933-1942 von Gerhard Vibrans aus seinem Familien- und Freundeskreis und von Dietrich Bonhoeffer* (Münich: Chr. Kaiser Verlag, 1995), p. 181. They now are displayed in Bonhoeffer's old rooms in *Marienburger Allee* 43 in Berlin. The single composition of this pair of paintings is typically called *The Four Apostles* or *The Four Holy Men*; it hangs today in the Alte Pinakothek in Münich. For a digital image, see: http://www.pinakothek.de/alte-pinakothek/sammlung/rundgang/rundgang_inc .php?inc=bild&which=7614. For brief histories of the paintings, see A. Ottino della Chiesa, *The Complete Paintings of Dürer* (London: Weidenfeld and Nicolson, 1971), plates 181A and 181B; and Wolfram Prinz, *Dürer* (New York: Smithmark, 1998), p. 138. For a longer, detailed treatment, see David Hotchkiss Price, *Albrecht Dürer's Renaissance: Humanism, Reformation, and the Art of Faith* (Ann Arbor: University of Michigan Press, 2003), pp. 258-73.

left, John and Peter; to the right, Mark and Paul. Though intended from
the start for display in magistrates' buildings, both the subject matter
and monumental size of the images are redolent of a painted altarpiece.
At the base of each, Dürer had inscribed the text of four biblical passages
in Luther's translation from 2 Peter 2:1-2, 1 John 4:1-3, Mark 12:38-40 and
2 Timothy 3:1-7.[26] At the head of these scriptural verses, he had the cal-
ligrapher set this preface: "In these dangerous times all worldly rulers
should take care that they do not mistake human seduction for the word
of God. For God wants nothing to be taken from or added to it. Therefore,
hear these four excellent men, Peter, John, Paul and Mark."[27]

In its original polemical context, the paintings constituted a "Reformation broadside" aimed to refute "both visually and verbally" Catholic
and enthusiastic challenges to the principle of *sola scriptura*.[28] In the
different but no less polemical context of the German church struggle,
Bonhoeffer's decision to set up these same images prominently at the
heart of the seminary at Finkenwalde is no less a "broadside." It is of
course aimed squarely at the German Evangelical Church as instrumentalized by the Nazis, the German Christian movement and, later, also
toward the "compromise" party within the Confessing Church itself. It
is aimed, in short, at the opponents of Barmen/Dahlem for the sake of
affirming what was confessed by these two synods. Bonhoeffer was
deeply convicted by the evangelical truths of Barmen and their radical
implications for church order and governance drawn out at Dahlem,
and his position in debates surrounding them was "radically and un-
compromisingly one-sided."[29] It was Bonhoeffer's bold conviction that

---

[26]These texts were sawed off the works in 1627 when the paintings were moved from Protestant
Nuremberg to Catholic München, though later restored to their place in 1922. For the com-
plete text of the original German inscriptions, see ed. H. Rupprich, *Dürer Schriftlicher
Nachlaß*, Bände 1 (Berlin: Deutscher Verein für Kunstwissenschaft, 1956), pp. 210-13.

[27]Rupprich, *Dürer Schriftlicher Nachlaß*, p. 210, referencing Revelation 22:18.

[28]Price, *Albrecht Dürer's Renaissance*, p. 273.

[29]Wolf Krötke, "Kein Zurück hinter Barmen: Die Barmer Theologische Erklärung im Denken
Dietrich Bonhoeffer," in *Barmen—Barth—Bonhoeffer. Beiträge zu einer zeitgemäßen chris-
tozentrischen Theologie* (Bielefeld: Luther-Verlag, 2009), p. 46. Bonhoeffer's most sustained
presentations of his view are in the essay, "Zur Frage nach der Kirchengemeinschaft" (April
1935) and the subsequent published reply to critics in Bonhoeffer, DBW 14:655-80, 691-700
(partially translated into English in Dietrich Bonhoeffer, *The Way to Freedom*, trans. E. Robertson [London: SCM, 1966], pp. 75-96) and an address to the *Bruderrats der Bekennenden
Kirche* in Pommerania in October 1938: "Lecture on the Path of the Young Illegal Theolo-

the Holy Spirit had stirred the church to "join the battle at a specific place," brought about a "true confession of the Lord Jesus Christ," and thus acted to preserve the true church. As he said, "We can no longer go back behind Barmen and Dahlem, because we can no longer go back behind the Word of God."[30]

As the depiction of the crucifixion from Grünewald's Isenheim altarpiece is taken to express something of the essence of Karl Barth's theological endeavors,[31] so Dürer's *Four Apostles* together with its inscription may be taken to epitomize both "visually and verbally" Bonhoeffer's theological program during the years of the church struggle. His writing and teaching, especially after 1933, is a single sustained effort to "hear these four excellent men;" that is, to suffer the full force of the promise and claim of the gospel attested in Scripture, and as a corollary, to summon the Christian church to "take care . . . not [to] mistake human seduction for the word of God." In the same letter in which he mentions Dürer's painting, Bonhoeffer makes this clear, explaining to his correspondent that "the Bible stands at the focal point of our labor. For us, it has become once more the starting point and the center of our theological endeavor and all our Christian action. Here, we have learned to read the Bible prayerfully once again."[32]

Bonhoeffer works out his allegiance to Barmen in no small part by advocating relentlessly for the centrality and exclusivity of the biblical witness as the locus of Christ's self-presentation to and for the Christian congregation. His concern is ever with the force of the first article of the declaration, which confesses that "Jesus Christ, as he is attested for us in Holy Scripture, is the one Word of God which we have to hear and which we have to trust and obey in life and in death." It is no doubt true

---

gians of the Confessing Church," *Theological Education Underground: 1937-1940,* DBWE 15:416-37. For recent assessments of Bonhoeffer's relation to Barmen, see Krötke, "Kein Zurück hinter Barmen," pp. 45-62; and Robert W. Bertram, *A Time for Confessing,* ed. Michael Hoy (Grand Rapids: Eerdmans, 2008), pp. 65-95.

[30]Bonhoeffer, *Way to Freedom,* pp. 83, 110, 86-87.

[31]See Eberhard Busch, *Karl Barth: His Life from Letters and Autobiographical Texts* (London: SCM Press, 1976), pp. 116, 408; Joseph Mangina, *Karl Barth: Theologian of Christian Witness* (Louisville: Westminster John Knox, 2004), p. 12; and, exhaustively, Reiner Marquard, *Karl Barth und der Isenheimer Altar* (Stuttgart: Calwer, 1995).

[32]Bonhoeffer, DBW 14:91.

and important, as John de Gruchy and others have argued, that Bonhoeffer served the cause of Barmen by drawing out very concretely its
practical implications for the church in the Third Reich and that, in so
doing, he made himself "one the main links" between that confession of
faith and contemporary struggles for justice and peace in the world.[33]
And it is also true that Bonhoeffer's involvement with the nascent organs
of the ecumenical movement helped to bring the ecclesiological substance of Barmen into view both at the time and since.[34] Yet at the heart
of all this was an even more basic struggle, namely the struggle to hear,
to trust and to obey the one Word of God attested in Scripture, Jesus
Christ, as God's unparalleled assurance of our forgiveness and royal
claim on our whole life, as the second Barmen article has it.[35] It is em-
blematic of the utter seriousness of Bonhoeffer's concern on this score
that he should have redundantly amended in his own hand the *dam-
natus* clause of the first article on his personal copy of the text of the
Barmen Declaration to read: "We reject the false doctrine that the
Church could and should acknowledge *as a source of revelation* and its
proclamation, beyond and besides this one Word of God, yet other
events, powers, historical figures, and truths as God's revelation."[36] Franz
Hildebrandt certainly understood himself to speak on behalf of his lost
friend when he remarked in 1984 that all of the social, political, ecclesiastical and ecumenical implications of Barmen, even the "stor[y] of the
church under the cross, are but footnotes and commentaries on the es-

---

[33]John W. de Gruchy, "Barmen: Symbol of Contemporary Liberation?" *Journal of Theology for
Southern Africa* 47 (1984): 69. This view is echoed in several of the essays in the special issue
of *The Ecumenical Review* 61, no. 1 (2009), dedicated to reflecting on Barmen and its legacy
on the occasion of its seventy-fifth anniversary. The latter point is often made with reference
to the question of the churches and Judaism—see, for example, Victoria Barnett, "Transcending Barmen: Confessing in Word and Deed," *Christian Century* (May 11, 1994): 495-96.
[34]See Bonhoeffer, "The Confessing Church and the Ecumenical Movement," in *No Rusty
Swords*, pp. 321-39. Keith Clements makes much of Bonhoeffer's ecumenical role in "Barmen
and the Ecumenical Movement," *The Ecumenical Review* 61/1 (2009): 6. For Barmen's decisive ecclesiological importance, see Rolf Ahlers, "The Community of Brethren: The Contemporary Significance of Barmen III," *Calvin Theological Journal* 20/1 (1985): 7-32.
[35]Article two reads, "As Jesus Christ is God's assurance of the forgiveness of all our sins, so, in
the same way and with the same seriousness he is also God's mighty claim upon our whole
life. Through him befalls us a joyful deliverance from the godless fetters of this world for a
free, grateful service to his creatures."
[36]A photograph of this can be seen in *Dietrich Bonhoeffer: A Life in Pictures*, ed. R. Bethge and
C. Gremmels (Minneapolis: Fortress, 2005), p. 145.

sential message: the Word, the whole Word, nothing but the Word."[37]

If it is not too much to claim that the "record of Finkenwalde" repre-sents an essential part of Bonhoeffer's "responsible interpretation" of Barmen, then we should find this radical concern for the Word at the heart of the church to be borne out in texts from this period.[38] And so we do. These works evince that Bonhoeffer understood that the question put to the church at Barmen was first and foremost the question of the *truth* of the Word of God. In allegiance to this confession, this question, that is, the question of the truth that Jesus Christ is and the "formative power of its particularity"[39] for church *and* world—became Bonhoef-fer's central concern.[40] Some few examples may suffice to demonstrate that this is the case.

On the eve of the start of the first course at Finkenwalde, Bonhoeffer addressed a Confessing Church gathering in Saxony on the theme of the interpretation of the New Testament. In his programmatic lecture, Bon-hoeffer sets the struggle for the truth of the living and present witness of Christ through his appointed witness, namely the Scriptures, over against all efforts to justify Christianity to the present age.[41] The church *qua* church cannot forfeit its proper concern for evangelical truth in favor of an overriding concern for relevance. As he says, "where the question of relevance becomes the *theme of theology*, we can be certain that the cause has already been betrayed and sold out."[42] Why should this be? Programmatic concern for relevance grants to the world, rather than the Word, the status of *decisive* reality; it effectively "fetters" the properly unfettered word of God and affords the present—in Bonhoef-fer's case the so-called "German hour of the church"—*de facto* status as "another source" of divine promise and claim which delimits the hearing

---

[37]Franz Hildebrandt, "Barmen: What to Learn and What Not to Learn" in *The Barmen Confes-sion: Papers from the Seattle Assembly,* ed. H. G. Locke (Lewiston/Queenston: Edwin Mellon Press, 1986), p. 287.

[38]Betram, *Time for Confessing,* p. 76.

[39]The phrase is Paul L. Lehmann's in "The Formative Power of Particularity," *Union Seminary Quarterly Review* 18, no. 3 (1963): 306-19.

[40]See Krötke, "Kein Zurück hinter Barmen," pp. 46-47.

[41]Bonhoeffer, *No Rusty Swords,* pp. 308-9.

[42]Ibid., pp. 309-10. He takes as examples of this fate then recent works by Paul Althaus and Adolf Schlatter on the "Germanness" of the church.

of the Word and channels the church's message.[43] Put otherwise, to pursue "relevant theology" in this sense is to confess the perspicacity of our social-political contexts and the obscurity of the Scriptures.

Against this, Bonhoeffer avers that what is truly relevant "is and begins where God himself is in his Word." The "relevant fact" is the present presence of the Spirit, who as the "subject of [biblical] interpretation," commits the church to attend afresh to the biblical witness as the "sole and exclusive means" by which Christ speaks. The Word of God is present to the church in the power of the Spirit, and Christ comes on his people in the proclamation of the gospel with the power to "judge, command and forgive."[44] The Word provides the really relevant criterion for discerning the truth of the present situation, such that it will be the alien gospel which comes upon the world from beyond and over against it *(extra nos)* that will prove itself to be supremely relevant in each and every case.

The "one Word of God" which the church has to hear will thus not be a religio-ethical programme or application arrived at by its contextual domestication.[45] What makes Christian truth relevant—and this for Bonhoeffer means concrete, rampant and critical, able to arrest, turn around and sanctify women and men—is the same thing which makes it formative and effective, namely that it is the real and eloquent presence of "Christ himself as the Lord, the Judge and the Savior." He writes,

> Precisely because the so-called concrete situation of the congregation is *not taken with the utmost seriousness* there is room to see the true situation of [humanity] before God. God does not ask us about our being men or women or National Socialists, he asks about our faith in him and his forgiving love and our obedience towards the Word which is witnessed in the Bible.[46]

In short, in as much as the church in its listening to Scripture "really takes this text as a testimony to the living Christ" it will discover "every-

---

[43]The phrase is the title of an indicative work by Paul Althaus, *The German Hour of the Church.* For discussion, see Robert P. Ericksen, *Theologians Under Hitler* (New Haven: Yale University Press, 1986), pp. 79-119.

[44]Bonhoeffer, *No Rusty Swords*, p. 316.

[45]Ibid., p. 309.

[46]Ibid., p. 316.

thing is here."[47] The view Bonhoeffer advances here—in which the most effective and concretely relevant engagement with the world is a function of our exposure to the Word of God attested in Scripture—is of course redolent of Barth's famous injunction about the salutary merit of "doing theology as if nothing had happened." And like Barth's tract, Bonhoeffer's aim is to heighten the human and political significance of Christian theology precisely by demanding that it "mind its own business."[48] But its business, of course, is to keep abreast in thought and speech with the Word of God which is pressing on the entire world over which Christ is Lord. Hence,

> the Bible knows nothing of the pathos and problem of [the question] about "our path." Our path follows self-evidently, plainly and necessarily from the truth that is witnessed to. Our path does not have its own weight, its own problem, and certainly not its own particular tragic aspect. It is simply "doing the truth" (John 3:21), whereby the emphasis is entirely on the truth.[49]

What is critical in all this is, as Bonhoeffer says, that "through the Bible in its fragility, God comes to meet us as the Risen One."[50] Such a view of the centrality and exclusivity of the truth of Scriptures in the life of the church is only credible when the biblical witness is understood to be at the disposal of Jesus Christ, the living Word of God, present in the present, addressing himself to his people with his word of freedom and direction. As such, the Scriptures never provide a cognitive "guarantee" for the course of our actions, because it is the work of the biblical witness to call Christians "to faith and obedience to the truth once acknowledged in Jesus Christ." Outside of such a robust theology of the living Word, Bonhoeffer's exclusive privileging of the Scriptures would dissolve into an evidentialist obscurantism which in its longing to be spared the need for faith is all-too readily instrumentalized by the

---

[47]Ibid.

[48]Ibid., p. 317. "The polemic lies in the exegesis of the text itself!" Karl Barth, *Theological Existence Today!* See Eberhard Busch, "'Doing Theology as if Nothing Had Happened'—The Freedom of Theology and the Question of Its Involvement in Politics," *Studies in Religion* 16, no. 4 (1987): 459-71.

[49]Bonhoeffer, *Theological Education Underground: 1937-1940*, DBWE 15:419-20.

[50]Bonhoeffer, *No Rusty Swords*, p. 312.

powers of the age. But to listen for the one Word of God attested in the Scriptures is to harken unto the voice of the Risen One himself, who summons us to the venture of faith and obedience and then also strengthens us in it by the power of his Spirit.[51] Precisely this is the motive force behind Bonhoeffer's provocative remark that a doctrine of verbal inspiration is "a poor surrogate for the resurrection."[52]

With origins reaching back as far as Bonhoeffer's time at Union Seminary in 1929-1930, his *Discipleship* published in 1937 can rightly be read as an exemplary iteration of his theological concerns during these most intense years of the church struggle.[53] Like the occasional pieces considered to this point, it is also a work which clearly displays the depth of Bonhoeffer's commitment to achieving a "responsible interpretation" of the Barmen Declaration. Further, it continues to demonstrate the priority over all other matters Bonhoeffer gives to the truth of the gospel understood as a fruit of the living Word of God attested in the Scriptures. Here we will attend briefly to the two short prefaces Bonhoeffer set at the beginning of parts one and two of the work. These prefaces are late compositions written it seems during the summer of 1937 just prior to the closure of the seminary at Finkenwalde.[54] They breathe the same polemical air as other works from these years of crisis within the Confessing Church and concentrate just as clearly on the themes we have been canvassing.

One might be forgiven for thinking that the opening words of *Discipleship* are the famous programmatic claim: "Cheap grace is the mortal enemy of our church. Our struggle is for costly grace."[55] In fact, the discussion of grace is preceded by introductory remarks whose brevity belies their significance. The opening words of the book are in fact these:

---

[51]Bonhoeffer, *Theological Education Underground*, DBWE 15:420.

[52]Bonhoeffer, *Berlin*, DBWE 12:331: "Verbal inspiration means to deny the Christ who alone is present as the Risen One. Inspiration from the literal words [Verbalinspiration] is a poor surrogate for the resurrection. It eternizes the historical, instead of recognizing the historical as coming from God's eternity and God's resurrection."

[53]For discussion see Philip G. Ziegler, "'Not to Abolish but to Fulfil'—The Person of the Preacher and the Claim of the Sermon on the Mount," *Studies in Christian Ethics* 22, no. 3 (2009): 275-89.

[54]See the editors' introduction, Dietrich Bonhoeffer, *Discipleship*, DBWE 4:27-28.

[55]Ibid., p. 43.

"In times of church renewal, holy scripture naturally becomes richer in content for us." Addressing himself explicitly to the church struggle—and echoing the inscription of Dürer's great portrait of the evangelists—Bonhoeffer says that the most basic labor of the Christian community is also its most important one, namely, to brush aside the "many dissonant sounds, so many human, harsh words, and so many false hopes and consolations, which still obscure the pure word of Jesus."[56] There is but one hope to see this done, and Bonhoeffer trumpets it here: "Let us be led back to scripture, to the word and call of Jesus Christ himself," for the only sure defense against the enemies of the gospel is "the overpowering and winning word of the gospel" itself. Only this same word is able to lift us out of the "poverty and narrowness of our own convictions and questions" and to set our feet down once again in that "broad place" (Psalm 37) opened up by the calling and promise of the living Lord. Once again, Bonhoeffer sees that the Word of God must overtake and overreach the putative demands of our "situation" in order for truth and freedom for faithfulness, that is, for discipleship, to emerge. The crucial discrimination he goes on to draw out between cheap and costly grace is one which can only be discerned in a fresh hearing of the gracious voice of Jesus Christ, or not at all.

In the second short preface set at the head of his discussion of Pauline ecclesiological texts in the final part of *Discipleship,* Bonhoeffer points out once again a cardinal error that underwrites the frantic pursuit of contextual relevance for Christianity. What all anxious questioning about the appropriateness, applicability and force of the gospel bespeak is the fact that "we place ourselves outside the living presence of the Christ"; our handling of Scripture evinces all too clearly that "we refuse to take seriously that Jesus Christ is not dead but alive and still speaking to us today through the testimony of scripture." But Christ *is* present calling his people to discipleship. And just as by the Spirit the first disciples looked to their Master, believed and followed Christ, so too for us: "we hear the word and believe in Christ."[57] Held firmly within context of the reality of Christ's present presence, the Scriptures are understood to

---

[56]For the text of the first preface cited in this paragraph, see ibid., pp. 37-40.
[57]Ibid., p. 202.

bear the "clear word and command" of the Lord himself, and they become *the* means by which we are encountered by him. So heeding the call to discipleship demands that the follower first and foremost "listen" to the proclaimed word because "the Christ who is present with us is the Christ to whom the whole of scripture testifies."[58] Faith together with discipleship comes through hearing, as Paul said, and hearing comes through the word of Christ (Romans 10:17).

In such remarks as these, we hear once again the distinctive echoes of the Barmen Declaration. And these prefaces specify the "*one* Word of God" as the single basis for the gripping account of the Christian life and controversial ecclesiology Bonhoeffer develops in the rest of *Discipleship.* Although the themes of discipleship and church community are often taken to be Bonhoeffer's primary concerns, it is no small thing to keep in view that their importance is in fact derivative, following from a finally more basic concern with the hearing of the one Word of God, the present address of the living Lord Jesus Christ in the church.

A THEOLOGY OF THE WORD OF GOD

What kind of theologian was Dietrich Bonhoeffer? I have endeavored to show that one important answer to this question is a theologian of the Word of God. This category registers his formative indebtedness and living dialogue with the theologies of Martin Luther and Karl Barth, as well as his unstinting allegiance to the radical application of the evangelical confession of the Barmen Declaration within the German church struggle. Materially, it draws attention to the central and abiding role played in Bonhoeffer's theology by the utterly gracious and concrete self-revelation of God in Jesus Christ. As the Word of God incarnate, Jesus Christ represents the very enactment of God's transcendence, not its forfeiture or compromise. In him God addresses himself to the fallen world of Adam with saving effect, bringing about a new reality, namely the one reality of the world reconciled and made new. With Luther, Bonhoeffer radically concentrates Christian attention solely on the person of Jesus Christ because in him God declares himself to be *utterly*

---

[58]Ibid., p. 206.

for us. As he wrote, "what we imagine a God could and should do—the God of Jesus Christ has nothing to do with all that. We must immerse ourselves again and again, for a long time and quite calmly, in Jesus's life, his sayings, actions, suffering, and dying in order to recognize what God promises and fulfils."[59] Christian dogmatics must therefore cleave to the confession that Jesus Christ *is* God and admit that "the *is* may not be interpreted any further" for having been established in the incarnation it must stand as "the premise of all our thinking and not be subject to any further constructions."[60]

The evangelical promise always addresses us from outside through the appointed witness of the Scriptures which stand fully in the service of the risen and crucified One, who is uniquely present in the power of his person as God's word of forgiveness, claim and direction. In the spirit of Dürer's painting of the four apostles, Bonhoeffer's theology pursues relevance by an ever greater concentration on listening for Christ's voice as attested in the manifold biblical witness, and by discerning it over against "the voice of the stranger." As Bonhoeffer himself put it,

> God's Spirit battles only through the Word of Scripture and of confession and only where my insights are overwhelmed by Scripture and confession can I know myself to be overwhelmed by the Spirit of God. . . . At such moments of responsible decision our attention must remain directed solely towards the truth of the Word of God.[61]

To focus on the Word in such an exclusive way, Bonhoeffer contends, does not abstract or distract from reality, but quite the opposite. For what is really going on amidst what is taking place in the world around us wins whatever reality it has only by reference to Christ, who is present as its Lord, conforming it to his gracious will and ways through the humble power of divine love. The work of the present Word is always

---

[59]Bonhoeffer, *Letters and Papers,* DBWE 8:515.
[60]Bonhoeffer, *Berlin,* DBWE 12:350. Bonhoeffer aims to defend the graciousness and provenience of God's contingent self-revelation in Christ by "in effect . . . doubling down on the 'exclusive "Jesus Christ"'-pit of the Lutherans'" as Karl Barth had once characterized it—so DeJonge, *Bonhoeffer's Theological Formation,* p. 105. The cited phrase is from an April 1924 letter from Barth to his friend Eduard Thurneysen.
[61]Bonhoeffer, *No Rusty Swords,* pp. 305-6 (DBW 14:111).

world-making. Theology becomes of worldly use precisely by discerning and keeping pace with this work of the Word in its own thought and speech. As it does this, it need not adopt an apologetic posture, either positive or negative. This last point became increasingly clear to Bonhoeffer in his last years: Christian theology does not need to disparage the world or aggravate the neediness of women and men for the sake of trying to display the relevance of the gospel. As he put it, "the Word of God does not ally itself with this rebellion of mistrust [of humanity]. . . . Instead, it reigns."[62]

The struggle for true Christian community and life is thus fought by renewed devotion to receiving the truth of the gospel from the hand of the living Lord of the church. Ingredient in the witness made by the faithfulness, obedience, message and order of the church will be its supreme confidence in the Word of God which has come on it. In Bonhoeffer's own words,

> In all speaking and acting in the church I am concerned with the primacy, with the sole honour and truth of the Word of God. There is no greater service of love than to put men in the light of the truth of this Word, even where it brings sorrow. The Word of God separates the spirits. There is . . . only the humble and dismayed recognition of the way which God himself will go with his Word in his church.[63]

And the hallmark of a church gathered in faith around the self-presenting Word of God in this way will be its evangelical *freedom*. The liberty of the church from the "godless fetters" of this age is a function of the effective presence of its Lord, and naught else beside. The acuity with which Bonhoeffer perceived, practiced and attested this fact is arresting. Writing in the summer of 1939 Bonhoeffer explained,

> The freedom of the church is not where it has possibilities, but only where the gospel is truly effective in its own power to create space for itself on earth, even and especially when there are no such possibilities for the church. The essential freedom of the church is not a gift of the world to the church but the freedom of the word of God to make itself heard. . . .

---

[62]Bonhoeffer, *Letters and Papers*, DBWE 8:457.
[63]Bonhoeffer, *No Rusty Swords*, pp. 304-5 (DBW 14:110).

Only where this word can be concretely proclaimed in the midst of historical reality as judgment, commandment, gracious salvation of the sinner, and deliverance from all human ordinances is there freedom of the church.[64]

On Bonhoeffer's account, when the Word of God gains such a hearing for itself it does so solely for the sake of the salvation of this world of ours: the church's freedom arises from the Word and as such takes shape in concrete service to the gospel's cause in the world. Writing from prison in the Spring of 1944 Bonhoeffer explained,

What matters is not the beyond of this world, how it is created and preserved, is given laws, reconciled, and renewed. What is beyond this world is meant, in the gospel, to be there for this world—not in the anthropocentric sense of liberal, mystical, pietistic, ethical theology, but in the biblical sense of the creation and the incarnation, crucifixion and resurrection of Jesus Christ.[65]

The point of a theology of the Word of God is that Christian faith is concerned solely with what is given in the gospel, and what is given in the gospel is God for us in Jesus Christ. At the heart of Bonhoeffer's theological legacy is his powerful witness to the identity of the God of Jesus Christ as attested in Scripture, a God who, coming low to us in humility to save, rightly becomes and ever remains our highest concern, the very basis, measure and goal of life itself.[66]

---

[64]Bonhoeffer, *Theological Education Underground*, DBWE 15:448-9.
[65]Bonhoeffer, *Letters and Papers*, DBWE 8:373.
[66]See Eberhard Bethge, "Wer ist Jesus von Nazaret für mich? (1973)" in *Am gegebenen Ort: Aufsätze und Reden* (Münich: Chr. Kaiser Verlag, 1979), p. 289.

2

THE EVANGELICAL RECEPTION
OF DIETRICH BONHOEFFER

TIMOTHY LARSEN

DICK VAN DYKE, IN HIS SHOWBIZ MEMOIR *My Lucky Life,* remarks, in a chapter titled, "Never a Dull Moment," on how much he
enjoyed reading John A. T. Robinson's *Honest to God* (1963).[1] He was so
impressed he wrote the bishop a fan letter and even looked him up
when he was in England to film *Chitty Chitty Bang Bang.* Van Dyke had
a genius for physical comedy which was founded on his astonishing
flexibility, and as the bishop was no less flexible in his own chosen
calling, Robinson and Van Dyke got along famously—even doing a
radio program in which they pontificated on how the church needs to
change in the light of modern thought. We may take Dick Van Dyke's
enthusing over *Honest to God* as illustrative of just how big a splash that
book made. It sold over a million copies and became an inescapable
point of discussion for anyone interested in contemporary Christianity.
It was also a controversial book which set out to decommission traditional Christian beliefs and to commend liberal or radical theological
moves in their stead. Robinson mentions by name C. S. Lewis and
Dorothy Sayers as figures still writing in the old, traditional way that he
thinks is no longer tenable and needs to be replaced.[2] In order to

---

[1]Dick Van Dyke, *My Lucky Life* (New York: Crown Archetype, 2011), p. 162.
[2]John A. T. Robinson, *Honest to God* (London: SCM Press, 1963; 1969 reprint), p. 15.

achieve these ends, Robinson attempted to popularize the thought of three theologians: Paul Tillich, Rudolf Bultmann and Dietrich Bonhoeffer. The bishop of Woolwich proceeded on the assumption that Bultmann's dictum that one cannot both use electricity and believe in miracles was a profound insight rather than a self-flattering non sequitur. Following Tillich, Robinson revealed breathlessly that God is not actually "up there" but rather "the ground of our being" (theologians having hitherto lacked spatial reasoning). Bonhoeffer was drawn on for his musings on "religionless Christianity" in the posthumously published *Letters and Papers from Prison.*

Until then the theology of Dietrich Bonhoeffer had not been widely noticed let alone much discussed in the English-speaking world. At the time of the publication of *Honest to God,* the conventional assumption was that Bonhoeffer was not nearly as important to modern theology as Bultmann or Tillich. Bonhoeffer then quickly became a hero of iconoclastic radicals—most notoriously the attention-grabbing death-of-god theologians. It is not biased to claim that these theologians fundamentally misrepresented and distorted Bonhoeffer when they drafted him for their own secular agenda. One of their own prophets, William Hamilton—professor of systematic theology at Colgate Rochester Divinity School, coauthor of *Radical Theology and the Death of God* (1966), and the generally acknowledged leader of this school of thought—admitted it, "We made creative misuse use of Bonhoeffer!"[3] It is also important to bear in mind that this was a wider cultural atmosphere and concern and not merely an insider scholarly trend by tenure-and-promotion seeking academic theologians. *Time* magazine famously ran a cover on April 8, 1966 which was predominantly pure black set off with a border in imitation of traditional mourning paper and accompanied by the stark question in red, "Is God Dead?" In other words, for most evangelicals the conversation about Bonhoeffer's thought began in 1963 and was therefore from the very beginning completely enmeshed in unorthodox contexts in which he was portrayed as part of the same theological cause and trajectory as Bultmann and as a

---

[3]Martin E. Marty, *Dietrich Bonhoeffer's "Letters and Papers from Prison": A Biography,* Lives of Great Religious Books (Princeton: Princeton University Press, 2011), p. 75.

herald and champion of the triumph of secularism.[4]

Stephen R. Haynes, who has written the most about evangelical reactions to Bonhoeffer, has observed: "Bonhoeffer appeared on the radar of lay evangelicals about 1965."[5] In his book, *The Bonhoeffer Phenomenon*, Haynes begins the story of evangelical reactions with an article in *Christianity Today* in 1966—that is, three years after the sensation of *Honest to God*. That article, however, as well as one that same year in *Moody Monthly*, were both informed by a book that Haynes does not mention. *The Abolition of Religion: A Study in "Religionless Christianity"* was written by the evangelical Leon Morris and published by InterVarsity Press.[6] It refers to *Honest to God* in the very first sentence and, as it appeared in 1964, Morris and InterVarsity Press were quick off the mark indeed. In it Morris argues that Bonhoeffer had both radical and conservative thoughts. Morris's judgment on this diversity in the Bonhoeffer corpus is that they are "contradictory ideas, ideas which I see no way of harmonizing."[7] Nevertheless, Morris emphasizes that it was unfair to lump Bonhoeffer together with either Tillich or Bultmann. Morris approved of *The Cost of Discipleship* and *Ethics* and therefore argued a discontinuity thesis: that is, some of the statements in the *Letters* are new departures that are incompatible with Bonhoeffer's earlier writings. Morris sought to be fair and charitable to Bonhoeffer and to affirm what he is able to affirm, even in the *Letters*. Notably—and particularly in the context of that time I think Morris should get full credit for his perceptiveness and openness—he conceded that evangelicals do need to repent of sometimes adopting a god-of-the-gaps mentality. Nevertheless, as the subtitle of his study suggests, Morris was mainly perplexed and perturbed by the concept of "religionless Christianity." He took it to mean

---

[4]For my definition of evangelicalism, see Timothy Larsen, "Defining and Locating Evangelicalism," in Timothy Larsen and Daniel J. Treier, *The Cambridge Companion to Evangelical Theology* (Cambridge: Cambridge University Press, 2007).

[5]Stephen R. Haynes, "Between Fundamentalism and Secularism: The American Evangelical Love Affair with Dietrich Bonhoeffer," in *Dietrich Bonhoeffer's Theology Today: A Way Between Fundamentalism and Secularism?* John W. de Gruchy, Stephen Plant and Christiane Tietz, eds. (Müchen: Güterslosher Verlagshaus, 2009), p. 219.

[6]Leon Morris, *The Abolition of Religion: A Study in "Religionless Christianity"* (Chicago: InterVarsity Press, 1964).

[7]Morris, *Abolition*, p. 5.

that Bonhoeffer was calling for an abandonment of corporate worship and other explicitly Christian practices such as evangelism. The argument of *The Abolition of Religion* is essentially that Christianity cannot be sustained without these disciplines, however, and therefore religionless Christianity is wrongheaded and dangerous.

The 1966 article in *Christianity Today* had the unpropitious title, "Religionless Christianity: Is It a New Form of Gnosticism?"[8] It opened by identifying "religionless Christianity" as one of "the current theological fads," thus once again situating the conversation in the light of the radical (mis)appropriation of Bonhoeffer. The author, the philosopher Milton D. Hunnex, was even more emphatic than Morris in assuming that religionless Christianity was a program for "the abandonment of the Church, of personal piety, and even of personal salvation" as well as "holy living, evangelism, and substantive Bible beliefs." Hunnex was so committed to retaining the category of "religion" that he even commended Tillich as more conservative than Bonhoeffer because the American theologian assumed human beings are inherently religious. The article in *Moody Monthly* in 1966 was notably more sympathetic and nuanced than the one in *Christianity Today*. It was written by Charles Horne, a professor of theology at Moody Bible Institute, and was given the much less tendentious title, "What Is Bonhoeffer Theology?"[9] (It might help, however, to recall what era of evangelicalism we are exploring here. The other article asking a probing question in the same issue was entitled, "Is 'Beat' Music Eroding Our Youth?") Horne goes out of his way to praise *The Cost of Discipleship* as a book that draws attention to the need for us to have a faithful Christian "walk," as the evangelical dialect called it. His only disclaimer is that there are lots of litmus test issues that Bonhoeffer does not address in *The Cost of Discipleship* and therefore just because we might find every word of it true and right, "We must not be deceived into thinking that he writes as a fundamentalist." (*Fundamentalist,* of course, is being used here as a term of appro-

---

[8]Milton D. Hunnex, "Religionless Christianity: Is It a New Form of Gnosticism?" *Christianity Today,* January 7, 1966, pp. 7-9. I am grateful to my former research assistant, Eric T. Brandt, for his help in securing sources for this article.
[9]Charles Horne, "What Is Bonhoeffer Theology?" *Moody Monthly,* May 1966, pp. 40-42.

bation—in other words, according to Horne, we must not imagine that the early Bonhoeffer who wrote this admirable book would have agreed with conservative evangelicals on all theological or ecclesiastical questions.) Horne even conceded that the perplexing phrase from the *Letters* could be used in a fitting way because "religion" can be defined pejoratively: "When the term religion is used to denote a mere outward profession rather than a genuine Christianity, we would gladly plead for this kind of 'religionless Christianity.'" Horne then quotes Isaiah 1:11-13 as a biblical example of this kind of a critique of religiosity. Nevertheless, he rather astutely reflects that the movement that has latched onto Bonhoeffer's phrase might actually be establishing a "non-religious religion." (I think evangelicals ought to know whereof Horne speaks as our movement has had a tendency to produce non-denominational denominations.) Horne concluded by asserting that true religion is a category that cannot be dispensed with by Christians, echoing James 1:27 (KJV: "Pure religion and undefiled before God and the Father is this") as a parting proof-text shot.

A 1967 article in *Christianity Today* was entitled, "The Old 'New Worldliness.'"[10] It was written by Harold B. Kuhn of Asbury Seminary. Kuhn opens by grumbling that the only kind of theology that now sells is trendy, radical theology. He references Harvey Cox's *The Secular City* (which, like *Honest to God*, was also a bestseller) and, once again, it is clear that this unnerving contemporary movement is the primary concern rather than the actual thoughts of the historic Bonhoeffer. Nevertheless, Lutherans have always been much better at gleaning insight through paradox than low-church evangelicals, and if evangelicalism as a whole in the 1960s was not ready to view "religion" as a bad thing, it was certainly not ready for Bonhoeffer's attempts in the *Letters* to redeem "worldliness" as a concept to be embraced and affirmed by Christians. The question about a Christian's "walk," after all, was largely about whether or not he or she was being tempted into "worldly" patterns of thought and behavior. Kuhn therefore assumed that affirming worldliness was tantamount to tolerating immorality. There could be no

---

[10]Harold B. Kuhn, "The Old 'New Worldliness,'" *Christianity Today*, December 8, 1967, p. 56.

clearer indication that traditional evangelical concerns with lifestyle issues were trumping any attempt to read Bonhoeffer on his own terms than when Kuhn even went so far as to mention Hugh Hefner as an ostensibly germane case in point. For 1960s American evangelicals, the notion of "worldliness" could not conjure up, as it did for Bonhoeffer, "the profound this-worldliness, characterized by discipline and the constant knowledge of death and resurrection,"[11] but rather simply images of drunken businessmen leering at playboy bunnies.

The most negative early response to Bonhoeffer's thought that I have found by an evangelical is a review essay by Cornelius Van Til which was published in the *Westminster Theological Review* in 1972. As Van Til fought bravely and sacrificially in the fundamentalist-modernist conflict of the 1920s and '30s, one may therefore charitably surmise that this maniacal and deranged attack on Bonhoeffer was a manifestation of posttraumatic stress disorder. The decidedly pro-Bonhoeffer wave was already rising within evangelicalism, however, and thus a part of Van Til's rage was prompted by very positive comments about Bonhoeffer's theology that had been made in *The Banner,* an official publication of the solidly theologically conservative Christian Reformed Church.[12] On the discontinuity question, Van Til argued for continuity in the Bonhoeffer corpus, with the twist that it was unorthodox rather than orthodox from beginning to end. There are philosophical underpinnings, Van Til averred, which make Bonhoeffer's Christology "not the Christ of the Scriptures" even though this is not apparent on the surface of his writings.[13] Van Til saw a polarization between the forces of good and evil, with Kant as the father of the evil faction and Bonhoeffer as one of his heirs in this unfaithful lineage. Attempts to see part of Bonhoeffer's thought as having affinities with orthodoxy are not only misleading, they are deadly: there are superficial similarities, Van Til analogized, between

---

[11]See the letter to Eberhard Bethge, July 21, 1944, in Dietrich Bonhoeffer, *Letters and Papers from Prison* (New York: Touchstone, 1997), p. 369.

[12]Cornelius Van Til, "Dietrich Bonhoeffer: A Review Article," *Westminster Theological Journal* 34, no. 2 (May 1972): 152-73.

[13]In his own hostile way, Van Til was participating in a wider trend: "During the 1970s the dominant concern centred around Bonhoeffer's philosophical roots." John W. de Gruchy, "The Reception of Bonhoeffer's Theology," in *The Cambridge Companion to Dietrich Bonhoeffer,* ed. John W. de Gruchy (Cambridge: Cambridge University Press, 1999), p. 99.

north Vietnamese and south Vietnamese soldiers, but this should not be allowed to obfuscate the fact that one is your ally and the other your sworn enemy. Bonhoeffer's thought is on the side of the enemies of Christ: "It is the battle of Armageddon that is now being waged between them, and every man is involved in it." I have seen a fair number of feisty conference sessions in my day and as scholarly critiques go, I take saying that a theologian is on the wrong side in the battle of Armageddon as fairly thorough-going.

Van Til's position of rejecting Bonhoeffer's theology *in toto* as pernicious is championed today by Richard Weikart, a historian at California State University. In 1997 he published a rather obscure book by a thoroughly obscure press, *The Myth of Dietrich Bonhoeffer: Is His Theology Evangelical?*[14] Weikart tells a kind of personal deconversion narrative from the pro-Bonhoeffer camp. As a young evangelical, he had been blessed by reading *The Cost of Discipleship* and *Life Together* and therefore was naively in favor of Bonhoeffer's theology. He was then shocked when he read *Letters and Papers from Prison*. Weikart resolved this dissonance by constructing his own continuity thesis which is very similar to, if not identical with, Van Til's (whom he curiously does not cite). Bonhoeffer's thought, Weikart asserts, is based in philosophical assumptions which are incompatible with orthodox Christianity and thus even the early works are unsound. Evangelicals do not notice how dangerous these books are because their Bible reading habits have accustomed them to taking texts literally. Bonhoeffer, however, uses orthodox words and phrases but does not mean orthodox things by them. Weikart explicitly claims that it is not safe to allow believers to read even *Life Together* or *The Cost of Discipleship*. Weikart has since continued to advance this position, including in a 2011 article in *Trinity Journal,* "So Many Different Dietrich Bonhoeffers," which is partially an attempt to expose Eric Metaxas's biography as presenting a portrait of Bonhoeffer that is too evangelical-friendly. In this recent article, Weikart again warns that a seemingly pious veneer covers a rotten foundation: "Neither Bonhoeffer nor most German theologians be-

---

[14]Richard Weikart, *The Myth of Dietrich Bonhoeffer: Is His Theology Evangelical?* (San Francisco: International Scholars Publications, 1997).

lieved in such things as propositional truths, timeless or universal morality, and absolutes."[15] Weikart, of course, is decidedly untypical as the evangelical movement today is overwhelmingly marked by euphoric Bonhoeffer-mania.

Stephen R. Haynes has rightly identified what he calls "the American evangelical love affair with Dietrich Bonhoeffer."[16] Haynes first documents the trend of Bonhoeffer's "growing popularity among tens of millions of American evangelicals for whom he has become a hero, theological guide, or privileged critic."[17] Extolling Bonhoeffer now consistently happens across a remarkably wide spectrum of the evangelical movement. Emergents do it. Leaders of the Christian Right do it. Even Southern Baptists do it. From a variety of surveys and clues, it is clear that for evangelicals today Dietrich Bonhoeffer is the most widely cited and respected twentieth-century theologian. When in the year 2000 *Christianity Today* announced the "books of the century" for the hundred years that had just passed, it listed C. S. Lewis's *Mere Christianity* as number one and Bonhoeffer's *The Cost of Discipleship* as number two.[18] After the top ten, books were listed in alphabetical order by author rather than ranked for importance, and Bonhoeffer's *Letters and Papers from Prison* was in that wider list. By contrast, a range of leading evangelical theologians did not make it unto this list of one hundred "classics that have shaped contemporary religious thought" including Bernard Ramm, Donald Bloesch, Clark Pinnock, Thomas Oden and Millard Erickson. Perhaps it would not be too mischievous to notice that another person who did not make the list was Cornelius Van Til. As for popular authors, even Francis Schaeffer was not included.

Moreover, the twentieth century restriction is actually too limiting. It seems clear that for evangelicals today Dietrich Bonhoeffer is the most widely cited and respected theologian of the last four hundred years or

---

[15]Richard Weikart, "So Many Different Dietrich Bonhoeffers," *Trinity Journal* 32 (2011): 81.

[16]Haynes, "Between Fundamentalism and Secularism." I found some of these sources independently and will carry the story forward, especially in regard to the Eric Metaxas biography, and even backward further than Haynes, but still I must acknowledge that I am grateful for and to a certain extent dependent on Haynes's work.

[17]Haynes, "Between Fundamentalism and Secularism," p. 201.

[18]"Books of the Century," *Christianity Today*, April 24, 2000, www.christianitytoday.com /ct/2000/april24/5.92.html.

more since the era of the Protestant Reformers. Evangelicals are apt to include *The Cost of Discipleship* (and perhaps *Life Together* as well) in their canon of the greatest Christian spiritual classics of all time, so that they happily rub shoulders with fellow hall-of-fame legends from across the ages in short lists which also include works such as Augustine's *Confessions* and Bunyan's *Pilgrim's Progress*. A recent publication is entitled *25 Books Every Christian Should Read: A Guide to the Essential Spiritual Classics*. The books on the list were chosen by a dozen-strong editorial board that included such leading evangelical figures as Dallas Willard, Richard J. Foster and the editor of *Books & Culture*, John Wilson. The roughly chronological list begins with Athanasius' *On the Incarnation* and progresses through authors such as Augustine, Dante, Calvin, Pascal and Bunyan before reaching *The Cost of Discipleship*.[19] It is suggestive that when Wheaton College launched a One College, One Book program, the first title it invited its entire community to attend to for a year was *Life Together*, because Bonhoeffer was a safe choice for creating unified support and approval around a single text across this evangelical community.

Beyond an institution of higher education, Bonhoeffer also finds his way into even the most popular of evangelical formats. For example, in 1997 Focus on the Family Radio Theatre made a compelling, award-winning drama of his life called *The Cost of Freedom*. A possible contemporary application of this inspiring story was made by the president of Focus on the Family himself, James Dobson, in a 1999 article in *Christianity Today* titled, "The New Cost of Discipleship."[20] Dobson admonished evangelicals who had become weary in the culture wars that they had to stick to their posts even when fighting a losing battle: "Since when did being outnumbered and underpowered justify silence in response to evil? Dietrich Bonhoeffer, a Lutheran pastor and theologian, stood against the Nazi regime and its oppression of the Jews, for which he paid with his life."[21] Another example is Bethany House's popular Men of Faith series. These books are specifically designed for home-

---

[19]Renovaré, *25 Books Every Christian Should Read: A Guide to the Essential Spiritual Classics*, ed. Julia L. Roller (New York: HarperOne, 2011).
[20]James Dobson, "The New Cost of Discipleship," *Christianity Today*, September 6, 1999, pp. 56-58.
[21]Dobson, "New Cost," p. 57.

schoolers and are marketed as stories which "provide an inspiring example of a man dedicated to living fully for God." Besides volumes on Martin Luther and John Calvin, every title in the over forty books in this series so far is on a figure from the eighteenth century to the present and, with two exceptions, they are all clearly evangelicals. The two exceptions are C. S. Lewis and Dietrich Bonhoeffer. Other figures in the series include Jim Elliot, George Müller, D. L. Moody, Charles Spurgeon, Charles Finney, Oswald Chambers, Billy Graham and Charles Colson. There is even a volume titled *Francis and Edith Schaeffer,* with Edith apparently being given honorary status as a man for the purpose of inclusion in the "Men of Faith" pantheon.[22] To take one more example, in his autobiography *Just As I Am*, Billy Graham identified Martin Luther and Dietrich Bonhoeffer as the two "great heroes" of church history from Germany.[23]

Another sign of the times is a recent *New York Times* bestselling book, Eric Metaxas's *Bonhoeffer: Pastor, Martyr, Prophet, Spy* (2010). Metaxas is himself an evangelical. His previous *New York Times* bestselling biography was of the eminent evangelical opponent of the slave trade, William Wilberforce, and Metaxas judged rightly that Bonhoeffer is a hero for evangelicals at the same rarefied height as Wilberforce. Metaxas's *Bonhoeffer* has a foreword by evangelical pastor Timothy J. Keller, which serves as another way of signaling that this is a story written by an evangelical for evangelicals.

This conservative Protestant passion for Bonhoeffer has started to rattle mainline and liberal Christians who have begun to complain that the German theologian has been distorted, misrepresented and co-opted by evangelicals. Haynes's article trying to explain this phenomenon was in an edited collection published in 2009, titled *Dietrich Bonhoeffer's Theology Today: A Way Between Fundamentalism and Secularism?* You can hear the structure of the concern in that title: while admittedly the secularist death-of-god theologians initially twisted Bonhoeffer's thought into serving their own cause, the more recent

---

[22]I looked at a complete list of the titles printed so far in this series through a WorldCat series search. The language describing the scope and goal of the series came from the page on the series on the publisher's website: www.bethanyhouse.com. The Bonhoeffer book is by Susan Martins Miller, *Dietrich Bonhoeffer* (Minneapolis: Bethany House, 2002).
[23]Billy Graham, *Just As I Am* (New York: HarperOne, 2007), p. 515.

danger of such behavior is from the conservative end of the spectrum, and the task today must be to find a way to get Bonhoeffer back where he belongs in the mainline middle. Even more recently, preeminent mainline church historian Martin E. Marty has written a book on the reception of *Letters and Papers from Prison* which has as its implicit structure this same argument. In other words, Marty has secularists and evangelicals as foils on opposite ends, while mainliners are presented as the faithful interpreters and true proprietors of the Bonhoeffer legacy:

> Questions like this have drawn the energies of the people I think of as my own generation, some would say "mainstream Protestants and Catholics" who have not been sidetracked and now abandoned with the Marxist or "honest to God" or "death of God" interpreters *or* taken the path of re-action against them all in new fundamentalisms.[24]

A desire to rescue Bonhoeffer from his Walmart-shopping, weak-coffee-drinking, praise-chorus-singing admirers has been particularly on display in reactions to Metaxas's biography. A particularly mean-spirited and full-blooded example of this was the review of Metaxas's book by Clifford Green, professor emeritus of theology at Hartford Seminary, in *Christian Century,* the leading journal of mainline Protestant thought in America. Here is how it ends: "Given all this, the most descriptive and honest title for Metaxas's book would perhaps be *Bonhoeffer Co-opted.* Or better: *Bonhoeffer Hijacked.*"[25] This review was posted online with an opportunity for adding comments, and these remarks are heavily populated by readers who were grateful that someone had the courage to snatch their hero out of the grubby hands of the evangelicals. One curious theme was that it was inappropriate to have Tim Keller write the foreword, ostensibly because he is a pastor and not a Bonhoeffer scholar. One cannot imagine such concerns being raised if the foreword had been written, for example, by Desmond Tutu.

And so we move to evaluating this critique. I myself have written a review of Metaxas's book in which I also document ways that, around

[24]Marty, *Letters,* p. 241.
[25]Clifford Green, "Hijacking Bonhoeffer," *Christian Century,* October 5, 2010, www.christian century.org/reviews/2010-09/hijacking-bonhoeffer.

the edges, I think that he has skewed things in an evangelical direction.
Here is a portion of that review:

> More subtly, an American evangelical obsession with evolution leaps out at
> odd places. Metaxas describes the portrayal of the theology of *Letters and
> Papers from Prison* by radicals as "a theological Piltdown man." He describes
> Nazi racist ideology as a new form of "Darwinism" (not even "Social Dar-
> winism"). Most regrettably and bizarrely, he analogizes that Harnack was to
> Barth as "strict Darwinian evolutionists" are to advocates of Intelligent
> Design. Methinks that another part of Metaxas's brain that has nothing to
> do with Bonhoeffer is trying to work out its relationship to evolution.[26]

Moreover, Green did find an interview in which Metaxas referred to
Bonhoeffer as an evangelical.

Nevertheless, my own view is that the charge that evangelicals have
co-opted Bonhoeffer is, by and large, inaccurate and unfair. It is not
standard for evangelicals to claim that Bonhoeffer was himself an evangelical (and it is significant that even Metaxas does not do so in his well-
nigh six-hundred-page biography). It is true that evangelicals have emphasized certain parts of the Bonhoeffer story and corpus, but every
group interested in the German theologian does this. Moreover, these
parts had often been downplayed or neglected hitherto and they are
authentic pieces of the Bonhoeffer puzzle. For example, leaders of the
Christian Right citing Bonhoeffer approvingly seems particularly to get
up the noses of mainliners. Nevertheless, it is a deployment but not a
distortion for the pro-life movement to evoke Dietrich Bonhoeffer. After
all, he did declare in *Ethics*: "Destruction of the embryo in the mother's
womb is a violation of the right to live which God has bestowed upon
this nascent life. . . . And that is nothing but murder."[27] Mainline Christians were thrilled with the way that Bonhoeffer's thought was utilized
in the anti-apartheid movement in South Africa and it is not at all clear
how one could justify this while simultaneously condemning the pro-
life use of Bonhoeffer as inappropriate.[28]

---

[26]Timothy Larsen, review of *Bonhoeffer* by Eric Metaxas, *Fides et Historia* 43, no. 2 (2011): 138-41.
[27]Dietrich Bonhoeffer, *Ethics,* ed. Eberhard Bethge (London: SCM Press, 1955), pp. 130-31.
[28]An example of this appropriation is John W. de Gruchy, *Bonhoeffer and South Africa: Theology in Dialogue* (Grand Rapids: Eerdmans, 1984).

Mainliners are also annoyed by the suggestion that Bonhoeffer had a conversion experience in 1931. Haynes writes, "Ironically, Eberhard Bethge supplies impetus for an evangelical reading of this experience by describing it under the heading 'the theologian becomes a Christian.'"[29] This is just plain odd. Bonhoeffer himself had described his state before this experience which changed "everything" for him by saying, "I had not yet become a Christian."[30] Bethge's heading is a descriptive one which, far from editorializing, merely uses Bonhoeffer's own language. If others are not comfortable with it, their discomfort is not with Bonhoeffer's interpreters but rather with his own testimony in his own words. It is of course also true that evangelicals have their own parts of Bonhoeffer's life and thought that they tend to downplay or ignore, but once again this is true for all groups interested in the German theologian. (To give just one, rather mischievous example, Bonhoeffer's suggestion in the *Letters* that one response to our secular age should be that ministers no longer receive a salary certainly did not inspire John A. T. Robinson to forfeit his income as a bishop.) Evangelicals have been able to provide valuable correctives that present a more accurate picture of a complex man and theological legacy. Rather than thinking in terms of co-opting, I would argue that the evangelical attitude toward Dietrich Bonhoeffer is analogous to the evangelical attitude toward Augustine of Hippo. Evangelicals like and admire Augustine's life, thought and writings, but they do not pretend that he was an evangelical in the contemporary American sense of that term. They are aware that they disagree with Augustine on some issues of doctrine and practice, but they tend to focus on what they admire.

One way this analogy breaks down, of course, is that it would be anachronistic to think of Augustine as an evangelical, while the evangelical movement in the contemporary American sense did exist in Bonhoeffer's day. So why then do evangelicals so admire Bonhoeffer? One clue is that evangelicals are fond of describing him as a "pastor." *Pastor,* after all, is the first descriptor in Metaxas's subtitle. (It is also the

---

[29]Stephen R. Haynes, *The Bonhoeffer Phenomenon: Portraits of a Protestant Saint* (Minneapolis: Fortress, 2004) p. 79.

[30]Eberhard Bethge, *Dietrich Bonhoeffer: A Biography*, trans. Victoria Barnett, rev. ed. (Minneapolis: Fortress, 2000), pp. 202-5.

first noun James Dobson used to identify Bonhoeffer in his article, "The New Cost of Discipleship.") Likewise when Billy Graham did a whole section on the theme of the cost of discipleship in his book *Hope for the Troubled Heart,* he introduced Bonhoeffer as "a brilliant young German pastor."[31] A sympathetic article in *Christianity Today* in 1969 entitled "Bonhoeffer the Man" was already emphasizing this point: "His theology is not purely academic; he accepted the challenge of the pastorate, wherein he related the insights of the scholar to the needs of the common man."[32] In other words, evangelicals tend to have less respect for the kind of professorial theologian who sends out theories with little awareness of or concern for what their effect might be on the church and the faithful, while they respect someone who rolls up their sleeves and puts their hands to the plough in the work of ministry. Even the fact that Bonhoeffer chose to teach Sunday school to inner-city youths is a significant and telling biographical detail for evangelicals.

Another clue is the second descriptor in Metaxas's subtitle: *martyr.* In the past, evangelicals often tended somewhat unconsciously to identify the separation of the sheep and the goats as evangelicals versus non-evangelicals but even in those days this could sometimes be re-aligned more ecumenically so that the two categories are real Christians versus merely nominal, formal or cultural Christians. Fifty years ago evangelicals were all too quick to assume that the adherents of huge branches of Christianity—not least Roman Catholicism and Eastern Orthodoxy—were in the latter category. A willingness to risk life and livelihood and to endure persecution for the cause of Christ, however, has often allowed evangelicals to discern an authentic Christian faith in members of these communions. The costly, faithful actions of Catholic and Orthodox priests, religious and lay people in communist countries, for example, often prompted American evangelicals to see them not only as authentic Christians but even as heroes of the faith and inspiring martyrs. In the 1970s and beyond, for example, American evangelicals frequently spoke glowingly of the Russian Orthodox layman Aleksandr Solzhenitsyn as a noble, heroic

---

[31]Billy Graham, *Hope for the Troubled Heart* (Dallas: Word, 1991), p. 40.
[32]J. Murray Marshall, "Bonhoeffer the Man," *Christianity Today,* October 10, 1969, pp. 28-29.

Christian and a true spokesman for the cause of Christ even though they did not imagine he was an evangelical. Bonhoeffer is a similar case in point. The fact that he was a German Lutheran working in mainline institutional and ecumenical contexts who spoke well of Adolf von Harnack is overcome by the greater fact that his life bore witness to his living faith. Even Bonhoeffer's most thoroughgoing evangelical opponents have been cowed by his personal willingness to endure the cost of discipleship. No less a critic than Cornelius Van Til conceded that Bonhoeffer's brave actions in the church struggle meant that he "could not help comparing him" to his fundamentalist hero, J. Gresham Machen.[33] Leon Morris humbly acknowledged: "In common I am sure with many others, I have felt the tepidity of my faith rebuked as I have read his burning letters from prison, and have caught revealing glimpses of a man who stood firm and was faithful even unto death. One who lives in easy circumstances has no business to complain about the martyrs."[34] Van Til and Morris, of course, still felt the need to sound the alarm that Bonhoeffer's theology was dangerous, but evangelicals increasingly came to believe that the life informs the writings and therefore they have had a growing predisposition to read them in an orthodox way if two opposing interpretations both seem reasonably possible.

The situation has changed significantly since the context in which Morris and Van Til wrote. Most obviously death-of-god theology is now itself dead and so worries about getting sucked into a radical, unorthodox, contemporary movement no longer loom large. More specifically, between the 1960s and the present evangelicals themselves have turned the word *religion* into a pejorative term. It has become an almost ubiquitous evangelical slogan to say that Christianity is relationship not a religion. To take a random example, my nephew who attends a public, secular university in Britain was recently telling me about the evangelical student group on campus. They were organized into outreach small groups something along the lines of the Alpha model. These groups have as their theme, "Jesus without religion." Indeed, *Jesus Without Religion* is the title of a 2007 book published by

---

[33]Van Til, "Bonhoeffer," p. 152.
[34]Morris, *Abolition*, p. 89.

InterVarsity, revealing that forty years on from that press's *The Abolition of Religion* the connotations of that term have changed, as it were, radically, for evangelicals.[35] Jefferson Bethke, an evangelist from Mark Driscoll's Mars Hill Church in Seattle, has created a YouTube video entitled, "Why I Hate Religion, but Love Jesus," which received 21.1 million views in its first four months—a sure sign that evangelicals have well and truly wrested trendiness and popularity back from the death-of-god theologians. These examples, of course, might be a long way from what Bonhoeffer himself meant by "religionless Christianity," but the point is that evangelicals are now positively attracted by, rather than allergic to, that formulation—and they certainly no longer assume that James 1:27 means that they need to defend rather than decry the category of religion. From 1990 through 2002, I assigned *Letters and Papers from Prison* every year to classes of students at evangelical institutions of higher education, first in Britain then in Canada, and I did not find that they were repulsed by Bonhoeffer's comments about religionless Christianity. Proving their true evangelical credentials, however, I never ceased to be amazed at how often students were shaken to discover in the letters that the great Christian Dietrich Bonhoeffer was a smoker. (I wish I had a hundred dollars for every anti-smoking rant I have read in a Bonhoeffer paper!) Moreover, even the early commentators who assumed that religionless Christianity meant the end of Christian practices were aware that Bonhoeffer had also spoken about maintaining spiritual disciplines in secret, *disciplina arcani,* and that the letters themselves as well as the testimony of others bore witness that Bonheoffer continued to pray, read his Bible, sing hymns, lead worship and otherwise provide explicitly spiritual ministry to his fellow prisoners even while he was advocating religionless Christianity.[36] This was therefore seen as an inconsistency by figures such as Morris, but increasingly evangelicals decided that the latter statements and practices meant that it was a misreading of

---

[35]Rick James, *Jesus Without Religion* (Downers Grove, Ill.: InterVarsity Press, 2007).

[36]For a source at around the start of the turning of the tide of evangelical reactions that particularly emphasizes this point, see Vernon C. Grounds, "Pacesetters for the Radical Theologians of the Sixties and Seventies," in *Tensions in Contemporary Theology,* ed. Stanley N. Gundry and Alan F. Johnson (Chicago: Moody Press, 1979), pp. 74-75.

religionless Christianity to see it as a call for the abandonment of spiritual disciplines.

Not least in the reasons why the reception of Bonhoeffer by evangelicals has become so positive is the simple fact that evangelicals have always appreciated *The Cost of Discipleship*. If *worldliness* was a word that had wide currency in the evangelical subculture as pejorative, conversely evangelicals had maintained the language of *discipleship* even though it had dropped out of fashion in many other Christian circles. From its founding to the present, the evangelical movement has always been concerned about the problem of nominal Christianity, and *The Cost of Discipleship* was a forthright, biblical attack on that woeful spiritual state. Neither *Life Together* nor *The Cost of Discipleship* have the technical, inaccessible, stodgy and pretentious feel of many writings by modern, academic theologians, but rather are devotional, edifying and focused on Christian living rather than theorizing. That is to say, the genre of these writings is one that evangelicals particularly value.

Having attempted to explain the widespread evangelical enthusiasm for Bonhoeffer today, I would like to return now to his early reception by evangelicals in order to introduce a couple additional sources that I think are suggestive. The first is a sympathetic and perceptive article titled, "Dietrich Bonhoeffer: The Man and His Beliefs," which was written by Klaas Runia, principal of Reformed Theological College in Australia, and published in *Eternity* magazine in 1965.[37] Runia commends some of Bonhoeffer's writings, especially *The Cost of Discipleship* but also *Ethics* as "real gems" that "make for very profitable reading." He goes on to explore *Letters and Papers from Prison,* providing an astute synopsis of the main theological themes that are presented therein. He then thoughtfully evaluates this material—without either accepting or rejecting the controversial strains *in toto*. Runia argues that Bonhoeffer is on to something in his negative stance toward religion, going so far as to muse: "It is striking, indeed, how little the New Testament speaks in 'religious' terms." On the other hand, he avers that Bonhoeffer's determination to greet the world come of age with joyful enthusiasm, while partially correct, was unbal-

---

[37]Klaas Runia, "Dietrich Bonhoeffer: The Man and His Beliefs," *Eternity*, December 1965, pp. 11-13, 29-30.

anced: "He leaves no room whatever for the *tragic* aspects in this process of secularization." Runia goes on to document Bonhoeffer's ongoing spiritual practices to demonstrate that he did not mean by religionless Christianity an abandonment of a life of prayer and devotion. This 1965 article, even in such a popular venue as *Eternity* magazine, reveals a thoughtful evangelicalism that had not been thrown off balance by liberal and radical appropriations of Bonhoeffer.

My real hope as I waded into researching this project, however, was not to have to start the story of the evangelical reception of Bonhoeffer in 1965 as Stephen R. Haynes has done, but rather to find an early evangelical voice prior to, and therefore unclouded by, *Honest to God* and its aftermath. This quest was fulfilled when I hit upon a book which Haynes had not found—nor had Marty or anyone else discussing the evangelical reception of Bonhoeffer. *Brothers of the Faith* was published by Abingdon Press in 1960.[38] The author was the evangelical Anglican missionary to India and then bishop, Stephen C. Neill. In *Brothers of the Faith,* Neill dedicated an entire chapter to "Dietrich Bonhoeffer and Worldly Christianity." Here he provided a very evangelical-friendly reading of Bonhoeffer's life and thought—and one that focused on *Letters and Papers from Prison.* If this was co-opting it was done naively without any sense that this is a contested legacy over which one needs to fight. In complete contrast to the hopes of Bishop Robinson and the fears of figures such as Richard Weikart which would all come later, Neill viewed Bonhoeffer as a man of absolute principles who therefore provides the antidote for the contemporary climate of relativism. The Confessing Church is presented as almost a kind of protest against liberal or radical attempts to update Christian thought as their agenda is described as standing fast "by the great Confessions of Faith of the period of the Reformation."[39] Bonhoeffer was a man of principle because of a deep, living faith: "What was the secret of his power? . . . A reality of inward life, which is often lacking in the professed and professional servants of the church."[40]

Far from being embarrassed or perplexed by the controversial pas-

---

[38]Stephen C. Neill, *Brothers of the Faith* (Nashville: Abingdon, 1960).
[39]Ibid., p. 123.
[40]Ibid., p. 126.

sages in the *Letters*—let alone alarmed by them—Neill quotes them with relish. His reading of them was that in getting to know working-class people in prison, Bonhoeffer the academic had become inflamed with an evangelistic concern that there was an "appalling distance that separates the churches and their members from the way in which ordinary men think and live their lives and make their decisions."[41] The theology of the *Letters* was a call to replace "a pale and unproductive pietism" with a form of Christianity that was robust enough to meet the real needs of real people.[42] Again, if that sounds like a misreading, it was an innocent one. Neill did not need to make a chapter of his book about Bonhoeffer, nor did he need to focus on the *Letters* when writing about Bonhoeffer, nor did he need to help people who had already been disturbed by Bonhoeffer's thought in the hands of liberals and radicals to learn to assess it aright. This chapter was simply there because of Neill's own exuberance for Bonhoeffer and his ideas, including his late, startling ones. As a general comment which can be applied to Neill's defense, it should also be observed that as Bonhoeffer was being a provocateur playing with paradoxes in these sayings and reflections in the *Letters,* it is not easy for anyone to interpret them without either domesticating them or taking them too literally. Moreover, Neill had a prescient sense that Bonhoeffer would emerge from his status as a minor theologian into a major voice in contemporary theology: "Perhaps like Søren Kierkegaard he will come into his own only long after his death."[43] After a turbulent period in the 1960s and '70s, Neill's prophecy has proved exceedingly, abundantly true for the evangelical community.

---

[41]Ibid., p. 128.
[42]Ibid.
[43]Ibid., p. 120.

3

DIETRICH BONHOEFFER, THE HARLEM RENAISSANCE AND THE BLACK CHRIST

REGGIE L. WILLIAMS

SPRING 1931 WAS THE SECOND SEMESTER of Dietrich Bonhoeffer's Sloane Fellowship. That spring, he took a course with Dr. Reinhold Niebuhr called Ethical Viewpoints in Modern Literature.[1] In his end-of-the-year summary to the Church Federation Office in Germany, he described the course in the following way: "In a lecture course by Dr. Niebuhr, the social and Christian problem was discussed in the context of modern American literature. That was extremely informative. I learned much from my own experiences in Harlem."[2] That class was one in a collection of classes he took that spring, in a course schedule that reflected an interest in a different engagement with theology than he had in the fall. His altered course schedule was not the only change between the semesters. In the fall, he didn't have much positive to say about his academic experience at all. For example, in December of his fall semester, he wrote these words to his church superintendent about his experience in America thus far:

> There is no theology here. Although I am basically taking classes and

---

[1]Dietrich Bonhoeffer, *Barcelona, Berlin, New York: 1928-1931*, DBWE 10:318, 420.
[2]Ibid., p. 318.

lectures in dogmatics and philosophy of religion, the impression is overwhelmingly negative. They talk a blue streak without the slightest substantive foundation and with no evidence of any criteria. The students—
on the average twenty-five to thirty years old—are completely clueless.[3]

But his description of his second semester courses was very different.
The difference indicated a noticeable interest in the social performance
of theology and in Christian ethics. It is a difference that I will argue was
influenced in part by the experiences he was having in Harlem.

Bonhoeffer's description of Niebuhr's class, along with the other positive language he used to describe classes that semester with Ward and
Webber, may tell us something about the personal significance of this
time in New York for his Christian development. What was this learning
that he was referring to in Harlem? We can answer that question by
paying attention to what was going on in Harlem at the time of his
Sloane Fellowship. Bonhoeffer was a Sloane fellow studying at Union
Seminary during the Harlem Renaissance. This meant that his accounts
of his involvement in African American life in 1930-1931 were occurring
in this critical moment in African American history. Bonhoeffer experienced this influential moment in the same year that he turned twenty-
four, while he was still young and impressionable.

In New York, the Harlem Renaissance consisted of the formation of a
"new negro" with regard to perspectives on politics and the economy
along with the creation of a culture that was to be a public declaration of
an authentic black self-perception. It involved the migration of thousands of African Americans from rural spaces like southern farm fields
or the Caribbean to urban and metropolitan areas. Harlem was the destination of choice. Consequently, the time period can also be understood as the urbanization of black life, when old pejorative perceptions
of black people were exchanged for the sophisticated, educated and cultured urban black. Additionally, this self-perception worked to animate
a seedling of a theology of civil disobedience. It was an interim moment
with a nascent social theology—post–Civil War, pre–Civil Rights—that
expressed the already-present black definition of Christ the suffering

---

[3]Ibid., p. 265.

servant for the reclaiming of African American humanity and self-worth. Yet, during the Harlem Renaissance, this theology also included a theologically informed engagement with social expectations by reclaiming Christ in the face of human suffering. As a movement, the Harlem Renaissance is generally understood to have involved at least two stages, beginning around the time of the First World War and lasting well into the global great depression that was ravishing Harlem during Bonhoeffer's fellowship year.

Bonhoeffer's practice of an incarnational ethic, with his notion of Christ as *Stellvertreter,*[4] had been a working part of his theology since his first dissertation, and it equipped him to enter into the evolving Harlem world as an engaged learner—and even a participant—through his relationship with his African American friend Frank Fisher. His theological practice of incarnational ethics equipped him for that encounter by helping him see the concrete needs for justice as they were perceived by the people within the communities gathered in Harlem during his time there. That incarnational practice thickened his interpretation of the way of Jesus and also equipped him for the prophetic stance that he took in the Confessing Church. His desire for a pastorate in poor communities prior to the church struggle;[5] his unique position early on as perhaps the only German theologian to argue that the Jewish question was *the* problem for Christians in Germany,[6] indeed a *status confessionis* for the church;[7] his insistence on the importance of solidarity with those in suffering;[8] and his claim in his 1933 Christology lectures that proletariat Christians separate Christ from the constructs

---

[4]*Stellvertretung* is usually translated "representing" or "vicariously representing," but this does not adequately portray the incarnational emphasis of Bonhoeffer's theology. One can "represent" another from a distance, and Bonhoeffer often uses the term *eintreten,* "entering in" or "stepping in," to portray God's entering into the midst of our lives in Christ. This incarnational "entering in" to human life captures the meaning of the term. See the translator's note in Christine Schliesser, *Guilt by Doing Right? Responsible Conduct According to Dietrich Bonhoeffer,* trans. David Stassen (Louisville: Westminster John Knox Press, forthcoming).

[5]Dietrich Bonhoeffer, *Berlin: 1932-1933,* DBWE 12:22.

[6]Eberhard Bethge, *Dietrich Bonhoeffer: A Biography,* trans. Victoria Barnett, rev. ed. (Minneapolis: Fortress, 2000), pp. 325-26.

[7]Bonhoeffer, *Berlin,* DBWE 12:371.

[8]This is representative of his efforts in poor Germany and his advocacy for Jewish Christians. See Dietrich Bonhoeffer, *London, 1933-1935,* DBWE 13:22.

to which the bourgeois church and its religion have confined him can all be recognized as inspired by his Harlem-world experiences in 1930-1931.

This chapter will examine Bonhoeffer's exposure to the Harlem Renaissance by focusing on his theological encounter with the race divide, particularly in his interaction with Countee Cullen's 1929 poem, "The Black Christ." The goal will be to show that Bonhoeffer's exposure to the race divide in Harlem was a vital piece of his later politically inflected Christian witness in Germany. Along the way, we also will unpack three important tropes that one can see in Bonhoeffer's writing and advocacy that arose out of the year of his Sloane Fellowship: his interpretation of W. E. B. Dubois's notions of "the veil" and "the color-line," and their respective roles in the further development of his interpretation of Martin Luther's notion of the *theologia crucis*.

The Harlem Renaissance community provided Bonhoeffer with a unique perspective on the racial divide within American Christianity by allowing him to see the distortion that occurs with Christianity when it becomes blended with oppressive power structures. In Harlem, he began to see some of what that community saw operating within the dominant white, Christian worldview. From this vantage point, he observed a worldview that nurtured a racial imagination arising from a diseased practice of Christian discipleship. Historically, the theology of that discipleship worked to legitimate white supremacy as the accepted God-given norm, shaping whites and blacks to be obedient disciples of its dictates. But in the Harlem Renaissance community, as Cullen's poem indicates, Bonhoeffer was exposed to a theological critique of race from within, as he put it, "a rather hidden perspective."[9] That perspective gave him insights into the theological ability of an oppressed group to deflect popular yet harmful ideology.

In his end-of-the-year report to the Church Federation Office, written at the end of his spring semester 1931, Bonhoeffer borrowed from Dubois to describe some of what he learned during his brief sojourn as a Sloane fellow. His description demonstrated some familiarity with this prominent Harlem Renaissance scholar when he said: "Here one gets to

---

[9]Bonhoeffer, *Barcelona, Berlin, New York*, DBWE 10:314.

see something of the real face of America, something that is hidden *behind the veil* of words in the American constitution saying that 'all men are created equal.'"[10] The reference to "the veil" was clearly borrowed from Dubois's seminal work *The Souls of Black Folks* (1903). The veil is a construct that describes racialization; it is the forced attribution of racial identity by whites on black bodies that works like a projector screen. Dubois argued that real black selves are hidden "behind the veil." That is also the reason for double consciousness: blacks know themselves as whites see them in addition to their knowledge of their real black selves. In *Souls,* Dubois described "double consciousness" and "the veil" as hermeneutical keys to the interpretation of the black-white encounter. This framework is vital to understand his theological critique of race.

Dubois claimed that the problem of the twentieth century was the problem of the color line. The color line is a power structure that belts the planet, subjugating people of color to whites-only power structures. It is reinforced by an abstract theology that gives theological support to an ideal humanity by placing real life and social interaction in the column of *adiaphora,* or things indifferent. Bonhoeffer gained the ability to see that the color line is a Christian problem, and most importantly for what he was to face at home, to see how the color line passed through Germany in the form of *die judenfrage,* or the Jewish question.

We see his engagement with the color line at the very beginning of the church struggle. Bonhoeffer quickly rebuked his colleagues in the Pastor's Emergency League for their willingness to ignore what he saw was the heart of the problem with the Nazi Christians: their racism. Early in the struggle, the majority of his colleagues viewed their conflict with the Nazi-sympathizing German Christians much the same way that Martin Niemöller did—by resisting government intrusion in church affairs and viewing the Jewish question as *adiaphora.*[11] For Niemöller, the Jewish question was not a church issue, but for Bonhoeffer, it was *the* church issue, even to the point of being a *status confessionis* for the church. He rebuked his colleagues for their inability to see that the priv-

---

[10]Ibid., p. 321.
[11]Bethge, *Dietrich Bonhoeffer*, p. 306.

ileges of the "Aryans only" power structure in the church, which they were willing to accept, fundamentally changed the nature of Christian discipleship:

> The German Christians' demands destroy the substance of the ministry by making certain members of the Christian community into members with lesser rights, second-class Christians. The rest, those who remain privileged members, should prefer to stand by those with lesser rights rather than to benefit from a privileged status in the church. They must see their own true service, which they can still perform for their church, in resigning from this *office of pastor as a privilege,* which is now what it has become.[12]

Early in the struggle, Bonhoeffer stood alone in his opposition to what he described as "fatal privilege," having come to recognize the color line that he saw from the "hidden perspective" of oppressed blacks in Harlem, passing through Germany in the shape of the Jewish question.[13]

These two pieces—his interaction with the hermeneutical key of the black experience in America and his criticism of the color line in Germany—are important to Bonhoeffer's deepening understanding of Luther's *theologia crucis.* This shift in his thinking is vital to our understanding of Bonhoeffer after New York in 1930-1931. His language about the hiddenness of God was deepened from an emphasis on Christ's hiddenness and our acceptance of grace bestowed upon Christians who are ambivalent to Scripture—that is, Christ hidden in the world in the lives of Christians who cannot be distinguished from non-Christians[14]—to an emphasis on concrete obedience to Christ's commandments. Bonhoeffer's insistence on costly grace became the fruit of this development as it resulted from his emphasis on the revelation of Christ who cannot be hidden in a likeness to the world, as is the case in cheap grace.[15] From this basis, Bonhoeffer also began to insist on our solidarity with outcasts, because Christ is *hidden in suffering.* It is this Christ that Bonhoeffer came

[12]Bonhoeffer, *Berlin,* DBWE 12:431.
[13]Bethge, *Dietrich Bonhoeffer,* p. 306.
[14]Bonhoeffer, *Barcelona, Berlin, New York,* DBWE 10:353.
[15]Bonhoeffer, *Berlin,* DBWE 12:260.

to see within the hidden perspective of Harlem through his exposure to the critique of the problem of race during the Harlem Renaissance.

Bonhoeffer regularly wrote home describing what he was learning about the "race problem" in America.[16] He was learning about the race-based division within American Christianity at a time when the notion of race was being critically analyzed in the dynamic engagement with race, religion and politics by African American artists and intellectuals. He may have even personally met some of the prominent literary shapers of the Harlem Renaissance. In November of 1930, Frank Fisher brought his German friend with him to visit his alma mater Howard College, now called Howard University, in Washington, D.C. At the time of their visit, Alain Locke, the author whose monumental book *The New Negro* named the movement, was a well-known faculty member of the college and the chair of its philosophy department. Locke and Dubois are still recognized as the two foremost intellectual architects of the New Negro movement. Of that visit to Howard with Fisher, Bonhoeffer claimed: "I was introduced not only to the leaders of the young Negro movement at Howard College in Washington, but also in Harlem, the Negro quarter in New York."[17] We know that he read some work from both Locke and Dubois along with other prominent Harlem Renaissance intellectuals in Niebuhr's spring course, and he also wrote an essay on the works of Harlem Renaissance writers, many of whom he was voraciously studying even apart from assigned reading.[18]

In addition, Bonhoeffer became aware of the very public dispute between Booker T. Washington and Dubois over the role that blacks must embrace for themselves in a white racist society. Washington's perspective was understood by some to be an "Old Negro" type of black accommodation of white supremacy. From their perspective, Washington represented an assimilated white racist perspective of black people, one that was absorbed into a black self-perception and formed an internalized mandate for an inferior black existence. Dubois had a different perspective. Bonhoeffer would have read the following when

---

[16]Bonhoeffer, *Barcelona, Berlin, New York*, DBWE 10:321.
[17]Ibid.
[18]Bonhoeffer, *Berlin*, DBWE 12:95.

he read Dubois's book *Souls of Black Folk:* "Mr. Washington represents
in thought the old attitude of adjustment and submission. . . . Mr. Washington's program practically accepts the alleged inferiority of the Negro
races."[19] Dubois and his students rejected Washington's model of black
engagement with white racism. Rather than "adjustment and submission," Dubois's model can be described as a resistance model of engagement with racism. The resistance model seems to have been attractive to the young Bonhoeffer. Regarding the conflict between Dubois
and Washington, Bonhoeffer said the following: "B. T. Washington
preaches the gospel of working, with regard to the white people separate
like the fingers and one like the hand." This is a reference to Washington's famous Atlanta Compromise speech delivered in 1895, in which he
encouraged blacks to accommodate a white racist worldview by accepting segregation and their second-class citizenship for the ad-
vancement of humankind. Bonhoeffer continued: "Du Bois criticizes
Washington sharply, accuses W. to agree with the statement of inferiority of the black race. More race-proud!"[20] His emphasis on Dubois's
race-pride sounds as though he is affirming it. That is not surprising
given what he came to learn about the reception of Washington's perspective within the communities of young participants in the Renaissance among whom he was gathering friendships. Indeed, some interpreted black leaders who succumbed to this submission-to-racism
perspective to be pawns of white racist leadership.[21] Within the black
community at Abyssinian Baptist, in classes at Union, and at Howard,
Bonhoeffer would have learned that this perspective was particularly
problematic for younger blacks, because it housed a theological justification of racial inferiority that was leading young blacks away from
Christianity. They reasoned, as Bonhoeffer observed, that "it made their
fathers meek in the face of their incomparably harsh fate."[22] Put differently, Christianity, to them, served merely as an opiate.

We can see the young blacks' theological critique of Christianity in

---

[19]W. E. B. Dubois, *The Souls of Black Folk* (New York: Penguin Books 1989), p. 43.
[20]Bonhoeffer, *Barcelona, Berlin, New York,* DBWE 10:421.
[21]C. Eric Lincoln and Lawrence H. Mamiya, *The Black Church in the African-American Experience* (Durham, NC: Duke University Press, 1990), p. 15.
[22]Bonhoeffer, *Barcelona, Berlin, New York,* DBWE 10:315.

Cullen's "The Black Christ," a poem to which Bonhoeffer referred by name. Cullen was Dubois's son-in-law and it is likely that Bonhoeffer encountered his work in his spring-semester course with Niebuhr. He was the "young Negro poet" that Bonhoeffer was referring to when he commented on the racial condition of American Christianity: "If it has come about that today the 'black Christ' has to be led into the field against the 'white Christ' by a young Negro poet, then a deep cleft in the church of Jesus Christ is indicated."[23] Bonhoeffer also referred to the black Christ with explicit reference to the American Christian problem of race:

> American Protestantism presents the image of a church torn by race. The severe destruction of the Church is demonstrated by the fact that the white Christ is confronted by a black Christ. It is the guilt of the Church that the ambitious young generation of African-Americans turns away in general from the faith of the older ones with its strong eschatological tendencies.[24]

The "strong eschatological tendencies" that Bonhoeffer was referring to were the opiate features of oppressive religion that were being rejected by the younger blacks. Cullen's "Black Christ" was indicative of that rejecting process. That this process was performed in the context of a critical analysis of race and religion was unique to the Harlem Renaissance. "The Black Christ" is representative of what James Cone describes as Harlem Renaissance "lynching parables." The lynching parables were poems by black intellectuals of the Renaissance that placed Christ in the lived experience of race-terror as a "colored" victim, to provide a theological critique of race and African American suffering in a white supremacist society. Their efforts can also be understood by what womanist ethicist Emilie Townes suggests as a distinction between suffering and pain. Townes references Audre Lorde when she describes suffering as cycles of inescapable, unscrutinized pain.[25] Yet, in an experience

---

[23]Dietrich Bonhoeffer, *No Rusty Swords: Letters, Lectures and Notes, 1928-1936*, trans. Edwin H. Robertson and John Bowden, ed. Edwin H. Robertson (London: Collins, 1965), p. 112.

[24]Cited in *Andreas Pangritz, "Who Is Jesus Christ, for Us, Today?" in The Cambridge Companion to Dietrich Bonhoeffer*, ed. John W. de Gruchy (New York: Cambridge University Press, 1999), p. 144.

[25]See Emilie Townes, *A Troubling in My Soul: Womanist Perspectives on Evil and Suffering* (Maryknoll, NY: Orbis, 1993), pp. 78-91.

similar to what Dubois describes as lifting the veil, the pain becomes something different when it is highlighted. It is extracted from the un-determined, vicious and inescapable cycles and changed into an experience that is recognized, named and then used for transformation. This means that our responsibility in the face of human suffering is to resist it by moving from suffering to pain. Pain, as Townes describes it, is a constituent of the struggle against injustice. We may interpret the goal of the lynching parables in this light: they represent critical theological analyses by Harlem Renaissance intellectuals of religion and black suffering in an effort to move from suffering to pain.

Dubois wrote numerous lynching parables as well. One in particular placed a Jewish Jesus in Waco, Texas, where he was encountered by pious Christian whites so aghast at his "colored" appearance that he ends up a victim of a lynching.[26] "Jesus Christ in Texas" represents the color line as an ironic, Christological tragedy: in a white-centered world, the Son of God becomes a frightening disruption and simply one more inhabitant of the racialized communities that are intimately familiar with white Christian scorn. They are the people Howard Thurman described as "the disinherited," until white Christians come to recognize Christ's natural, physical identification with the subjugated and disinherited who comprise the populations on the unfavorable side of the color line.

That Cullen's poem is also this kind of critical engagement with race is indicated by the audience to whom Cullen dedicates it: "Hopefully dedicated to white America."[27] In the poem, the historical Jesus becomes the first lynched victim of an evil mob in a succession of lynched victims that includes African Americans:

How Calvary in Palestine,
Extending down to me and mine,
Was but the first leaf in a line,
Of trees on which a Man should swing
World without end, in suffering.[28]

---

[26]See W. E. B. DuBois, *Darkwater: Voices from Within the Veil* (Mineola, N.Y.: Dover, 1999), pp. 70-77.

[27]Countee Cullen, *The Black Christ & Other Poems* (New York: Harper and Brothers, 1929), p. 67.

[28]Ibid., p. 69.

The poem consists of three main characters: a Job-like, pious Christian mother and her two young-adult sons who function in a role resembling Job's accusatory friends. Both of these young men—the younger brother Jim and an unnamed older brother— wrestle with questions of theodicy. Since his childhood, Jim has doubted the existence of God because of white cruelty and innocent suffering:

> "A man was lynched last night."
> "Why?" Jim would ask, his eyes star-bright.
> "A white man struck him; he showed fight.
> Maybe God thinks such things are right."
> "Maybe God never thinks at all—
> Of us," and Jim would clench his small,
> Hard fingers tight into a ball.
> "Likely there ain't no God at all . . .
> God could not be if he deemed right,
> The grief that ever met our sight."[29]

Initially this language used in conversation about God is problematic for the older brother, who has been introduced as friendly toward the religion of his mother. But we soon learn of his growing concern for the safety of his smart, handsome younger brother. This concern leads to bitter words of fear and anguish over the role of God in black suffering. Why is it dangerous for Jim, the younger brother, to exist as an intelligent, handsome and self-confident black man? This gets to the theological critique in Cullen's depiction of race: it is the problem of discipleship and obedience within the racialized structure of Christianity and a vital insight on the intersection of race religion and oppression in white power structures.

This perspective likely would have proven enlightening for Bonhoeffer, as he saw white Christians turn Christ into the representative of white cultural longing and a fetish of idealized humanity. This was a Christ who did not guide daily interaction with one's neighbor or command that we must do unto others as we would have them do to us; rather, he had become a policeman on the borders of white racial

---

[29]Ibid., pp. 77-78.

identity and a theological justification for dehumanizing real people in the name of an ideal Christian community. Discipleship to Jesus, in this view, had become training in hatred. This was the white Christ that Bonhoeffer was referring to in his letters home that year as the source of the cheap grace active within the fatal privilege he was protesting in the church struggle.[30] He also noticed that this Christ was the repellent driving young blacks in Harlem away from Christianity.

Jim represents this youthful resistance model of race critique within the Harlem Renaissance: proud, intelligent, good-looking and no longer silent. He strikes an assaultive, racist white man, and this act results in his death-by-lynching at the hands of an angry white mob at his home, in front of his mother and brother. His elder brother is devastated, and his emotional state is exaggerated by the sight of his mother on her knees in prayer to white Christ:

> "Call on him now," I mocked, "and try
> Your faith against His deed, while I
> With intent equally as sane,
> Searching a motive for this pain,
> Will hold a little stone on high
> And seek of it a reason why.
> Which, stone or God, will first reply…?
> What has He done for you who spent
> A bleeding life for His content?
> Or is white Christ, too, distraught
> By these dark skins His Father wrought?"[31]

The white Christ does nothing for their family's well-being except hurt, humiliate and kill them. But here is the heart of Cullen's critique; the religion of the pious, black Christian mother has nothing to do with the religious representation of white racism. She is not praying to a white Christ. Rather, the Christ she worships betrays the lethal nature of the mixture of race-terror and Christianity that white racist Christians force society to drink. This mixture is lethal for victims and perpetrators alike. Her faith in Christ extracts him from that lethal concoction, and

---

[30]Bethge, *Dietrich Bonhoeffer,* p. 306.
[31]Cullen, *Black Christ,* pp. 103-5.

disassociates him from the structures that fail to acknowledge his life in solidarity with the oppressed. Her Jesus is very different from the Christ who is co-opted by forces that turn him into a weapon wielded against marginalized people. With her, Jesus becomes a contradiction to the way in which white racist Christians construct society. Her Jesus cannot be found in the domination and race-based privileges of racialized communities, for she knows that Christ is hidden from racists in and amongst their victims—with those whom Bonhoeffer in his ethics would later describe as "the poorest of our brothers and sisters."[32] Indeed, Christ was hidden even from her own son, who did not know that Jesus was there among them until he came to recognize him in his brother's suffering. *This* is the poem's admonition to us, and only at this recognition did the elder brother come to know Christ and proclaim him as the "form immaculately born, betrayed a thousand times each morn, as many times each night denied, surrendered, tortured, crucified!"[33] Cullen's black Christ exists in solidarity with this suffering black family, because he is one of them.

Christ entering into the suffering of the outcasts and marginalized is a theme that resonates with Bonhoeffer's Christology as he would develop it in the years ahead. Upon his return to Germany, Bonhoeffer not only agreed with this christological theme as the mode of Christ's existence in the world but also with the ethical imperative for real Christian discipleship. It is this form of Christ-centered Christianity that Bonhoeffer saw expressed with zeal at Abyssinian Baptist:

> I heard the gospel preached in the Negro churches. . . . Here one really could still hear someone talk in a Christian sense about sin and grace and the love of God and ultimate hope, albeit in a form different from that to which we are accustomed. *In contrast to the often lecture-like character of the white Christ, the "black Christ" is preached with captivating passion and vividness.*[34]

The captivating passion of the black Christ was invigorating and a source through which he came to identify with African Americans in

---

[32]Dietrich Bonhoeffer, *Ethics,* DBWE 6:253.
[33]Cullen, *Black Christ,* p. 108.
[34]Bonhoeffer, *Barcelona, Berlin, New York,* DBWE 10:315.

the spirituals he loved so much that spoke of grace in suffering. One Sunday, during that spring semester of 1931, one of Bonhoeffer's fellow students observed Bonhoeffer returning to his seminary lodging from Abyssinian Baptist, where he had become a lay leader. Bonhoeffer lingered for a time, excited to talk about that day at church. To Horton's surprise, Bonhoeffer was quite emotional. This was out of character for Bonhoeffer's typically logical, unemotional temperament. Horton remembered Bonhoeffer claiming that "the only time he had experienced true religion in the United States, was in black churches, and he was convinced that it was only among blacks who were oppressed that there could be any real religion in this country." As Horton recalled: "Perhaps that Sunday afternoon . . . I witnessed a beginning of his identification with the oppressed which played a role in the decision that led to his death."[35] Indeed, Horton *was* right. Bonhoeffer's identification with the resistance model of Christ who knew and accepted suffering in America placed him in solidarity with the outcast and the marginalized in Germany. It led him to drink the full measure of the cup of Christ's suffering, like the lynching parables of the Harlem Renaissance described it, at the gallows at Flossenbürg concentration camp in the morning hours of April 9, 1945.[36]

---

[35]Bonhoeffer, *Barcelona, Berlin, New York*, DBWE 10:31.
[36]This paper was originally presented at the conference *Bonhoeffer for the Coming Generations,* which commemorated the Bonhoeffer Lectures in Public Ethics and the Dietrich Bonhoeffer Works English Edition, that was held at Union Theological Seminary, New York, in November, 2011.

4

THE EVANGELIZATION
OF RULERS

Bonhoeffer's Political Theology

STEPHEN J. PLANT

BONHOEFFER'S CHAPLAINCY TO STUDENTS at the Charlottenburg
Technical College in Berlin was always an uphill struggle. He had been
assigned the role following his ordination and his first semester in the
post, in his own words, had the appearance of being "almost completely
unsuccessful."[1] In November 1932 Bonhoeffer pinned to his notice board
a plaintive note addressed to the joker who had three times removed the
chaplaincy program for the term.[2] In the winter semester Bonhoeffer
tried Bible studies on current topics, but with no greater success. Yet the
four services he conducted for students at Trinity Church were, as he
put it in his end of year report, "conspicuously well attended by students."[3]

On February 26, 1933, therefore, as Bonhoeffer began the service
marking the end of the winter semester, he may have had a sense of occasion. It had been an eventful term, one that had begun in the dying
days of the Weimar Republic and was ending as the Third Reich was
being born. Bonhoeffer's sermon was based on several verses from

---

[1]See Bonhoeffer's annual report to the Berlin Consistory in Dietrich Bonhoeffer, *Berlin: 1932-1933,* DBWE 12:118-20.
[2]Ibid., p. 69.
[3]Ibid., p. 119.

chapters 6, 7 and 8 of the book of Judges that condense the story of Gideon. It would have been plain to his student congregation that these Bible verses were concerned with the politics of Israel in the period of the Judges. Less plain was that his sermon was also an exercise in political theology understood, using Oliver O'Donovan's definition, as a reflective practice whose task "is to shed light from the Christian faith upon the intricate challenge of thinking about living in late-modern Western society."[4] In the first part of this paper, I ask what light this sermon sheds from the Christian faith on the political challenges Bonhoeffer and his students faced. In the second part, I explore the sources from which Bonhoeffer's political theology draws and identify two of his key insights.

To grasp what Bonhoeffer is doing in his sermon we must first take note of the significance of the date on which he preached it. From the late 1920s the Nazi party had become increasingly successful in elections to the German *Reichstag*.[5] The rule of law hung in the balance and politically motivated violence became commonplace. In one incident, several Nazis beat a communist sympathizer to death in Potempa, a Silesian village, and were condemned to death. Hitler sent the men a telegram expressing his solidarity with them and a Nazi newspaper reported that one of the condemned men had said: "This telegram and his [Hitler's] picture will be the small altar before which I shall pray daily."[6] In presidential elections Hindenburg proved hard to beat, but in April 1932 Hitler polled 37 percent of votes to Hindenburg's 53 percent. After declining Chancellor Papen's offer of the vice-chancellorship, Hitler endured a frustrating winter until Hindenburg finally appointed him chancellor on January 30, 1933. Most Germans were delighted. That evening the Brown-shirts and the S.S., groups with a history of internecine conflict, marched together through Berlin. Within weeks of

---

[4]Oliver O'Donovan, *The Ways of Judgment* (Grand Rapids: Eerdmans, 2005), p. x. I am also indebted to O'Donovan's *The Desire of the Nations* (Cambridge: Cambridge University Press, 1996) for the phrase "the evangelization of rulers."

[5]For details of the historical events discussed in this section see Ian Kershaw, *Hitler 1889-1936: Hubris* (London: Allen Lane, 1998), pp. 314-495.

[6]See Bonhoeffer, *Berlin*, DBWE 12:462n6, and Klaus Scholder, *The Churches and the Third Reich, Volume 1: 1918-1934* (London: SCM Press, 1977), p. 180.

taking office Hitler freed the killers from Potempa. Still many, including the theologian Karl Barth, initially judged Hitler's appointment to be an inconsequential shuffling of the deck of right-of-center leaders.[7] But the Bonhoeffer family saw immediately that the consequences of Hitler's appointment were serious. On the evening of January 30, Dietrich's brother-in-law Rüdiger Schleicher, on arriving home, announced: "This means war!"[8] The following day Bonhoeffer made his own views public in a radio broadcast on the "younger generation's altered view of the concept of the Führer." Unfortunately, Bonhoeffer overran his allotted time and the broadcast was cut off with the result that the theological conclusion was lost. His full script concluded: "The leader points to the office; leader and office, however [point] to the ultimate authority itself before which Reich and state are penultimate authorities. Leader and office that turn themselves into gods mock God."[9] It is the same insight Bonhoeffer would glean from the story of Gideon.

In the weeks that followed Hitler's appointment, the Nazis moved with astonishing speed and organizational skill to fix themselves in a position of complete power. A key moment was the burning of the *Reichstag,* the national parliament building in Berlin, on the evening of February 27. The fire was started by Dutchman Marinus van der Lubbe, whose lapsed communist party membership enabled Hitler to portray his arson as an attack on the state. On February 28, Hitler enacted his "Order for the Protection of People and State." It was the first of several legal moves giving Hitler total power.

Such detailing helps situate Bonhoeffer's sermon in its context, a month after Hitler took office as Reich Chancellor and forty-eight hours before the first of the legal acts that would replace the Weimar Republic with the Nazi Third Reich. In spite of what we know to be Bonhoeffer's political views, his sermon makes no explicit mention of Hitler. We may

---

[7]Karl Barth to Anna Katharina Barth, February 1, 1933, cited in Klaus Scholder, *Churches and the Third Reich, Volume One: 1918-1934*, pp. 221, 624.

[8]Eberhard Bethge, *Dietrich Bonhoeffer: A Biography*, trans. Victoria Barnett, rev. ed. (Minneapolis: Fortress, 2000), p. 237.

[9]Bonhoeffer, *Berlin*, DBWE 12:281-82. See also Bonhoeffer's circular note to friends explaining that he had run over his time limit and that this distorted what he aimed to say (p. 91); the incident has sometimes been misrepresented as if Bonhoeffer was cut off by a producer put out by the anti-Nazi tenor of the address.

assume that many of the students in his congregation were Nazis, but it was not reluctance to offend that accounts for why Bonhoeffer does not name Hitler in his sermon. When preaching Bonhoeffer preferred to let the Bible do its own work theologically and politically.[10] In times of crisis or confusion, Bonhoeffer instead urged theologians and preachers to "go back to the very beginning, to our wellsprings, to the true Bible, to the true Luther," as he put it in November 1933, adding that "one should keep on, ever more undaunted and joyfully becoming a theologian 'aletheuntes en agape' [speaking the truth in love]."[11]

Bonhoeffer carefully prepared for his sermon. In his copy of the *Lutherbibel* he has underlined the key verses and at one point (Judges 7:2) he substituted Luther's phrasing with his own translation in such a way as to emphasize God's reluctance to let Israel take credit for its victory.[12] He begins with a summary of his main point: "This is a passionate story about God's derision for all those who are fearful and have little faith. . . . It is a story of God's mocking human might, a story of doubt and faith in this God who mocks human beings, who wins them over with this mockery and with love."[13]

If Gideon is a "hero," he is not, for Bonhoeffer, a Teutonic hero like Wagner's Siegfried, who succeeds by cunning and the power of his own arm. Gideon is merely a creature, called to do God's will, coaxed round by teasing and love to obedience to God. In a side swipe at the Nazi killer from Potempa worshipping Hitler at his small altar, Bonhoeffer insists that the church has only one altar: the altar of the Most High, the Almighty, the Creator, the Lord. If we grasp only one thing of Bonhoeffer's theopolitics, let it be this: "Anyone who wants to build an altar to himself or to any other human is mocking God."[14] Faith, Bonhoeffer tells his student congregation, has the quality of pointing away from oneself to the one we obey.

---

[10]See Bethge's comment on Bonhoeffer's preaching in *Dietrich Bonhoeffer*, p. 235: "Though he took liberties with his text, he avoided modernist tricks that twisted the meaning, and did not comment directly on current political or church events."

[11]Bonhoeffer, *Berlin*, DBWE 12:435.

[12]See ibid., p. 461n1, which reports Bonhoeffer's handwritten marginal note in his copy of the *Lutherbibel*.

[13]Ibid., 461-62.

[14]Ibid., p. 463.

In a neat rhetorical move, Bonhoeffer turns next from Gideon as a historical figure, to one whose situation is recognizable in his own context. Bonhoeffer offers his congregation Gideon as a type or figure for the Protestant church, called to proclaim God to the nation, but in every way without influence, powerless and undistinguished. What can such a church do? His answer is that the church is able to follow its calling simply because "God is with us." To make the point, God orders Gideon to dismiss the army he has assembled and, in doing so, Gideon gives God the glory. In a conclusion that points a way toward the coming church struggle with the Nazi state, Bonhoeffer says, "it does seem crazy, doesn't it, that the church should not defend itself by every means possible in the face of terrible threats coming at it from every side."[15] The basic insight here is Pauline: God's grace is sufficient for us, for God's power is made perfect in weakness (2 Corinthians 12:9). The insight is a refraction backward through time of the one Bonhoeffer would articulate from prison in the phrase "only a suffering God can help." God's lordship, God's rule, God's politics, God's power are seen most clearly in Jesus' nailed and outstretched hands: "The cross of Jesus Christ—that means God's bitter mockery of all human grandeur and God's bitter suffering in all human misery, God's lordship over all the world."[16]

What are we to infer from the Gideon sermon about Bonhoeffer's political theology? I want to turn first to the sources of Bonhoeffer's thinking, before exploring two of its key elements. I present these points in sequence, but they may also be conceived as a rudimentary systematically interrelated political theology, with each point informing the others.

"WELLSPRINGS"

On March 5, a few days after his end-of-semester service, Bonhoeffer went with his friend Franz Hildebrandt to the polls for the *Reichstag* elections. Hildebrandt, ever the convinced Protestant, voted for the Protestant Christian People's Party; but Bonhoeffer voted for the Catholic Center Party on the pragmatic basis that it was the only party

---

[15]Ibid., p. 466.
[16]Ibid., p. 467.

with half a chance of standing up to Hitler.[17] If Lutheran perspectives shaped Bonhoeffer's politics they did not do so in a *tribal* fashion, as if his ecclesial community were simply one more political party whose interests he was duty-bound to defend. Yet, as we have already noted, Bonhoeffer wrote at the end of 1933 that periods of crisis should drive theologians "back to the very beginning, to our wellsprings, to the true Bible, to the true Luther."[18] The Gideon sermon tells us several things about how the Bible sheds light on unfolding political events. A first point to note is that the Bible, for Bonhoeffer, meant both the Old and New Testaments, which together constitute the Bible as the church's book.[19] This may seem obvious to most Christians, but it was by no means so obvious in Bonhoeffer's context, in which a strong Marcionite tendency existed in liberal Protestantism that judged the New Testament to be superior to the Old, which consequently was virtually excluded from theological discourse. By 1933 this liberal prejudice was already being used to warrant a denial of the Old Testament as Christian Scripture on far uglier anti-Semitic grounds.

It is, therefore, all the more striking that so many of Bonhoeffer's biblical studies with a political flavor from 1933 to 1945 were based on Old Testament texts: Genesis 1–3 is used to reveal the basis on which human life is preserved; a study of the Psalms treats political themes such as law, kingship and the punishment of enemies; another on Ezra and Nehemiah sees in the rebuilding of a wall around Jerusalem an analogy of the theological axiom that *extra ecclesiam nulla salus*—outside the church there is no salvation. One consequence of Bonhoeffer's attentiveness to Old Testament as well as New Testament texts may be to balance a tendency observable in some Christian political theologians who proceed more narrowly on New Testament texts alone.[20] New Testament texts reflect contexts in which the early church was a minority without political power; they either perceive authorities as beastly per-

---

[17]Bethge, *Dietrich Bonhoeffer*, p. 266.

[18]Bonhoeffer, *Berlin*, DBWE 12:435.

[19]See Martin Kuske, *The Old Testament as the Book of Christ* (Philadelphia: Westminster Press, 1976).

[20]I am thinking here of John Howard Yoder's influential *The Politics of Jesus* (Grand Rapids: Eerdmans, 1972).

secutors or as established by God but without being godly. While some Old Testament texts likewise reflect an experience of political exile, others, like the book of Judges, wrestle with the messier experience of the exercise of power by God's servants: Gideon, Samuel, Saul, David and Nehemiah, who, with their compromises and frailties, lived out their political lives within the penultimate in ways that directed the eyes of their people to the ultimate.

A second point of note concerning Bonhoeffer's political use of biblical texts is his expectation that in the Bible God really does speak to the church about concrete contemporary situations. Bonhoeffer does not discern in the Bible—as, for example, did the Anabaptist revolutionaries at Münster between 1532 and 1535—a blueprint drawn by God for a theocracy that can and should be built by Christians now on earth; but he does believe that an authentically Christian politics is one that seeks to discern God's will for today in Scripture.

The second wellspring Bonhoeffer identified as central for theologians facing a crisis is the theology of Martin Luther. Making sense of Luther's political theology is challenging, not least because the treatises from which his political thought is mainly derived were responsive to particular and very different challenges. This has two consequences: first, it makes knowledge of context important for an intelligent understanding of any particular treatise written by Luther; second, it makes it hard to derive a consistent theopolitical position based on Luther's writings.[21] To add to these challenges, from 1933 pro-Nazi Lutheran theologians began to debase the currency of Lutheran theopolitical vocabulary by claiming Luther as father of German nationhood, a promoter of Christian anti-Semitism,[22] and crucially as author of an understanding of a human society described in terms of inviolable orders of creation. Nonetheless, Bonhoeffer's political theology is shaped by Luther in four ways.

---

[21]As examples, see the contrast between the 1520 treatise *To the Christian Nobility of the German Nation,* which defends temporal rulers against papal interference in the exercise of their responsibilities and the 1523 treatise, *Temporal Authority: To What Extent It Should Be Obeyed,* which sets limits to the rights of temporal rulers to interfere with freedom of religious conscience.

[22]Alas, not in this case without justification.

- Bonhoeffer shares with Luther a fundamentally Augustinian concep-
  tualization[23] of politics structured by two realms: a temporal realm
  and a spiritual realm. For Luther, the spiritual realm comprises Christians only but the temporal realm comprises both Christians and
  non-Christians. Crucially, the authority of both realms is derived
  from God.

- The two realms place limits on each other's authority. Temporal authority only extends to bodily life; the life of faith should be free of
  interference by temporal rulers. But the converse is also true: spiritual
  authority, while it may offer counsel to a godly temporal ruler, has no
  authority to impede the state in the exercise of its authority over
  bodily life.

- Luther—like Augustine developing his political theology under the
  shadow of political chaos and violence—affirmed the value of political order. Like Augustine, but unlike Thomas Aquinas, Luther understood political authority as a remedy for sin: if all the world were
  genuinely Christian, there would be no need for temporal authorities,
  such as soldiers, police or magistrates at all, since Christians do not
  make war, murder, rape or steal.

- Luther bulked out his understanding of the two realms with a political theology he, indeed, thought rather more important: a theology of orders of creation and preservation, to which he sometimes
  gave the alternate term the three estates. The first estate is the church,
  since one is claimed by God before one has any other relationship.
  The second estate is the household, which includes not simply marriage and the relationship of parents and children, but in the broadest
  sense economic life, i.e., all that is needed for the sustenance of life—
  farming, commerce, work. The third estate is government, under-

---

[23]Opinion divides over what Augustine's two-cities theology intends, between those who
think Augustine means that citizens of the earthly and the heavenly cities *cooperate* in a
limited sense, or whether all Augustine's talk of intermingling is merely a qualification of the
fundamental point, which is that the two cities are in *competition* with each other. For a
representative of the first approach see R. A. Markus, *Saeculum: History and Society in the
Theology of Augustine* (Cambridge: Cambridge University Press, 1970). For an advocate of
the second, more "combative" approach, see Gregory W. Lee, "Republics and Their Loves:
Rereading *City of God* 19," *Modern Theology* 27, no. 4 (2011): 553-81.

stood broadly as princes and rulers and the magistrates and soldiers and tax collectors who do their bidding.

We can grasp little of Bonhoeffer's originality until we see it essentially as biblical exegesis undertaken from within a confessionally Augustinian and Lutheran tradition.

Bonhoeffer is explicit about these two wellsprings; but there is a third that we must take note of: Bonhoeffer's political roots in a very particular culture and family within a broader German context. That culture is nowhere better displayed than in Bonhoeffer's attempts while in prison to turn his hand to writing fiction. While imprisoned in Tegel Bonhoeffer began to write a drama, a novel and a short story. In his letter to Eberhard Bethge of November 18, 1943, Bonhoeffer describes his intention in these fragments as being "to rehabilitate middle-class life as we know it in our families, specifically from the Christian perspective."[24] For our purposes, what we must take note of is that it was this same middle class, family-based culture, undergirded by roots in a Christian culture both Protestant and Catholic, that characterized those with whom Bonhoeffer cooperated in the anti-Nazi resistance. The central figure in the hub of resistance in which Bonhoeffer played a relatively minor role was Admiral Wilhelm Canaris the head of the Abwehr, German military intelligence, with whom Bonhoeffer would later be hanged. The conspirators who belonged to the so-called Canaris conspiracy held common values and political views rooted, like Bonhoeffer, in the German middle class.[25] By the time Germany invaded Poland in September 1939, the Nazis had successfully expunged most opponents on the political left: socialists, communists and trades unionists. Josef Goebbels's process of conforming all German social life to Nazi forms, a policy termed *Gleichschaltung* ("coordination" or "bringing into line"), had destroyed all possible centers of anti-Nazi opposition. Only the German military retained any degree of autonomy. There, among the officer class, there remained a few individuals with serious doubts about the course on which Hitler had steered the German nation. Though Bon-

---

[24]For this link, see Dietrich Bonhoeffer, *Fiction from Tegel Prison*, DBWE 7:200n18.
[25]For the term "Canaris conspiracy" and a historical study of the resistance group to which Bonhoeffer belonged, see Roger Maxwell and Heinrich Fraenkel, *The Canaris Conspiracy: The Secret Resistance to Hitler in the German Army* (London: Heinemann, 1969).

hoeffer's immediate family did not include military officers, contact was established through his brother-in-law Hans von Dohnanyi, who became a lawyer in Canaris' office. Unsurprisingly, the conspirators were cagey about writing down their political views; but from what Bonhoeffer's sister and other survivors have written, certain core values and political commitments emerge. They include a commitment to the rule of law, a sense of the importance to government of a lively civil society and roots in Catholic and Protestant moral traditions. They were suspicious of liberal democracy because it placed too much trust in the will of the people. On the evidence of the popularity of the Nazis they judged that popular political opinion was not always in the best interests of the nation or of the people. They understood political authority to derive not from the people but from God. Some considered a restoration of a monarchy desirable. They distrusted revolutionary change, and, following the manifest failings of the Weimar Republic, judged that political democracy was not likely to be viable in Germany for years, possibly decades, after the end of war. Their preference was for an interim government by the military, giving way steadily to government by a civilian elite. This preferred political system reflected their conviction that of those to whom much had been given much was expected; political service, like resistance to tyrants, was a question of serving the common good.

Like many first attempts at creative writing individual characters in the writing fragments are recognisably based on Bonhoeffer's immediate circle, his family and friends, or are composites of several of them. In the drama the character of Christoph is based on Bonhoeffer himself. To Christoph, another character, Heinrich explains the basis of Christoph's moral and political values, so at odds with the rootlessness of Nazi revolutionaries:

> People like you have a foundation, you have ground under your feet, you have a place in the world. There are things you take for granted, that you stand up for, and for which you are willing to put your head on the line, because you know your roots go so deep that they'll sprout new growth again. The only thing that counts for you is to keep your feet on the ground.[26]

---

[26]Bonhoeffer, *Fiction*, DBWE 7:68.

Bonhoeffer's political theology, then, draws from these sources: Bible, Luther and cultural tradition. We turn now to two key elements in Bonhoeffer's theopolitical thinking, both discernible in his Gideon sermon, but developed more fully in the unfinished fragments written by Bonhoeffer toward an *Ethics* between 1940 and 1943.

THE STRUCTURE OF RESPONSIBLE LIFE

The first is Bonhoeffer's understanding of what from the beginning of 1942 he had come to term the "structure of responsible life." In his end of term sermon almost a decade earlier Bonhoeffer was already clear about where Gideon's authority to exercise political office came from: it came from God. Any pretence that the source of Gideon's authority came from his own greatness or from his tribe is mocked by God and, at the end of the story, Gideon rejects attempts by the Israelites to redirect his authority into a hereditary monarchy. Though Samuel would eventually find Israelite pressure to anoint a hereditary monarch irresistible, Bonhoeffer's exegetical conclusion here is that the exercise of political authority comes from God and is therefore ultimately accountable to God.

In *Ethics* Bonhoeffer continued to maintain that conviction, but now in a more sophisticated way, holding accountability to God in tension with taking full responsibility for one's own actions. In the second draft of his section on "History and Good" Bonhoeffer writes that in acting responsibly "primarily . . . I do not take responsibility for myself, for my actions; I do not justify myself (2 Corinthians 12:19). Rather, I take responsibility and answer for Jesus Christ, and with that I naturally also take responsibility for the commission I have been charged with by him (1 Corinthians 9:3)."[27] He continues that responsibility means responsibility exercised in concrete social and political relationships: "Responsibility is based on vicarious representative action *[Stellvertretung]*. This is most evident in those relationships in which a person is literally required to act on behalf of others, for example, as a father, as a statesman, or as the instructor of an apprentice."[28] The examples are not randomly chosen; one is from a domestic context, the next political, and the third socio-

---

[27]Dietrich Bonhoeffer, *Ethics*, DBWE 6:255.
[28]Ibid., p. 257.

economic. A year later, when retracing his steps in reflecting on vicarious representative action, Bonhoeffer gives three slightly different examples of social structures in which it is undertaken: "a church, a family, or a government."[29] The examples employed have in common that the one who stands in the place of, or who acts for another, is in a social relationship in which God is encountered "within an earthly relationship of authority, within an order that is clearly determined by above and below."[30] Understanding that such apparently hierarchical forms of relating may be misunderstood and abused, Bonhoeffer sharpened his definition by insisting that the divine authority for such social structures may not be invoked by those above to enforce obedience on those below, or that such structures exist in the interests of those above. Crucially, such relations were always between people. The nature of this final clarification is visible in the warmth of relationship in the examples Bonhoeffer uses to unpack his thinking about relations between an office holder and those he (and Bonhoeffer typically means *he*) is responsible for: "A father acts on behalf of his children by working, providing, intervening, struggling, and suffering for them. In doing so he stands in their place."[31] Within such relationships too, the one who is "below" also has obligations; thus, for example, as Bonhoeffer wrote in a study of truth telling while a prisoner in Tegel, a son rightly denies his father is regularly drunk when asked about it by a teacher, because his relationship to his father requires loyalty.

A year later, in the section of his *Ethics* on which he was working when he was arrested in April 1943, Bonhoeffer reflects on the divinely commanded or mandated nature of the social structures in which vicarious representatives act. As we have seen, Bonhoeffer inherited from Luther a theological vocabulary concerning orders of creation. Bonhoeffer was still using that vocabulary in 1933 when he lectured on Genesis 1–3 at the Humboldt University in Berlin,[32] but was already

---

[29]Ibid., p. 391.
[30]Ibid. When Karl Barth, who never lost his social democratic instincts for all that he purified his theology of the social gospel, commented on Bonhoeffer's posthumously published *Ethics,* it was this he had in mind when he found a "suggestion of North-German patriarchalism." See Karl Barth, *Church Dogmatics* III/4, trans. G. W. Bromiley and T. F. Torrance (Edinburgh: T & T Clark, 1961), p. 22.
[31]Bonhoeffer, *Ethics*, DBWE 6:257-58.
[32]See Dietrich Bonhoeffer, *Creation and Fall*, DBWE 3.

beginning to refashion Luther's theological thinking in response to a misuse of this same vocabulary by pro-Nazi theologians who saw in the rise of Nazism a new revelation from God for the German people. By the time he worked on ethics during the war Bonhoeffer prefers to write in terms of "divine mandates"[33] that are implanted in the world from above and hold divine commissions. The mandates—church, marriage and family, culture and government (elsewhere Bonhoeffer includes work and friendship)—exist for and not in competition with one another. The authority and sphere of operation for each mandate is limited because God is the source of its authority; it is limited by each other mandate (such, for example, that government has no mandate to alter the institution of marriage); and it is also limited by those below within each mandate (children placing proper limits on their parents, a wife placing proper limits on her husband, a citizen placing proper limits on her government, and so on).

Bonhoeffer's understanding of social relationships was, even as he was writing about them, beginning to sound oddly archaic. But being out of date is not, of course, the same as being wrong. As one learns in any basic ethics course, an argument that argues that because things *are* this way they *ought* to be this way is logically fallacious. But at a simple level of interpretation, for many—perhaps most—contemporary people in Europe and in North America, steeped in the egalitarian language of human rights, Bonhoeffer's account of the responsibility of those above to act vicariously for those below within mandated social structures can seem like listening to a voice from a different era.

THE PENULTIMATE AND THE ULTIMATE

A second element in Bonhoeffer's theopolitics already discernible in the Gideon sermon, but developed most fully in the *Ethics,* concerns the relationship between penultimate and ultimate things. As we have seen, though Bonhoeffer does not use the terms "penultimate" and "ultimate" in his Gideon sermon, he had already linked them to politics in his radio talk on "The Younger Generation's Altered View of the Concept of

---

[33]Though he is explicit in saying that he is writing of "orders," see Bonhoeffer, *Ethics,* DBWE 6:390.

the Führer" a matter of hours after Hitler's appointment as Chancellor.
In the Gideon sermon, the penultimate and ultimate are clearly discernible beneath the surface.

It is tempting to think that the terms *penultimate* and *ultimate* can be
mapped straightforwardly onto politics by locating all politics in the
penultimate and the life of faith in the ultimate. But the simplicity of this
formula is deceptive. For a moment, consider a phrase lifted from the
middle of the Magnificat, Mary's joyous song in Luke's birth narrative
(Luke 1:52-53):

> He has brought down the powerful from their thrones,
>   and lifted up the lowly;
> he has filled the hungry with good things,
>   and sent the rich away empty.

The terms used by Mary are certainly political; but do they speak of
penultimate or ultimate things? In my view, they are both at once. On
the one hand, such political vocabulary may be articulated in purely
penultimate ways, speaking of a penultimate, this-worldly, political revolution. On the other, the same words used by Christians may speak of
a more than this-worldly, an ultimate turning of things on their head.
Like all theological language, that is, theopolitical words and concepts
work because, on the one hand, they are recognizably and intelligibly
similar to the ways we use the same words and concepts in day-to-day
political discourse while, on the other, these same words and concepts
are transformed when we use them theologically. Political and theopolitical words and concepts are not identical, but are analogously related.

In his *Ethics* Bonhoeffer does not couch his discussion in terms of the
grammar of political theology; yet his discussion of the ways in which
penultimate and ultimate things are related to each other provides a
good example of such a grammatical rule in operation. For Bonhoeffer,
grace alone, faith alone, are ultimate: "It is faith alone that sets life in a
new foundation, and only on this foundation can I live justified before
God."[34] God's grace and faith in God are ultimate things because they
alone consummate human life. They are ultimate qualitatively, in that

---

[34]Ibid., p. 147.

there is nothing beyond them and in that they mark a complete break with penultimate things. But they are also ultimate temporally in the sense that they are always preceded by penultimate things.[35] Penultimate things are not, Bonhoeffer continues, interesting therefore for their own sake, "as if they had some value of their own"; rather, theology speaks of penultimate things because they precede and in some way prepare for the coming of the ultimate in a Christian's life.[36]

For Bonhoeffer, Christians have often tended to relate the penultimate to the ultimate in one of two mistaken ways. Either they have solved the relation between the penultimate and the ultimate radically by seeing the ultimate as a complete break with penultimate things, or they have solved the relationship through a compromise in which the "ultimate stays completely beyond daily life," serving in the end as a kind of divine preservation or even validation of penultimate things rather than as a judgment on them. Bonhoeffer sees merit in both, but also error. His own solution is to understand penultimate things as a preparing of the way for ultimate ones. Radicalism would renounce the world, while compromise would embrace it. But the incarnation of Jesus Christ, Bonhoeffer continues, makes nonsense of both approaches. Time and eternity, the life of this world and the life of God, are brought together in Jesus Christ in whom God enters into the world, the ultimate entering into the penultimate. For this reason, the "Christian life neither destroys nor sanctions the penultimate,"[37] just as Christ's resurrection does not abolish the penultimate as long as life on earth continues, even though "eternal life, the new life, breaks ever more powerfully into earthly life and creates space for itself within it."[38] The perspective of this ultimate enables us to see what being authentically human looks like; the ultimate thus *empowers* life within the penultimate.

What light does this shed on how Christians engage with the world? Bonhoeffer spells out what he means in an extended example worth citing at some length:

---

[35]See ibid., pp. 149-50.
[36]Ibid., p. 151.
[37]Ibid., p. 159.
[38]Ibid., p. 158.

The hungry person needs bread, the homeless person needs community, the undisciplined one needs order, and the slave needs freedom. It would be blasphemy against God and our neighbour to leave the hungry unfed while saying that God is closest to those in need. We break bread with the hungry and share our home with them for the sake of Christ's love, which belongs to the hungry as it does to us. . . . To bring bread to the hungry is preparing the way for the coming of grace.

What happens here is something penultimate. To give the hungry bread is not yet to proclaim to them the grace of God and justification, and to receive bread does not yet mean to stand in faith.[39]

Bonhoeffer concludes that this does not mean that for Christians to prepare the way for Christ it is enough to give bread to the hungry or shelter to the homeless, since "everything depends on this action being a spiritual reality, since what is at stake is not the reform of worldly conditions but the coming of Christ."[40]

BONHOEFFER'S POLITICS AND OURS

Gideon was not, in Bonhoeffer's sermon, the savior of his people: God alone saves. Any delusions of grandeur Gideon had, religious, political or military, were lovingly and laughingly mocked by God. Yet that is not to say Gideon was unimportant to God, or played no role in the unfolding of God's purposes for Israel. Gideon took vicarious representative action on behalf of God's people in defending them against the Midianites. Further, in his obedience to God, Gideon prepared the way for God's self-proclamation by such an astonishing victory over his people's enemies.

The resistance hub in which Bonhoeffer played a part acted also for the common good. Those who hazarded their lives on the successful working of bomb fuses in Oberstleutnant Claus Schenk Graf von Stauffenberg's briefcase on July 20, 1944, acted in what they took to be the national interest; they were vicarious representatives acting, as they saw it, on behalf of the German people. Was their vicarious representative action also a preparation for Christ, or did it remain in the penultimate,

---

[39]Ibid., p. 163.
[40]Ibid., p. 164.

merely as paving the way for the end of Nazism in Germany? Their actions did not have the element of the proclamation of God's purposes that might permit us to view it as a preparation for the ultimate.

And what of Bonhoeffer— in whose place did he stand? Did his act of political resistance pave the way for God's ultimate word of grace? In the church struggle, Bonhoeffer was in earnest in resisting, on Lutheran grounds, state interference in the church's proclamation. But, like Gideon, he was aware of the loving teasing mockery of God for the poor church in its struggles; he recognized the importance of not taking oneself too seriously. When he became involved in the Canaris conspiracy, much was changed. Though he was a pastor who took his office very seriously, Bonhoeffer seems reluctant to see his actions as representing the church; he may have intended to resign after the war from his ecclesial office, precisely so as not to associate the Protestant church with his actions as a conspirator against the state. With his fellow conspirators he too viewed himself as standing in for other Germans. But the element of self-mockery, of *hilaritas,* is gone; indeed Bonhoeffer seems concerned that that involvement in conspiracy may have damaged the conspirators morally and politically, asking them in a privately circulated essay written in January 1943, "Are we still of any use?" Bonhoeffer lived this disturbing double life conscious of doing so under God's judgment and trusting in the power of God's ultimate word of forgiveness. In resisting Hitler he stood on the line limiting the state's authority over Germans and over the German church: "Here I stand, I can do no other." To do so was to proclaim the gospel of Christ. The Nazis were not listening; the church today still has both the need, and the time, to do so.

5

MODERNITY'S MACHINE

Technology Coming of Age in Bonhoeffer's
Apocalyptic Proverbs

DANIEL J. TREIER

CHRISTIANS WHO ENGAGE WITH MODERNITY, rather than
simply embracing or trying to evade it, cannot escape this challenge of
discernment: to what extent is technology the machine powering modernity, and who is Jesus Christ for those who live in this brave new
world? Churchly responses to this question are surprisingly few and
theologically thin. Of course many historical accounts of modernity incorporate theological factors. Various thinkers even write prescriptions
for the church's future into their historical narratives. Yet relatively few
treatments address modernity as theological subject matter in its own
right, and even fewer do so in light of its characteristically technological
rationality. Thus Dietrich Bonhoeffer's fragmentary musings, however
sporadic, may provide valuable insight since he began to treat such aspects of the modern condition themselves, and not just its epistemo-
logical or political dimensions, in theological terms.

Theologians typically speak of "modernity" in ways that are historically imprecise, a problem we simply have to concede and work around.
Somewhat similarly, the word "technology" has broader and narrower
meanings, with Bonhoeffer of little help in pursuing a precise definition.
Yet, at least in moving beyond what Albert Borgmann calls the "device

paradigm," Bonhoeffer can provide a theological stimulus for understanding modern technology.[1] Technological rationality goes beyond providing new machinery, reshaping the very practices that characterize modern life. A key engine driving modernity, in other words, is newfound commitment to critical and instrumental uses of reason based on a large-scale narrative of cultural progress. Is the grand idea that we are now "modern" invariably a kind of salvation history rivaling the gospel?[2] Thus Bonhoeffer confronts biblical Christians with the challenge of discerning the divine providence implied in speaking of modernity. Others who have taken up this challenge—whether modernist liberals (in the best sense of that term) who preceded Bonhoeffer, or death-of-God theologians who thought they succeeded him—capitulated too readily to new cultural norms.[3] Yet more conservative thinkers likewise can easily assume the Bible's silent authorization for aspects of modernity that actually deserve careful Christian scrutiny—not least, technology.

Bonhoeffer's comments on modernity are largely occasional but still vast, as are the debates they generate. So the first section of this essay cannot survey all the relevant material but rather moves straight into a four-point distillation of Bonhoeffer's key reflections. Then the second

---

[1] See especially Albert Borgmann, *Technology and the Character of Contemporary Life* (Chicago: University of Chicago Press, 1984), and, more popularly, *Power Failure: Christianity in the Culture of Technology* (Grand Rapids: Brazos, 2003).

[2] "To complicate matters further, every attempt on the part of modernity to get a fix on who we are and what is at issue in our practices has only perpetuated the endless expansion of calculative rationality and the mechanisms which are the bearers of such instrumental reasoning, resulting in the continuing subjection of ourselves, our neighbors, and our world to more precise manipulations and control"—key factors in modernity that need scrutiny in the first place; so Barry A. Harvey, "A Post-Critical Approach to a 'Religionless Christianity,'" in *Theology and the Practice of Responsibility: Essays on Dietrich Bonhoeffer*, ed. Wayne Whitson Floyd Jr. and Charles Marsh (Valley Forge, PA: Trinity Press International, 1994), p. 40.

[3] Early "secular" theological appropriations of Bonhoeffer are now criticized: most recently, see Martin E. Marty, *Dietrich Bonhoeffer's "Letters and Papers from Prison": A Biography*, Lives of Great Religious Books (Princeton, NJ: Princeton University Press, 2011). Such interpretations bypass Bonhoeffer's central emphasis on disciples following Jesus' way to the cross, according to Douglas John Hall, "*Ecclesia Crucis:* The Disciple Community and the Future of the Church in North America," in Floyd and Marsh, *Theology and the Practice of Responsibility*, pp. 66, 70. Illuminating surveys of Bonhoeffer's reception also appear in John W. de Gruchy, "The Reception of Bonhoeffer's Theology," in *The Cambridge Companion to Dietrich Bonhoeffer*, ed. John W. de Gruchy (Cambridge: Cambridge University Press, 1999), pp. 93-109; and Stephen R. Haynes, *The Bonhoeffer Phenomenon: Portraits of a Protestant Saint* (Minneapolis: Fortress, 2004).

section assesses the ongoing significance of these views in brief comparison with those of a near contemporary, Jacques Ellul. Historically speaking, we will see that technology has more enduring significance in Bonhoeffer's understanding of modernity than others have emphasized.[4] Thus, theologically, we have to challenge the technological fixations of contemporary North American Christianity by understanding more carefully why aspects of the world's coming of age do or do not merit biblical celebration.[5]

BONHOEFFER MUSING ON MODERNITY

To begin with, then, in what sense may we legitimately pursue a synthetic account of Bonhoeffer's musings on modernity? Of course they have decidedly unsystematic, even "impulsive,"[6] elements. So one would expect, given the nature of his life and writings. Nevertheless recurring motifs, along with the possibility of plotting their development in a coherent narrative, authorize our quest. Bonhoeffer was a relatively unique churchman and theologian in recognizing almost automatically that Hitler must be resisted.[7] Accordingly, without addressing specialized historical debates or assuming that Bonhoeffer is always right, we should ponder what overarching concepts fostered this perceptiveness. What follows is an admittedly constructive and partial account of four categories that stem from repeated emphases in his texts—categories through which we might read the signs of our own times more perceptively.

---

[4]For tracking this claim beyond sources cited elsewhere in this essay, see Jean Bethke Elshtain, "Freedom and Responsibility in a World Come of Age," in Floyd and Marsh, *Theology and the Practice of Responsibility*, pp. 269-81; and Andreas Pangritz, "Who is Jesus Christ, for Us, Today?" in de Gruchy, *Cambridge Companion to Bonhoeffer*, pp. 134-53.

[5]Bonhoeffer famously suggested that American Christianity still needs a genuine encounter with the Protestant Reformation. Beyond European and anti-Pietist prejudices this provides constructive criticism; see "Protestantism Without Reformation," in Dietrich Bonhoeffer, *No Rusty Swords: Letters, Lectures and Notes, 1928-1936*, trans. Edwin H. Robertson and John Bowden, ed. Edwin H. Robertson (London: Collins, 1965), pp. 92-118.

[6]See David H. Hopper, *A Dissent on Bonhoeffer* (Philadelphia: Westminster, 1975), p. 135. Bonhoeffer's prison reflections do bear very personal and aristocratic marks. Hopper's "dissent" also usefully highlights apparent tensions created by the coming-of-age motif vis-à-vis the Bible, whether or not one agrees that Bonhoeffer's understanding and criticism of existentialism were superficial (let alone other churlish claims).

[7]Heinz Eduard Tödt, *Authentic Faith: Bonhoeffer's Theological Ethics in Context*, trans. David Stassen and Ilse Tödt (Grand Rapids: Eerdmans, 2007), p. 288.

Reason's technological growth spurt. First, Bonhoeffer clearly associated modernity with machines, symbolic of the new power of technology. As early as 1928 he found society to be longing for stability and
needing solitude, yet instead pursuing entertainment to the point of dis-
traction.[8] The machine era is one of naïve enthusiasm regarding
progress,[9] while people have lost the ability to receive the natural
rhythms of their days as divine gifts.[10] It is not the use of tools that makes
this era new, but the violent spirit of mastery over nature that makes
technology an end in itself.[11] Ultimately this supposed mastery becomes
a new form of slavery.[12] As Bonhoeffer said later, "The benefits of technology pale beside its demonic powers."[13]

Bonhoeffer saw in the modern liberation of reason an absolute
pursuit of freedom that aped the biblical fall into sin.[14] He unflinchingly
insisted that for humans to deify themselves, to live as if autonomy were
everything, is to end in nihilism—to wind up with nothing.[15] To put
mechanization in the service of a vitalistic, romantic and nationalist
kind of humanly-defined "life" is actually to idolize death.[16] The concrete German situation that elicited some of these later thoughts should
not be disconnected from Bonhoeffer's earlier and persistent character-
izations of modernity vis-à-vis technology; to the contrary, the German

---

[8]See his juxtaposition of the cross and twentieth-century humanism in Dietrich Bonhoeffer,
Barcelona, Berlin, New York: 1928-1931, DBWE 10:359, as well as his sermon on Psalm 62,
"My soul is silent before God, who helps me" (pp. 500-505). A 1929 note from a sermon
manuscript vividly declares the world to be without peace in light of the machines' noise and
pace (p. 551n21). Reading notes from 1930-1931 connect the first world war to the industrial
system (p. 427). Other examples of concern for quiet in the face of modern life include comments on pursuit of quality in the prologue from Dietrich Bonhoeffer, *Letters and Papers
from Prison*, DBWE 8:48, and the May 1944 "Thoughts on the Day of Baptism of D. W. R.
Bethge" pp. 386-87.
[9]See a 1932-1933 memorandum on the social gospel in Dietrich Bonhoeffer, *Berlin: 1932-1933*,
DBWE 12:241-42. That same winter Bonhoeffer lectured on technology and religion, but
those manuscripts have been lost (p. 119). Notes from that time suggest, "Now the human is
in service to the machine" (p. 199).
[10]Dietrich Bonhoeffer, *Creation and Fall*, DBWE 3:48-49.
[11]Dietrich Bonhoeffer, *Ethics*, DBWE 6:116.
[12]"Technology, which was intended to master nature, had been turned against defenseless
humans and thus robbed of its essential meaning!" Bonhoeffer, *Berlin*, DBWE 12:271.
[13]Bonhoeffer, *Ethics*, DBWE 6:116.
[14]Ibid., p. 122.
[15]Ibid., p. 123.
[16]See, for example, ibid., pp. 91-92.

situation in its concreteness should heighten our concern over just the sort of observations he initially made. A sophisticated technological society can easily wind up walking an extremely tragic path.

Bonhoeffer did not reject the use of tools; he refused to denigrate modern technology pure and simple. Solely to recognize its human hubris and to reject the world's coming of age might be refusing to accept divine providence. But sinful humans do not necessarily recognize the proper ways in which God's gifts are well received, and Bonhoeffer worried that technology would direct our focus onto material rather than intellectual, relational and spiritual needs.[17] That judgment proves itself time and again.

Modernity's deadly decay. Thus, second, along with Bonhoeffer we must acknowledge decaying elements in modernity, deadly ironies accompanying technology's rational growth spurt. The inability of newly mature humanity to live in harmony with natural rhythms points to the hubris involved in using technological power for building a world opposed to the one God created. Beyond Nazi fanaticism, more generally Bonhoeffer saw technology in terms of war against and among the very peoples so passionately pursuing it. The nihilism that results from deifying humanity consists, in part, of technology's war on human being— its weapons involving human self and mass destruction.[18] Cultural and spiritual fragmentation is a specific form of the modern decaying unto death.[19] So too are new forms of individualism and privatization.[20] Autonomy from others and autonomy from God are mutually implicating, although Bonhoeffer dared to hope that such modern godlessness might actually bring people nearer to the true, biblical God precisely by taking them farther away from false, religious ones.[21]

---

[17]See the June 30, 1944, letter to Eberhard Bethge in Bonhoeffer, *Letters and Papers*, DBWE 8:449.
[18]On the masses, see Bonhoeffer, *Ethics*, DBWE 6:119-121. On connecting nihilism with idolatry, see the June 27, 1944, letter to Bethge in Bonhoeffer, *Letters and Papers*, DBWE 8:447.
[19]See letters to Bethge in Bonhoeffer, *Letters and Papers*, DBWE 8: February 23, 1944 (pp. 305-6) and May 29, 1944 (p. 405). Also relevant are texts pondering "polyphony."
[20]See letters to Bethge in Bonhoeffer, *Letters and Papers*, DBWE 8: May 5, 1944 (pp. 372-73) and July 8, 1944 (pp. 455-57).
[21]See Bonhoeffer, *Ethics*, DBWE 6:124, plus a July 18, 1944, letter to Bethge in Bonhoeffer, *Letters and Papers*, DBWE 8:482.

Secular maturity? This hope leads, third, to positive elements in Bonhoeffer's construal of modern secularization. Reason's technological growth signals early death in some ways but genuine, newfound human maturity in others. To be sure, Bonhoeffer did not define secularization very carefully; at least in his later context he could hardly be expected to examine carefully its precise origins.[22] It is easy to get mistaken impressions from reading the "secular" passages in the earlier English translation of *Letters and Papers from Prison*. In fact, Bonhoeffer rarely used the relevant German word there; the newer, critical translation helpfully switches from "secular" vocabulary to more accurate "worldly" terminology.[23] Even so, Bonhoeffer did embrace a secularization narrative, and a number of collocated items in various passages bring to light his basic understanding of how modernity can thereby prompt Christians toward true worldliness.[24]

A first related subtheme is the liberation of reason, which surfaced above during the initial discussion of technology. Here we should simply mark the positive place of modernity in such histories of human thought. The coming-of-age metaphor comes from Wilhelm Dilthey,[25] but could also have come from Immanuel Kant or others. Kant's famous essay "What Is Enlightenment?" trades on the resonances of that German

---

[22]As Gustavo Gutierrez highlights, Bonhoeffer's models are psychological rather than sociopolitical, ignoring colonialism and other factors such as reductionism, historical consciousness, and so forth; see Clifford Green, "Bonhoeffer, Modernity and Liberation Theology," in Floyd and March, *Theology and the Practice of Responsibility*, pp. 125-27.

[23]Clifford J. Green, "Sociality, Discipleship, and Worldly Theology in Bonhoeffer's Christian Humanism," in *Being Human, Becoming Human: Dietrich Bonhoeffer and Social Thought*, ed. Jens Zimmermann and Brian Gregor, Princeton Theological Monographs (Eugene, OR: Pickwick, 2010), p. 86.

[24]Among these key "coming-of-age" passages are the following 1944 letters to Bethge from Bonhoeffer, *Letters and Papers*, DBWE 8: March 9 (pp. 318-24); April 30 (pp. 361-67); May 5 (pp. 371-74); May 29 (pp. 404-7); June 8 (pp. 424-31); June 30 (pp. 448-51); July 8 (pp. 454-58); July 16/18 (pp. 473-82); July 21 (pp. 485-87). See also "Thoughts on the Day of Baptism of D. W. R. Bethge" (p. 390) and "Outline for a Book" (pp. 499-504).

[25]As detailed in Ernst Feil, *The Theology of Dietrich Bonhoeffer*, trans. Martin Rumscheidt, rev ed. (Minneapolis: Fortress, 1985). See also Green, "Bonhoeffer, Modernity and Liberation Theology," pp. 121-22; Wolfgang Huber, "Bonhoeffer and Modernity," in Floyd and Marsh, *Theology and the Practice of Responsibility*, p. 13; Ralf K. Wüstenberg, *A Theology of Life: Dietrich Bonhoeffer's Religionless Christianity*, trans. Doug Stott (Grand Rapids: Eerdmans, 1998), especially p. 70. For the range of those influencing Bonhoeffer, see Martin Rumscheidt, "The Formation of Bonhoeffer's Theology," in de Gruchy, *Cambridge Companion to Bonhoeffer*, pp. 50-70.

word with passing through puberty; broadly speaking, such coming of age seems to be the dominant European conception of modernity's place in intellectual history. This liberation into the adulthood of thinking for oneself treats churchly, governmental and creational authorities as shackles from which reason must gain its release. Bonhoeffer further shared with much early modern German thought the rejection of traditional metaphysics as too static, problematic in relation to modern science and associated with religious inwardness.[26]

Indeed, a second subtheme is liberation from dualism. Bonhoeffer saw medieval monasticism as the apex of earlier overemphasis on spiritual existence. The Reformation and its aftermath were an epoch of fence-straddling, trying to keep feet in both spiritual and material realms, without effective integration. With modernity along came cultural Protestantism, in which the church wound up overemphasizing worldly existence.[27] Bonhoeffer's worry across all these platforms involved privatization of religion, in which dualism focuses everything on individuals and their inward aims or eschatological destinies. Positively speaking, modern emphasis on worldly existence could lead the church away from earlier, overly spiritual, forms of dualism—again, if culturally Protestant ways of falling back into privatized religious inwardness could be resisted.

A third secularization sub-theme obviously came on the heels of re-

---

[26]See the letters to Bethge in Bonhoeffer, *Letters and Papers,* DBWE 8: April 30, 1944 (p. 364) and May 5, 1944 (p. 372); also, "Outline for a Book," DBWE 8:501. The importance of eschatological tension for resisting metaphysics is noted in Luca D'Isanto, "Bonhoeffer's Hermeneutical Model of Community," in Floyd and Marsh, *Theology and the Practice of Responsibility,* p. 145. On Bonhoeffer's relation to Martin Heidegger's ontology, see Robert P. Scharlemann, "Authenticity and Encounter: Bonhoeffer's Appropriation of Ontology," in Floyd and Marsh, pp. 253-65. On his resistance to metaphysics vis-à-vis its Enlightenment legitimation of autonomous subjects (though application of this worry to Alasdair MacIntyre's thought seems questionable), see Hans D. van Hoogstraten, "Ethics and the Problem of Metaphysics," in Floyd and Marsh, pp. 227-30. Walter Lowe suggests that Bonhoeffer unfortunately mirrors what he opposes, failing to escape the identification of reason with the human subject and therefore with instrumental reason, in "Bonhoeffer and Deconstruction: Toward a Theology of the Crucified Logos," p. 216 of the same volume. For an illuminating discussion of Bonhoeffer's (non-metaphysical) theology as nevertheless (vis-à-vis Barth in particular) "an account of the continuities of God's identity, as well as human identities, socially and personally considered, in Jesus Christ," see Charles Marsh, *Reclaiming Dietrich Bonhoeffer: The Promise of His Theology* (New York & Oxford: Oxford University Press, 1994), p. xi.
[27]Bonhoeffer, *Ethics,* DBWE 6:57-58.

sisting dualism, namely, losing religion. This loss was already happening before Christians could intentionally resist religion in any particular way. Bonhoeffer accepted secularization as a fact: not just more public unbelief and less churchly involvement, but also changes among those who would still regard themselves as religious.[28] Today this view faces criticisms in light of developments in the global South, differences between Europe and the United States, and disputes among scholarly accounts of secularization. But one can also find Bonhoeffer's assertions to be remarkably prescient regarding the trajectory of European Christendom, and if nothing else Americans would do well to ponder our own marks of secularization. Rather than merely disputing over large-scale scholarly narratives, we must discern *how* modernity plays out in particular contexts and whether those conditions ought to be theologically celebrated or criticized.

Charles Taylor's recent work traces the modern shift as

> one which takes us from a society in which it was virtually impossible not to believe in God, to one in which faith, even for the staunchest believer, is one human possibility among others. I may find it inconceivable that I would abandon my faith, but there are others, including possibly some very close to me, whose way of living I cannot in all honesty just dismiss as depraved, or blind, or unworthy, who have no faith (at least not in God, or the transcendent). Belief in God is no longer axiomatic. There are alternatives. And this will also likely mean that at least in certain milieux, it may be hard to sustain one's faith. There will be people who feel bound to give it up, even though they mourn its loss.[29]

This depiction of modern Western culture offers considerable explanatory power, consistent with Bonhoeffer's musings: "The great invention of the West was that of an immanent order in Nature, whose working could be systematically understood and explained on its own terms, leaving open the question whether this whole order had a deeper significance, and whether, if it did, we should infer a transcendent Creator

---

[28]See coming-of-age texts noted above, especially the April 30, 1944, letter to Bethge in Bonhoeffer, *Letters and Papers*, DBWE 8:362.

[29]Charles Taylor, *A Secular Age* (Cambridge, MA: Belknap, 2007), p. 3.

beyond it."[30] That quotation from Taylor could basically come from one of Bonhoeffer's technologically-oriented modernity passages.

The important point for our present purposes is not just that certain basic features of Bonhoeffer's musings have more sophisticated staying power than some people realize. Significant too is secularization's confrontation of not just unbelievers or society in general but also believers—affecting not just religious adherence at the beginning but ultimately ongoing ways of life.

Christ's centrality: Cross and blessing. Bonhoeffer, of course, interpreted religionlessness in theological terms. He lauded human strength and lambasted attempts—churchly or otherwise—to prey on weakness or place God in our gaps.[31] This emphasis on strength reflects his worries about Nietzschean critiques of Christianity more than knee-jerk class instincts.[32] Most decisive, then, as a fourth synthetic factor is Bonhoeffer's theology of the cross. His concept of Christ as the "center" really has to do with mediation. As mediator, Christ is the One "in" whom each of us finds true humanity, relating to God and each other. We have no immediate relationships—except to Christ, who mediates all others. This allowed Bonhoeffer radically to affirm human strength, on the one hand, yet not to accept modern godlessness as an ultimate reality, on the other. For even the lives of godless modern people hold together in Christ, whether they know it or not, and Bonhoeffer dared to hope that these godless ones might be especially close to finding the true God

---

[30]Taylor, *Secular Age*, p. 15.

[31]See, e.g., these 1944 letters to Bethge in Bonhoeffer, *Letters and Papers*, DBWE 8: April 30 (pp. 366-67); May 29 (pp. 404-7); June 8 (pp. 425-30); June 30 (p. 450); July 8 (pp. 455-57); July 16/18 (pp. 478-82); undated (pp. 514-16).

[32]"This sort of complaint arises because interpreters fail to distinguish between a nostalgic defense of class-indexed mannerisms and a moral exhortation to preserve and cultivate the self-reserve that is inseparable from genuine respect for the concrete existential presence of the truly other"—so Jean Bethke Elshtain, "Bonhoeffer on Modernity: *Sic et Non,*" *Journal of Religious Ethics* 29, no. 3 (2001): 355. Bonhoeffer's patrician tendencies need not be denied, but Elshtain highlights a relevant factor. Comparison with Alexis de Tocqueville in this regard is interesting, from Ruth Zerner, "Church, State and the 'Jewish Question,'" in de Gruchy, *Cambridge Companion to Bonhoeffer*, p. 202. Though resistant to psychological speculation, Clifford Green still finds Bonhoeffer's depiction of sin to be autobiographically informed, suggesting that one can interpret his (self-)portrait "as a figure, an 'ideal type,' especially a type characteristic of modernity, just as Luther was characteristic of a late-medieval person"; see Green, "Sociality, Discipleship, and Worldly Theology," p. 79.

because of their resistance to other forms of religious mediation. If the church would quit trying primarily to impress on these people their weakness, and instead point them to God regarding their strength, then they might recognize the reality of Christ.

Such mediation ultimately leads to the cross, without which Nietzschean worries could easily mislead us simply into valorizing human strength under theological headings. Bonhoeffer's Lutheran heritage resisted any human alternative to the most crucial divine self-revelation. Hence religion seemed to be a medieval and modern version of "law," by which we are only to be driven to the gospel. Bonhoeffer's theology of the cross then pushed farther regarding implications for the doctrine of God. Not simply glorying in the paradoxes of the death of God for us in Christ, Bonhoeffer also read the history of Western Christendom in this light, daring to suggest that God has chosen to suffer the loss of religion—that is, loss of the divine as an essential hypothesis for managing human life—to help us recognize our true situation.[33] On the one hand God's weakness helps us to recognize our human strength, yet on the other hand God's weakness becomes thereby a strangely powerful form of action. True, "only the suffering God can help," according to Bonhoeffer, but the passage surrounding that very quotation emphasizes that God does help; God *is* with us. Bonhoeffer's account of worldly maturity involves doing away with false understandings of God, not the One who is our mediator in Christ.

When depicting true worldliness according to theological ends for human life—that maturity toward which reason's growth spurt ought to be directed and in light of which we must resist modernity's deadly decay—first and foremost we must speak of the cross. But Bonhoeffer also referenced the Old Testament in a number of the key letters, resisting any antithesis between the cross and God's blessing.[34] According to this perspective there may be a shift of emphasis from the Old to the New Testament, but not a fundamentally new approach. The way by

---

[33]July 16, 1944, letter to Bethge in Bonhoeffer, *Letters and Papers*, DBWE 8:478-80.

[34]The most important letter references to the Old Testament include these 1943 letters to Bethge in Bonhoeffer, *Letters and Papers,* DBWE 8: second Sunday in Advent (pp. 213-14); May 20, 1944 (p. 394); undated, containing a note on the Song of Songs (p. 410); June 27, 1944 (pp. 446-48); July 28, 1944 (pp. 491-93).

which we mature in true worldliness involves suffering. Suffering is our
way to freedom, at least insofar as obedient discipleship makes suffering
inevitable. Learning to live in accord with true reality means learning to
follow Christ in being for others.[35] Only in that form of discipleship do
we grasp what authentic this-worldliness means—but precisely in such
obedience humans embrace the freedom and blessing for which God
made them.[36] Having thus sketched Bonhoeffer's musings on modernity
to this end of cruciform blessing, we must now ponder what we can
learn for our contemporary contexts.

Taking on Modernity with Bonhoeffer

Secondary literature on the coming-of-age texts is quite massive; any
one essay's claims about the subject must therefore remain modest.
Moreover, not only are Bonhoeffer's understandings of modernity and
secularization understandably dated,[37] but his resulting theological
moves are further tied to his Lutheran heritage and other contested
particularities. Bonhoeffer is not always correct or fully coherent, but
remains important precisely because he does not fit into typical categories or propound a systematic program that necessarily elicits straightforward acceptance or rejection. Hence, merely to join or oppose certain
contemporary forms of Bonhoeffer enthusiasm risks doing injustice to
the historical contingency and theological complexity involved.[38]

---

[35]See especially the letters to Bethge in Bonhoeffer, *Letters and Papers*, DBWE 8: July 16, 1944
(p. 480) and July 28, 1944 (p. 493). In Bonhoeffer's book outline, the projected first chapter
references technical organization conquering nature (through which man "has learned to
cope with everything except himself"); the planned second chapter insists that Jesus is only
there *for others;* the third chapter applies the same point to the church (pp. 500-504).

[36]On authentic worldliness see all the coming-of-age texts noted above, starting with the
March 9, 1944, letter in Bonhoeffer, *Letters and Papers*, DBWE 8:319-21.

[37]We must remember that "the processes that once defined early modern Europe . . . now are
characteristic features of Third World societies," as noted by Vinoth Ramachandra, "Learning from Modern European Secularism: A View from the Third World Church," *European
Journal of Theology* 12, no. 1 (2003): 36. Put differently, modernity means modernization,
which is a present, not just a past, process; on implications of its elitism for underdeveloped
peoples see, briefly, Otto A. Maduro, "The Modern Nightmare: A Latin American Christian
Indictment," in Floyd and Marsh, *Theology and the Practice of Responsibility*, especially p. 78.

[38]"As a 'modern' theologian who has nevertheless inherited the legacy of liberal theology, I feel
responsible to address these questions." So an August 3, 1944, letter to Bethge in Bonhoeffer,
Letters and Papers, DBWE 8:498-99. This sort of assertion renders recent evangelical appropriations of Bonhoeffer too tame. He may have been a "Christ-mystic" as suggested in Georg

It is better to let these extraordinary Bonhoeffer texts provoke extended questioning than to propose quick take-them-or-leave-them answers. Aside from the early, very technical works, the Bonhoeffer corpus may be read best as a source of apocalyptic proverbs. That is a paradoxical genre designation: apocalyptic literature shatters the traditional thoughts that proverbs typically convey. Yet, despite varying complexity, Bonhoeffer's writings present compelling aphorisms, the kinds of spellbinding sentences that leave readers pondering. They are proverbial in this punchy, memorable sense. Yet this proverbial character should be dialectically juxtaposed with their refusal to accept and transmit the standard wisdom of any particular theological or cultural party. Memorable sentences appear not just because they are short and pungently written, but because Bonhoeffer thought provocatively too. It is not that Bonhoeffer should be dismissed as an academic theologian and treated only as a poet or prophet, merely a source of one-liners. Yet the genius of his theology, especially in view of how life circumstances shaped what written output we have, lies in its unfinished quality, by which Bonhoeffer raises afresh so many of our own supposedly answered or long ignored questions.[39]

To refrain from conforming Bonhoeffer to contemporary agendas re-

---

Huntemann, *Dietrich Bonhoeffer: An Evangelical Reassessment* (Grand Rapids: Baker, 1996). He was certainly an extraordinary witness to the gospel in a culture that horribly devalued life, as compellingly narrated in Eric Metaxas, *Bonhoeffer: Pastor, Martyr, Prophet, Spy* (Nashville: Thomas Nelson, 2010). These evangelical readings mark progress beyond earlier ignorance and fearful neglect. Indeed today's evangelical interest may manifest a kind of gradual publishing triumph for select popular spiritual writings over potential alienation that is somewhat parallel to the spread of C. S. Lewis's influence. Nevertheless, the Bonhoeffer emerging from such evangelicals does not seem to be as intellectually complicated—or resistant to straightforwardly fitting agendas on any side—as the primary texts and secondary scholarly consensus demand. Though resonances with any such figure are selective, some evangelicals (like early secular theologians) slide beyond inevitable selectivity into self-indulgent hagiography.

[39]Style matches or even generates substance: the contingency of the epistolary form, in particular, fits the contingency of divine revelation, as explored in Wayne Whitson Floyd Jr., "Style and the Critique of Metaphysics: The Letter as Form in Bonhoeffer and Adorno," in Floyd and Marsh, *Theology and the Practice of Responsibility*, especially p. 248. The apparent disjunctions between affirmation of modernity and adherence to traditional Christian discipleship are precisely "the signs of the continuing capacity of the Dietrich Bonhoeffer of *Letters and Papers from Prison* to address humanity in our time," according to Peter Selby, "Christianity in a World Come of Age," in de Gruchy, *Cambridge Companion to Bonhoeffer*, p. 228.

quires theological restraint, the acceptance of his and our freedom before God. This very form of restraint, however, ironically requires that we "use" Bonhoeffer in discerning an appropriate response to our own contexts. For we could not slavishly follow all the paradoxical lines of his thought at once, even if we could somehow develop historically responsible contemporary directions for each. In that spirit, then, Bonhoeffer's apocalyptic proverbs point our present response to modernity in two basic directions.

Secularization and the Old Testament. To begin with, Bonhoeffer indicates the need to recover the Old Testament for theological reflection—not just elements of the Law to buttress culture wars, or Psalms to ring true spiritually, or Proverbs to provide moral formation, or prophetic writings to challenge social injustice, or Ecclesiastes to win over angst-ridden youth. More generally for Bonhoeffer the Old Testament conveys an earthy anthropology. This runs contrary to our intuitive suspicions about a clash between the Scriptures and humanity's coming of age. Obviously the possibility of overcoming such a clash depends on which aspects of modernity or what construal of true worldliness one celebrates, but Bonhoeffer's reading is particularly striking in the face of widespread denigration of the Old Testament in his time. Today we publicly scorn anti-Semitism, but our commitment to the Christian gospel can still shift into subtle anti-Judaism including neglect of the Old Testament's affirmation of ordinary life. We forget that the living Christ speaks through those very Scriptures of Israel that were active in shaping the human vocation Jesus fulfilled.

Being cross-centered may seem to clash with celebrating the goodness of creation. Moreover, when seeking to overcome unhealthy dualism, contemporary Christians may fail to acknowledge the extent of human fallenness or the importance of the church's redemptive mission. Bonhoeffer not only points to earthy material that is easy to neglect—for instance, affirmations of bodily delight in Ecclesiastes. More deeply, the whole of his corpus helps with the perceived tensions by juxtaposing celebration of created goods with calls to true life as self-giving for others. Against either one-sided recovery of earthly blessing or escapist notions of redemption, Bonhoeffer points to blessing by way of the cross. His account of true worldliness calls for more holistic reading of Scripture, not least regarding how cross and blessing are interwoven with both personal and communal relationships—in short, highlighting the fullness of the mediation of Christ.

Put differently, secularization transcends what people say they believe or affiliate with, and how that settles their eternal destinies.[40] To focus only on these dimensions of secularization, in Bonhoeffer's estimation, would be to linger in religious dualism. The question of personal salvation is vitally important, but should not be formulated solely in terms of individual futures or assessment of those futures using falsely "religious" criteria. Secularization could be a blessing to the degree that it helps us recover biblical worldliness—a matter of lived practices and not just confessed beliefs.

Such true worldliness further points toward an account of responsible church life. As Barry Harvey points out,

> The fact that Bonhoeffer refers time and again to Old Testament texts drawn almost exclusively from exilic and post-exilic books when discussing a world come of age, religionless Christianity, and living completely in this world suggests that a typological connection is starting to take shape for him between the fate of the people of Israel during and after the Babylonian exile and the church's mode of sociality in a world come of age.[41]

Bonhoeffer's analogy of relationship between Christ being with and for the church, and the church suffering for others, may not seem revolutionary now.[42] Yet, however preliminary Bonhoeffer's account of this reality may be, its potential weaknesses are less problematic and its strengths are more profound than many contemporary alternatives it anticipated. Bonhoeffer's version of sociality appeals to richer doctrines

---

[40]Ramachandra also critiques a number of the aforementioned readings of modernity for "over-intellectualiz[ing] the processes of unbelief" in "Learning from Modern European Secularism," p. 39.

[41]Barry Harvey, "The Narrow Path: Sociality, Ecclesiology, and the Polyphony of Life in the Thought of Dietrich Bonhoeffer," in Zimmermann and Gregor, Being Human, p. 118.

[42]Today one scholar comments, "not many will dispute a claim like Bonhoeffer's that the individual and sociality of the human person are in some way or other interwoven." Kirsten Busch Nielsen, "Community Turned Inside Out: Dietrich Bonhoeffer's Concept of the Church and of Humanity Reconsidered," in Zimmermann and Gregor, Being Human, p. 101.

of sin, the church and, most importantly, Christ.[43] That is due, in part, to the influence of the Old Testament over his understanding of human life.

Technology and true freedom in Christ. Aside from pointing back to the Old Testament and the cross, Bonhoeffer takes stock of modernity by pointing toward the machine. Rarely highlighted in the secondary literature, technology is sometimes marginalized by characterizing Bonhoeffer's treatment of modernity in diachronic terms: according to one account, Bonhoeffer thought in terms of decay early on, and coming of age later—somewhat incompatibly.[44]

Yet larger scholarly trends find basic continuity between the *Letters and Papers from Prison* and key motifs from earlier writings. Why then should we find Christological continuity throughout, and view the prison letters' newness largely in terms of deeper questioning on certain subjects, only to turn around and narrate a significant point of discontinuity concerning modern technological rationality? Moreover, as a Lutheran and—to some degree anyway—an admirer of Søren Kierkegaard, Bonhoeffer reveled in paradox, thinking dialectically in certain respects. Does it make sense to interpret his later affirmations of a new worldly spirit purely in straightforward terms, marginalizing contrary evidence from the rest of the corpus? Particularly if the prison letters express occasional reflection rather than settled argumentation, it seems best to treat their "yes" to elements of modernity in dialectical fashion with earlier traces of "no," even while acknowledging that Bonhoeffer did struggle afresh with emerging implications of earlier commitments. This hypothesis gets further support from echoes of earlier themes in later texts.

Of course, technology as such is not a major Bonhoeffer theme. Yet it is an easily neglected factor in his thought. Construing modernity in terms of technology, and technology in terms of the human spirit, provides a theological bulwark against sometimes unbridled enthusiasm over the

---

[43]Sociality is the key to Bonhoeffer's theology in Clifford Green, *Bonhoeffer: A Theology of Sociality* (Grand Rapids: Eerdmans, 1999). For a compact overview, see Clifford Green, "Human Sociality and Christian Community," in de Gruchy, *Cambridge Companion to Bonhoeffer*, pp. 113-33.

[44]Green, "Bonhoeffer, Modernity and Liberation Theology," pp. 120-21.

world come of age.[45] Bonhoeffer did not uncritically celebrate mastery over nature, nor naively hope that humans could master life apart from God.

Ironically, many North American Christians have verbally resisted the idea of modernity—first in fundamentalist terms, and more recently in terms of controversy over so-called postmodernism. But we have not wrestled enough with modernity in between. For many of these same Christians have been early adopters of technology. While our churches are often appalled at notions of the world not needing God, most are simultaneously willing to minister with the latest techniques and without special divine action as a restraining hypothesis. Our official message may insist on the centrality of Christ, while our methods may resist a theology of the cross.

Jacques Ellul (1912-1994), a French polymath roughly contemporaneous with Bonhoeffer, relentlessly critiqued technology for transcending merely material changes and altering the human spirit. Ellul is worth mentioning because he was able to pursue concerns over the technological spirit far more thoroughly than Bonhoeffer while being intriguingly similar: a dialectical thinker, influenced by Kierkegaard and Barth; an opponent of "metaphysics" and "religion"; and an author of a large-scale ethics focused on freedom.

Ellul insisted that Christians have failed to make good on the promise of freedom stemming from the incarnation, to such an extent that modern humanity's pursuit of freedom always involves negation—and not just negation in general, but revolt against Christianity in particular. In this context Ellul alludes to Bonhoeffer:

> We have only ourselves to blame for the present situation. The secular world is by no means a world come of age. It is in fact the most infantile of all worlds. But it is so because Christians have not come of age, because they do not live as free men, and because they do not show the world what freedom is. Because they

---

[45]Briefly treating technology in relation to Bonhoeffer's ethics is Larry Rasmussen, "The Ethics of Responsible Action," in de Gruchy, *Cambridge Companion to Bonhoeffer*, pp. 210-11. Briefly referencing Bonhoeffer while attempting to address technology is Peter Scott, "Imaging God: Creatureliness and Technology," *New Blackfriars* 79, no. 928 (June 1998): 260-74. Scott's appeal for considering spatiality and temporality alongside sociality is well-taken, but remains theoretically abstract despite its appeal for concreteness. More promising categories from Bonhoeffer himself might be rest and movement.

have not done this they have condemned themselves to be rejected by men and
they have condemned men to pursue indefinitely a figment of freedom.

⨎   For ultimately it has to be acknowledged that Christians have not taken   ∜
up the freedom of Christ. Individual Christians through the centuries have
been free men, but not the church. Throughout its history the church has
studiously avoided the question of freedom. It has put it in parentheses. It has
concealed and resisted it.[46]

On the surface Ellul directly contradicts Bonhoeffer's use of the
coming-of-age motif. Yet both see in the work of Christ epoch-making
significance for Western culture. Both see in Christ God's gift that makes
human freedom possible. Ellul focuses more tragically on churchly
failure and the cultural reactions to this. Bonhoeffer's prison musings
focus more positively on overcoming the churches' fall into religion and
on opening space for Western culture's repentant freedom. Ellul goes on
to speak at length of dealing with "reality," an important ethical theme
for Bonhoeffer.[47] Both thinkers criticize the seemingly inevitable confusion of technical means with teleological ends.

When addressing technology, Ellul asserts that it is a matter of "ob-
jective mechanisms of domination" being established,[48] and these means
are universal:

Technology has become a mediation in all actions and for all purposes.
The technological path has to be taken to do anything at all in the world.
Technology also has its own exclusive efficiency. This is what charac-
terizes it. It thus cuts off all recourse to other types of efficiency. One can
no longer say as Ambroise Paré did: "I bandaged him and God healed
him." One cannot say: "I pressed down the accelerator and God accel-
erated the car." The regularity of effects, the exclusiveness of means, and
generalized mediation leave no place at all for the concept of vocation.[49]

---

[46]Jacques Ellul, *The Ethics of Freedom,* trans. Geoffrey W. Bromiley (Grand Rapids: Eerdmans,
1976), pp. 288-89.

[47]A major treatment of Bonhoeffer's thought on the whole is structured around this theme:
Heinrich Ott, *Reality and Faith: The Theological Legacy of Dietrich Bonhoeffer,* trans. Alex A.
Morrison (Philadelphia: Fortress, 1972). Thus, unsurprisingly, Ellul refers favorably to Bon-
hoeffer's *Ethics* and its claim that Jesus did not come to solve temporal problems; so *Ethics of
Freedom,* p. 373.

[48]Ellul, *Ethics of Freedom,* p. 418n47.

[49]Ibid., p. 502.

This seems to be thoroughly compatible with Bonhoeffer's earlier comments on mechanization and later comments on living without God as a hypothesis. It is possible and fruitful to see in Ellul's work a more sophisticated, detailed pursuit of the broad direction in which Bonhoeffer's inchoate thoughts on modernity and technology could go. Technology should not be relegated to a minor early appearance in Bonhoeffer's thought, lamenting decay before later lauding modern maturity. Instead, Bonhoeffer's musings on the human spirit come of age can be read more dialectically, with technology a background element that remains significant throughout.

Ellul acknowledges that theologians might try to handle technology purely in terms of using neutral objects for good ends. But, he replies, "this simply reveals . . . ignorance of the reality of the technological phenomenon," which cannot be limited solely to objects, for it now embraces a "civilization whose orientation is radically different."[50] Ellul recognizes that ministering without the God hypothesis can move us beyond healthy critique of "religion" toward succumbing to another form of its embrace.[51] We can move away from depending on God in supposedly infantile fashion all the way to depending on impersonal divine blessing of human market forces. The caution that comes from Ellul, consistent with Bonhoeffer, is that Christians, not just "secular" others, might come of age without coming to be in Christ for their brothers and sisters.

Bonhoeffer's contribution remains distinctive, though, for he does not lose the good and focus only on the bad. Ellul's acknowledgment of our using technology seems always and only to concede the inevitable. Rather than seeing human hubris as the tragic side of a more providentially blessed phenomenon, Ellul insists that technology is evil in an important, even fundamental sense. He loses its robustly dialectical aspect, with the only goodness apparently involving necessary divine accommodation to the fallen way things are.

Of course, it is unclear how Bonhoeffer might have theorized fully about technology. But he is clearer than Ellul and other critics about the

---

[50]Ibid., pp. 310-11.
[51]See, e.g., the comment on pastoral vocation, ibid., p. 503.

good involved in the human spirit using created objects and "creating" some of its own means. Bonhoeffer's and Ellul's comments are broadly consistent regarding technology as a systemic set of powers both expressing and dominating the human spirit. But their subtle differences could be vital. Whereas Ellul apparently speaks of power as always evil, even when tragically ordained by God out of necessity, Bonhoeffer has theological resources for speaking of power as a divinely-ordained good. Such power may seem to be paradoxical, stemming as it does from Christ's divine self-giving on the cross. The power of being for others is made perfect in weakness; the disciple's obedience is likely a vocation of suffering. But, for all that, it is also a source of the divine blessing for which we were created. Ellul can never quite say this clearly.

By contrast, it is a goal of this essay to show that reason's growth spurt, by which technology became pervasive, is ingredient to Bonhoeffer's account of modernity; that Bonhoeffer's account of modernity rightly says yes to this coming of age whereby false religion is overcome in the name of human freedom, while also saying no to the hubris that turns such apparent freedom into new forms of God-denying and others-dominating necessity; and, finally, that Bonhoeffer's account of Christ-existing-as-church-community could provide the resources with which to develop the Christian ethics of power that Ellul lacks.

These two thinkers can challenge us to take more seriously the positive aspects of modernity and the negative aspects of technology. Ironically, by contrast, many North American Christians have lambasted modernity and lauded technology. Modernity is not just about machines, which we humans have nearly always had with us. But the modern spirit both intentionally and unintentionally interweaves humans and machines in new ways, with the rationality that produced modern machines coming increasingly to define humanity itself. In response, while deeply critical of Western Christendom, Bonhoeffer and Ellul indulge in neither cheap shots at its ecclesiastical tragedy nor naïve celebrations of its ethical triumph.[52] The challenge of technology is

---

[52]"I am convinced that Bonhoeffer would share Paul Ramsey's amazement that there are so many 'post-Constantinians' who (1) proclaim with joy the end of that era, yet (2) never hesitate to issue advice to states as if they were Christian kingdoms, and (3) continue to applaud

much broader than what our churches and ministries use: the larger question concerns what true human life means in the era of the machine and its mechanistic underlying spirit. Bonhoeffer does not provide all the answers, but he was one of the first theologians to pose this question, even in an occasional fashion.

Insofar as the technological spirit is a complicated legacy of the Protestant Reformation, among other developments, it definitely presents spiritual, and not just intellectual or material, conditions to address. It would be facile to conclude that, because biblical Christianity presents human maturity in terms of dependence on God, and the modern West obviously overreached with its coming-of-age self-definition, therefore we should just ignore Bonhoeffer's prison writings. Instead, I have argued, we may read his reflections as apocalyptic proverbs, with particular attention to Bonhoeffer's earlier worries about vitalism and the mechanization serving such distorted pursuits of freedom. Biblical human maturity involves not only dependence on God, but also physical and social delight along with appropriate rational leadership of creation. Dualistic Christians can come to embrace these latter elements as Bonhoeffer points them back to the Old Testament. But we also need his dose of wariness about the nihilistic spirit behind humanity's "coming of age."

These concerns over which forms of earthly life the Scriptures truly celebrate arise when for example a recent essay asks, "Is Facebook Making Us Lonely?" The answer is a qualified yes, with the essay detailing health and other problems that follow for isolated human beings whom God made for relationship. At one point the essayist makes a forceful assertion with much larger implications for how we approach technology in general: "The problem, then, is that we invite loneliness, even though it makes us miserable. The history of our use of technology is a history of isolation desired and achieved."[53]

Ultimately, therefore, the question posed by Bonhoeffer's work con-

---

the destruction of the remaining 'social space' that sustains the independence of educational and other church institutions that will be needed if the church is to be even an effective sect in today's world, capable of conveying Christian ethos, faith, and practice to our children's children"; so Harvey, "Narrow Path," p. 115.

[53]Stephen Marche, "Is Facebook Making Us Lonely?" *The Atlantic* 309, no. 4 (May 2012): 68.

cerns which of our machines, and the aspects of technological rationality they manifest and foster, promote the bodily and social delights
blessed in the Old Testament and redeemed at the cross of Christ. But
this question comes with a corollary: which appropriations of modernity's technological machine in general, and of any particular machine—
for precisely Bonhoeffer's same world-affirming reasons—require our
resistance? Bonhoeffer will not provide any universal principles by
which to determine whether you should or should not purchase an iPad.
Yet, read with greater attention to the phenomena of technology, his
thoughts about modernity can foster discerning, authentically Christian,
freedom. For his apocalyptic proverbs can surface questions about
means turning into ends, while deepening our understanding of how in
Christ we are called to be for others.

6

DEATH TOGETHER

Dietrich Bonhoeffer on Becoming
the Church for Others

JOEL D. LAWRENCE

W<small>E SEE THE PRISONER, LOCKED IN HIS CELL.</small> He sits at a small
desk, writing. Though he is bound, his ideas are running free. It is quite
an irony actually: the time in jail has become one of the most fruitful
periods of his life. Those who wished to quiet him have given him the
platform from which his voice will be heard for decades to come.

On this day, the prisoner is sketching an outline for a book he will
write when he is released from prison. The outline focuses on the church:
the church as it must be when the war is over; the church as it must be
in order to spread the word of God's grace; the church as it must be after
it has failed so badly in its task of living out the lordship of Christ against
all other lords. The prisoner is focused on the very nature of the people
who follow Jesus Christ. As he pushes toward a definition of this community, he writes a sentence that brings together so much of what he has
believed and lived out in the past, and hopes to believe and live out in
the future. The words that are left after the pencil has finished its stroke
declare, "The church is church only when it is there for others."[1]

This sentence has become one of the most famous sentences written
by Dietrich Bonhoeffer. Many who come to Bonhoeffer's theology have

---

[1] Dietrich Bonhoeffer, "Outline for a Book," in *Letters and Papers from Prison*, DBWE 8:503.

been captured by his notion of "the church for others." This call for the church to follow her Lord by living for others has had monumental effects in engaging unjust political and economic systems that have suppressed the poor and the weak.[2] The phrase has led people to reimagine the church as a people who are called to follow Jesus Christ in "being for others."

In our day, many are sighing a lament for a church that is failing to live for others, failing to be the true community of God on earth, failing to live out her calling in the world. Today the church is looking for guidance: guidance in living out our vocation; guidance in understanding our mission; guidance in engaging our world with the life-giving gospel of Jesus Christ. And today many are looking to Dietrich Bonhoeffer as a guide for our times, as one who can encourage and inspire the church to faithful action. Today many are convinced that Bonhoeffer has something to say to us.[3]

But what does Bonhoeffer have to say? We have already noted that many see Bonhoeffer as a man of action, and so in turning their attention to his ecclesiology look for guidance by asking Bonhoeffer, how should the church *act* if she is going to be there for others? While this is an important question, and Bonhoeffer has much to say to us in reply, I believe that there is a different question that we need to ask Bonhoeffer if he is going to guide us in becoming the church for others.

The question that I propose we need to ask Bonhoeffer is this: how does the church *become* the church for others? This is a more basic, more fundamental question, because if we have not heard Bonhoeffer's answer to this question, then we will not truly grasp his vision of the church for others. Consequently, my purpose in this essay is to ask Bonhoeffer this question, the answer which leads us to a largely unexplored avenue in Bonhoeffer's theology: his notion of ecclesial transformation,

[2]See especially Rüdiger Scholz, ed., *Kirche für die Welt: Aufsätze zur Theorie kirchlichen Handelns* (Munich: Geinhausen, 1981); John W. de Gruchy, *Bonhoeffer and South Africa: Theology in Dialogue* (London: Paternoster Press, 1984); Josiah Young, *No Difference in the Fare* (Grand Rapids: Eerdmans, 1998); and Jennifer M. McBride, *The Church for the World: A Theology of Public Witness* (Oxford: Oxford University Press, 2011).
[3]The growth in Bonhoeffer's popularity is evidenced by the fact that Eric Metaxas's biography on Bonhoeffer was a *New York Times* bestseller. See Eric Metaxas, *Bonhoeffer: Pastor, Martyr, Prophet, Spy* (Nashville: Thomas Nelson, 2010).

or *how the church becomes the church for others.*[4]

My proposal for understanding how the church becomes the church for others is as follows. Throughout his theology, Bonhoeffer proposes a vision of the followers of Jesus Christ who share life together in being for others. But how does this "life together" come about in the church? How does this life of loving God and neighbor come into being? The need for this question arises from the fact that there is also in Bonhoeffer's work a strong theology of sin, in which the human creature is placed into bondage to self and so unable to exist for others. Bonhoeffer refers to humanity in this condition as the *cor curvum in se*—the heart turned in on itself—a phrase he inherits from Luther and utilizes throughout his career.[5] How, according to Bonhoeffer, do humans move from this state of being bent in on themselves to being free for others? For Bonhoeffer, this only happens as the form of Christ is formed in the church. But again we must ask: how does this happen?

It is my proposal that life together in being for others must arise out of an ecclesial transformation from selfishness to selflessness through communal practices by which the church participates in Christ's death.[6] The process of participation in Christ's death is the process that I have termed *death together.* It is through the process of death together that the church is transformed into the image of Christ in her life together. In other words, *apart from the transformative work of death together, there is no life together in being for others.* My aim in these pages is to describe death together and the primary practice by which death together occurs, the confession of sin. Only when we understand this aspect of Bonhoeffer's thought can we live out Bonhoeffer's vision of the church for others.

This essay is organized into two parts. First, I briefly explore three important aspects of Bonhoeffer's theology: his anthropology, hamarti-

---

[4]Two studies that discuss transformation in Bonhoeffer are Clifford Green, *Bonhoeffer: A Theology of Sociality* (Grand Rapids: Eerdmans, 1999) and David Ford, "Bonhoeffer, Holiness and Ethics," in *Holiness Past and Present*, ed. Stephen Barton (London: T & T Clark, 2003), pp. 361-80.

[5]On Luther's conception of sin, see Martin Lohse, *Martin Luther's Theology*, ed. and trans. Roy A. Harrisville (Minneapolis: Fortress Press, 1999), pp. 248-57.

[6]For Bonhoeffer, the practices are baptism, the Lord's Supper and confession. In this essay, I will be focusing primarily on confession as the primary practice of death together.

ology and Christology, which provide us with a broad outline of Bonhoeffer's understanding of creation, fall and redemption. Here we discover that Bonhoeffer describes humanity as created to live in freedom, a freedom that is defined as freedom for others, but which is lost when humanity rebels against God, losing its nature as free for others and instead becoming entrapped in the self. But through Christ, "the human being for others,"[7] God redeems humanity from the heart turned in on itself as the form of Christ is formed in the church. Second, I will explore the theme of death together as the means by which Christ's life for others comes into existence in the church. Here our attention will be on Bonhoeffer's theology of confession of sin, which I will demonstrate is the practice at the heart of his understanding of ecclesial transformation, and so is the indispensable practice of the church that would experience death together and therefore have life together for others.

HUMANITY, SIN AND CHRIST

Bonhoeffer's anthropology: Freedom. To understand Bonhoeffer's anthropology, we turn to his lectures on Genesis 1–3, given at the University of Berlin in 1932-1933 and published as *Creation and Fall.*[8] In this work, we see Bonhoeffer outlining his understanding of "being for others" by defining God's creation intention for humanity as freedom, and defining freedom as "freedom for others."[9] Foundationally, human freedom is freedom for God: we are free to worship the Creator who has given us life. However, this freedom also means freedom for the other. From this it follows that freedom is not something that humans have as individuals, but only in relation to others. Bonhoeffer writes, "Freedom is not a quality that can be uncovered; it is not a possession, something to hand, an object, . . . it is a relation and nothing else."[10]

To explain this notion of freedom, Bonhoeffer turns to Genesis 2, which describes Yahweh placing Adam and Eve in the garden. Set in the middle of that garden are two trees, the tree of life and the tree of the

---

[7]Bonhoeffer, *Letters and Papers,* DBWE 8:501.
[8]Dietrich Bonhoeffer, *Creation and Fall,* DBWE 3.
[9]Ibid., p. 63.
[10]Ibid.

knowledge of good and evil. The Scriptures simply assert that the first tree, the tree of life, stands at the center. There is no prohibition, no other discussion of the tree.[11] Bonhoeffer states that the tree of life at the center means that God, who is the Creator and giver of life, gives life from the center. Adam receives this life by remaining oriented to God through obedience, but Adam's life does not take the center; instead, it remains outside the center while always being oriented to God.[12] Adam is free for God and neighbor only when God is at the center.

But there is another tree in the garden, the tree of the knowledge of good and evil. But why is this tree in the garden? Bonhoeffer states that the prohibition that Adam should not eat of the tree of the knowledge of good and evil is God's gracious act of giving Adam the freedom to be who he is.[13] By doing this, Bonhoeffer imagines that God is saying to Adam: "Adam, you are who you are because of me, your Creator; so now be what you are. You are a free creature, so now be that."[14]

These two trees stand at the center of the garden precisely because both indicate what it is to be human. Both life and limit are at the center of human existence. Limit is not something on the margins of human life but is a central aspect of living how God intended when he created his image on earth.[15] To be creature is to be free by being limited in being-free-for-others.[16]

Bonhoeffer's anthropology, then, has at its core a vision of life in which God and humanity live together in an unbroken union of loving relationality that is described as freedom for others. In expressing this vision of the human person-in-relation, Bonhoeffer orients human living outside the self in a way that doesn't erase the self, but expresses that human life can only be what God intends when humanity is not the center of its own existence, but remains oriented to God as the center. As such, for Bonhoeffer, to be human *is* to be for others.

---

[11] Ibid., p. 83. Emphasis in text.
[12] Ibid., p. 78.
[13] Ibid., p. 85. For more on this, see Ann L. Nickson, *Bonhoeffer on Freedom: Courageously Grasping Reality* (London: Ashgate, 2002), 67ff.
[14] Bonhoeffer, *Creation and Fall*, DBWE 3:85.
[15] Ibid.
[16] On this, Bonhoeffer writes, "The limit is grace because it is the basis of creatureliness and freedom; the boundary is the center." Ibid., p. 87.

Bonhoeffer's theology of sin: The heart turned in on itself. We turn
now to investigate Bonhoeffer's theology of sin, an aspect of his work
that has been given relatively little attention in Bonhoeffer studies but
is critical for our theme of death together and becoming the church
for others.

We have seen Bonhoeffer's description of created life as a freedom in
which humanity is oriented toward God at the center of existence, receiving life from God, and so free for God and neighbor. However, Bonhoeffer's hamartiology asserts that through Adam and Eve's rebellion, a
reversal occurs. According to Bonhoeffer, "the fall replaced love with
selfishness. This gave rise to the break in immediate community with
God, and likewise in human community. With this change of direction
the whole spiritual orientation of humanity was altered."[17] The result of
this is devastating: no longer do humans live a common life with God
and with neighbor, life together in being for others, but now each individual lives in isolation. Humanity has become the *cor curvum in se*,
trapped in the self and therefore no longer in unbroken community
with God and neighbor.

The act of disobedience in eating from the tree of the knowledge of
good and evil is the death of the creature. The creature rejects its creatureliness, instead becoming like God,[18] falling away from its origin and
so becoming its own origin, its own creator. The serpent's promise is
fulfilled: in eating of this tree the human has become like God, but this
is the death of humanity. To become like God by eating from the tree of
the knowledge of good and evil is to transgress the limit that God gra-
ciously gave to the creature. In doing so, the creature has, in fact, become
sicut deus—like God.

The result of this is that the creature must now live from its own resources. In this rebellion, the creature has stormed the center, and as
such, has made itself its own creator. Instead of living in continual dependence on God and receiving life as a gift, "now humankind stands in

---

[17]Dietrich Bonhoeffer, *Sanctorum Communio*, DBWE 1:107.
[18]In the text of *Creation and Fall*, Bonhoeffer uses the Latin term *sicut deus* to express this
   aspect of human fallenness, contrasting it with the *imago dei*. In other words, there are two
   ways of being human: humanity in the *imago dei*, which is the creation ideal, and humanity
   sicut deus, which is fallen humanity.

the middle, with no limit. Standing in the middle means living from its own resources and no longer from the center. Having no limits means being alone. To be in the center and to be alone means to be *sicut deus*."[19] Humanity has rejected the grace of the prohibition, receiving exactly what it desired: No longer the creature, we are now the creator. However, in being the creator of our own life we no longer receive the gift of life from God. Humanity will now live a fractured existence, defined by our knowledge of good and evil, which replaces the life giving Word of God. The life of unbroken obedience and communion with God and neighbor is no more. Now humanity lives, but lives out of its own resources.

To summarize, for Bonhoeffer, sin is truly death because it removes humanity from life oriented toward God as the center. With this, the creature who was created to receive life as a gift from God and to live for God and neighbor is now trapped in the *cor curvum in se*. Now humanity is in isolation, unable to live the life we were created to live because of our bending toward self, and in this state there is no possibility of being for others. In turning next to Bonhoeffer's Christology, we come to the way in which humanity is freed from the *cor curvum in se* to be once again set free for others.

Bonhoeffer's Christology: Jesus, the human being for others. In the same outline for a book in which Bonhoeffer defines the church as the church for others, he comes to his clearest definition of Jesus: "The human being for others."[20] This summarizes Bonhoeffer's mature thought on Christ, who is the one who has laid down his life for others in order to bring them out of the isolation of sin and restore them to life with God and neighbor. As we turn to Bonhoeffer's doctrine of Christ, we will see how his Christology impacts his ecclesiology, for the question that always concerns Bonhoeffer is how the form of Christ, the human being for others, takes concrete form in the world. Bonhoeffer is uninterested in theoretical issues of Christology; he is interested in explicating the nature of Christ and how that nature is concretized in history. And, as we will see, he states that this happens as the form of Christ, the human being for others, takes form in the church. It

---

[19]Bonhoeffer, *Sanctorum Communio*, DBWE 1:115.
[20]Bonhoeffer, *Letters and Papers*, DBWE 8:503.

is to this understanding of the relationship between Jesus and the church that we now turn.

Bonhoeffer builds the foundation for his understanding of the form of Christ taking form in the church in his doctoral dissertation *Sanctorum Communio*. There Bonhoeffer reworks the Hegelian phrase "God existing as community" by stating it in christocentric terms, "Christ existing as church-community."[21] In doing this, Bonhoeffer states the deep ontological connection between Christ and the church.[22] He makes this connection because he takes seriously the Pauline image of the body of Christ. Bonhoeffer does not interpret this as merely a metaphor: instead, he understands this to be a statement of the very nature of the church and its relationship to Christ. Jesus, the human being for others, is truly present in the church. We read, "Paul repeatedly identifies Christ and the church-community (1 Cor. 12:12, 6:15, 1:13). Where the body of Christ is, there Christ truly is. . . . The church is the presence of Christ in the same way that Christ is the presence of God."[23] While Bonhoeffer maintains a clear distinction between Jesus and the church, he does want to press into the image of the body of Christ and take seriously the idea that Christ is present in, with and through the church on earth.

As Bonhoeffer moves forward in *Sanctorum Communio,* he turns his attention to the church as the place where the new humanity of Christ is actualized—that is, comes into being—in history.[24] For Bonhoeffer, Jesus *is* the new humanity because through the death and resurrection of Jesus Christ, God has created the new humanity through the second Adam. But Bonhoeffer is not content to leave that new humanity in heaven at the right hand of God in the form of the resurrected Jesus Christ, only to be actualized at the in breaking of the eschaton. Instead, Bonhoeffer asserts that new humanity is being actualized in history through the work of the Holy Spirit *in the church*. Here the body of

[21]Bonhoeffer, *Sanctorum Communio*, DBWE 1:110.

[22]For more on the connection between Christ and the church, see chapter two of my *Bonhoeffer: A Guide for the Perplexed* (London: T & T Clark, 2010). Here I address the issue of the church as revelation that is contained in Bonhoeffer's notion of "Christ existing as church-community."

[23]Bonhoeffer, *Sanctorum Communio*, DBWE 1:140-41.

[24]For more on the realization and actualization dynamic, see Lawrence, *Bonhoeffer: A Guide for the Perplexed*, pp. 37-41.

Christ is being transformed into the image of the human being for others, with his nature taking the place of the nature of the *cor curvum in se*. In the church, there is an ecclesial transformation occurring in which the old humanity is being transformed into the new as the form of the resurrected Christ is taking form in the church.[25]

In this conception of the realization of the new humanity through Christ and the actualization of the new humanity in the church, the ontological relation between Christ, the human being for others and the being of the church for others becomes apparent. The church is the concrete form of Christ's life in the world, and this life is the life of the human for others. This occurs as people who are isolated in sin are transformed into a community that experiences life together as the Body of Christ, and as Christ's ontological form as the human for others takes form in the church, so making her the church for others.

Summary. Up to this point, we have traced in outline form the movement of Bonhoeffer's theology of creation, fall and redemption, looking at his anthropology, hamartiology and Christology. In the section on Christology, we have made the connection between Christ and the church: Bonhoeffer describes the ontological relation of the church to Christ through the notion of "Christ existing as church-community." The church is the community on earth that is being freed from the isolation of sin through the form of Christ taking form in the church. Through the formation of Christ's life in the church, the church is being renewed as the community who can be free for others.

Having established the theological movement of anthropology, hamartiology and Christology, we can now develop the proper object of our study, death together. The question we are asking Bonhoeffer is: *how* does the church become the church for others? To answer this question, we turn to Bonhoeffer's theology of confession of sin, the concrete discipline that is essential for the community who would move from the *cor curvum in se* to being for others. Bonhoeffer asserts that it is in the act of confession that the community, which would be in the form of Christ

---

[25]Bonhoeffer refers to Galatians 4:19, in which Paul speaks of Christ's life being formed in the church, at a number of places in his works. See especially, Dietrich Bonhoeffer, *Discipleship*, DBWE 4:222.

on earth, undergoes death together, a communal death that frees her for life together.

CONFESSION AS THE HEART OF DEATH TOGETHER

Bonhoeffer's theology of confession was most clearly developed during the mid-1930s, when Bonhoeffer acted as the leader of an illegal seminary, training ministers who would be pastors in the Confessing Church. During the earliest days of the seminary, while it was still located in the town of Zingst (before it found its permanent home in Finkenwalde), Bonhoeffer suggested that, in preparation for the first Eucharistic celebration in the community, the seminarians practice private confession with one another or with him. Eberhard Bethge reports that this suggestion created a sense of uneasiness among the seminarians. He writes, "Hardly anyone could bring himself to do this and the atmosphere was somewhat embarrassed and resentful," adding to this a wonderful understatement: "since that kind of thing was not usually done in the Protestant church."[26] Bonhoeffer did not force the students to engage in the practice, but he himself modeled his commitment to its importance by practicing it himself, at one point confessing his sins to "one who was quite inexperienced in such matters."[27] It is no coincidence that Bonhoeffer's deepest insights on confession come from the Finkenwalde years: he was leading a group of Christians in creating a true Christian community, and believed, as we will see, that without confession, this community would not truly take the form of Christ.

The two main places where we find Bonhoeffer's theology of confession are in his short work on pastoral care, *Spiritual Care,* and in *Life Together.* We will look at each of these in turn, getting an overview of Bonhoeffer's theology of confession from *Spiritual Care* and then exploring in more depth the dynamics of confession in *Life Together.*

Confession in "Spiritual Care": An overview of Bonhoeffer's view of confession. In *Spiritual Care,* Bonhoeffer titles his chapter on confession, "Confession as the Heart of Spiritual Care." Bonhoeffer begins this

---

[26]Eberhard Bethge, *Dietrich Bonhoeffer: A Biography,* trans. Victoria Barnett, rev. ed. (Minneapolis: Fortress, 2000), p. 465.
[27]Ibid.

section with the following statement: "The goal of all spiritual care is the confession that we are sinners. . . . The invitation to confession is the invitation to become a Christian."[28] The purpose of spiritual care is to call people to faith in Christ, a goal that can only be accomplished by breaking down the barriers of sin that block the person's faith. For Bonhoeffer, the call to confession is not a call to guilt, but a call to grace.

But confession is costly grace because confession means entering into suffering. It means bringing our darkened souls into the light. As Bonhoeffer writes, "Confession is not only a self-expression, but a liberation from that which destroys my very life, not along the lines of a self-transformation but through the forgiving means God has given."[29] One of the primary means of forgiveness that comes from God is the enunciation of this forgiveness by another person. In the act of confession, each person becomes Christ for the other. The word of forgiveness is truly the word of Christ, but this word comes to the one who confesses to a fellow human.

What is the grace that comes to us? It is the *grace of participating in Christ's death.* Here, the power of the death of Christ, putting to death the old Adam, is at work in the soul of the one who confesses. Confession to another human strikes a death-blow to our pride. As Bonhoeffer puts it, "Confession to another human being breaks this arrogance as nothing else can."[30] How is this arrogance overcome? In confession before another, "The old, prideful Adam dies a disgraceful death in great agony . . . in our degradation we find our portion in the disgrace of Christ, who was not ashamed to stand before the world as a sinner. Confession of sin before another person is an act of discipleship to the cross."[31] Confession is the act of the old Adam participating in the death of Christ, sharing in the cross. Confession, then, is the means by which Bonhoeffer understands that the *cor curvum in se* is confronted and crucified. This death is painful, but it is the gift of God.

---

[28]Dietrich Bonhoeffer, *Spiritual Care,* trans. Jay C. Rochelle (Minneapolis: Augsburg Fortress, 1985), p. 60. This is a paraphrase of Luther's statement, "Therefore, when I urge you to go to confession, I am urging you to be a Christian" (*Large Catechism* 32), which Bonhoeffer quotes in *Life Together,* DBWE 5:114.

[29]Bonhoeffer, *Spiritual Care,* p. 62.

[30]Ibid.

[31]Ibid.

The result of confession is twofold: First, confession brings freedom. "By confession we gain freedom from pride of flesh. . . . Complete self-surrender to the grace, help, and judgment of God occurs in confession. Everything is surrendered to God; we retain nothing of ourselves. Thus we become free of ourselves."[32] But this freedom from self is not a destruction of the self. It is the renewal of the self because confession is a conversion, and so as we confess regularly, we are regularly converted to Christ and to Christ's way of being. Confession is the death of Adam that sets us free to be our true selves for others.

Second, confession opens us up into true community. Bonhoeffer states, "Genuine community is not established before confession takes place."[33] This is a remarkable statement. *Without confession, there is no community.* Without the death of Adam that takes place in sharing in the cross of Christ through confession, there is no *true* church. The great importance of death for understanding Bonhoeffer's notion of the church for others is brought more clearly into focus. Confession is death and so confession leads to community. Bonhoeffer writes, "If anyone remains alone in his evil, he is completely alone despite camaraderie and friendship. If he has confessed, however, he will nevermore be alone."[34] He goes on to write, "Where people lament that there is no life in the church we might ask how that is connected to disregard for confession."[35] When there is no life, or life together, in the church, it is because there is no confession, no death together. There may be mutual associations, there may be warmth, there may even be moral acts of service that help others, but there is no true being for others. At the center of the community that truly lives life together in the full newness of the gospel there is participation in death together through confession.

As we turn now to Bonhoeffer's theology of confession in *Life Together* we will see some of the emphases from *Spiritual Care* repeated and stated in sharper and more forceful terms, and will also find new emphases that clarify the role of confession in ecclesial transformation.

---

[32]Ibid.

[33]Ibid., p. 63.

[34]Ibid.

[35]Ibid., p. 64.

"*Life Together*": *The four breakthroughs of confession.* The final chapter of *Life Together* is titled "Confession and Communion." In it we see Bonhoeffer delineate further the effects of confession. Here Bonhoeffer discusses four breakthroughs that occur in confession: The breakthrough to community, the breakthrough to the cross, the breakthrough to new life and the breakthrough to assurance. Let's look at each of these in turn.

First is the breakthrough to community. Bonhoeffer begins the chapter with a critique of the pious community that does not allow its member to be sinners. The main factor in keeping the community from becoming a real community, a community that is the renewed community in faith, is the failure to get past the pious façade to the reality of *sin* underneath. Piety is the lack of faith in the message of the gospel that we are sinners. "The grace of the gospel, which is so hard for the pious to comprehend, confronts us with the truth. It says to us, you are a sinner, a great, unholy sinner."[36] But the grace of God calls us not merely to our sin, but to God's love that justifies the sinner. "Now come, as the sinner that you are, to your God who loves you."[37] The grace of God in Jesus Christ means that "you don't have to go on lying to yourself and to other Christians as if you were without sin. You are allowed to be a sinner."[38] What should mark the church of Jesus Christ, then, is that it is the one community that is allowed to be a community of sinners. The community that God desires is a community of those who confess their sin before one another, and thus before God, in order to know the grace of God that frees from sin. The community is not allowed to be sinful in order to remain in sin, it is allowed to be sinful in order to be freed from sin through confession.[39]

This, then, is the breakthrough to community. I bring to the light who I am and who I am finds God's word of forgiveness. By bringing sin into the light the sinner is released from the individuating power of sin, and thus is brought out of the *cor curvum in se* and established in community.

---

[36]Bonhoeffer, *Life Together,* DBWE 5:108.
[37]Ibid.
[38]Ibid.
[39]Ibid., p. 109.

Bonhoeffer writes, "The sinner has been relieved of sin's burden. Now the sinner stands in the community of sinners who live by the grace of God in the cross of Jesus Christ. Now one is allowed to be a sinner and still enjoy the grace of God."[40]

But as we have seen in *Spiritual Care,* this breakthrough to community is a painful breakthrough, because it requires the second breakthrough Bonhoeffer describes in this chapter: the breakthrough to the cross. Bonhoeffer here reaffirms his teaching from *Creation and Fall* that pride is the desire of human beings "to be like God."[41] But in confession, pride is faced and countered. "Confession in the presence of another believer is the most profound kind of humiliation."[42] And this humiliation is participation in the cross of Christ: "By confessing actual sins the old self dies a painful, humiliating death before the eyes of another Christian. Because this humiliation is so difficult, we keep thinking we can avoid confessing to one another. Our eyes are so blinded that they no longer see the promise and the glory of such humiliation."[43]

Humiliation as Bonhoeffer describes it follows the pattern of Christ: Christ was not afraid to be humiliated as a sinner before the world.[44] He endured the humiliation of the cross for the joy set before him.[45] Confession calls for the sinner to do the same, to endure the cross for the sake of the joy that comes through confession, the newness of life. But for newness of life to come, we must endure the cross in the concrete act of confession. This is the true means of death. Here the power of the death of Christ is at work. Confession, then, is the taking up of the cross in order to follow Jesus. We read, "In confession we break through to the genuine community of the cross of Jesus Christ; in confession we affirm our cross. In the profound spiritual and physical pain of humiliation

---

40Ibid.

41Ibid., p. 111.

42Ibid.

43Ibid. We must be careful to understand the sense in which Bonhoeffer speaks of humiliation. This is not the humiliation of another that seeks to dehumanize them. This is the willing humiliation of the self before another that partakes in the gracious humiliation of Christ's cross. This is a humiliation that is glorious because through it forgiveness and new life are to be found.

44Ibid.

45This is paraphrase of Hebrews 12:2.

before another believer, which means before God, we experience the cross of Jesus as our deliverance and salvation."[46] The promise is that death leads to life. But in order to know life, death must be experienced *concretely.* This is not bearing the cross as a general abiding under the sufferings of this imperfect world, but bearing the cross through the painful act of confession.

The third breakthrough is the breakthrough to new life. Because this notion has been contained in the first two breakthroughs, I will only comment on it briefly. The breakthrough to new life means "Life with Jesus and the community of faith has begun."[47] Through confession, "Christians begin to renounce their sins. The power of sin is broken. . . . We are delivered from darkness into the rule of Jesus Christ."[48] As a result, the humiliation of confession, the breakthrough to the cross, becomes the joy of confession, the breakthrough to new life. In confession, sin loses its power. Confession is the doorway on the path from death to life. It encompasses the pain and the joy.

The final breakthrough in *Life Together* is the breakthrough to assurance. Here Bonhoeffer asks, "Why is it often easier for us to acknowledge our sins before God than before another believer?"[49] Bonhoeffer suggests that if we find this to be the case then we should be concerned that perhaps we are not confessing to God at all, only to ourselves.[50] So how do we break this loop and be sure that we are in fact confessing our sin to God and not merely to ourselves, and so find the assurance of God's forgiveness? Ironically, we can only be sure that we are confessing to God if we confess to another human. This is because "the other believer breaks the circle of self-deception."[51] Consequently, confession provides the one who confesses the assurance that there is true forgiveness and true life, the restoration of the creature and the creation of true community.

Through our investigation of these four breakthroughs, we have seen

[46]Ibid., pp. 111-12.
[47]Ibid, p. 112.
[48]Ibid.
[49]Ibid.
[50]Ibid.
[51]Ibid.

the importance that Bonhoeffer gives confession of sin in the formation of life together. Without confession, there is no true life. In this essay, I am claiming that the act of confession is the central praxis of death together. But we must ask a final question: in what way is confession a death *together*? If confession is only between two individuals, how can this be understood as a communal death together? For Bonhoeffer, even though it occurs between two individuals, in confession the church community is present:

> A confession of sin in the presence of all the members of the congregation is not required to restore one to fellowship with the whole congregation. I meet the whole congregation in the one . . . to whom I confess my sins and who forgives my sins. . . . If the Christian is in the fellowship of confession with a brother he will never be alone again, anywhere.[52]

Confession is the death of solitude, which is why confession is at the heart of death together. It is the act in which the community of Christ dies and rises. It is through confession that the form of Christ takes form in the church, freeing the members of the church from the isolation of sin and instead being conformed to the image of Christ, the human being for others.

As such, confession is the hidden center of the true community. It is hidden because it happens in private, it happens in trust, and it happens in the pursuit of forgiveness and righteousness. It is the fountain of life springing from the pain of death, a fountain that is unseen from the outside but which waters the community and allows it to grow in vigorous health. Without this gracious gift of death, there is no life. Because of this, a church community that seeks to be "for others" must die to self through the painful act of confession. But through confession the church becomes the true community that God intended when he created humanity.

We have now the answer to the question that has occupied us in the essay: how does the church become the church for others? Through death together, the communal participation in the death of Christ that occurs in confession, and by which the church is freed from sin in order to live life together in being for others.

---

[52]Ibid., p. 110-11.

Conclusion: A Call to Death Together

Earlier we read a quote from Bonhoeffer: "Where people lament that there is no life in the church we might ask how that is connected to disregard for confession." Today, we hear the voices of many who are lamenting that there is no life in the church, and many of our own voices are a part of that chorus of lament. To correct this lack of life, many are encouraging the church to change her focus, to engage in different activities, to rethink her mission, or to restructure her polity. But we must ask with Bonhoeffer: Is the lack of life in the church today connected to disregard for confession? Is there no life today because there is no death? Are we stressing new activities and structures through which we hope to create the life of Christ in our churches while we are avoiding the work of the death of Christ in our churches? Are we failing to find true life together because we haven't been engaging in death together?

I believe that we need to hear this call to confession from Bonhoeffer. If we are going to have life together in living out the vocation of the church for others, we cannot avoid death together. The church doesn't exist to simply be active; the church exists to be the form of Christ on earth. It is time to reinvigorate our churches with a true theology of confession.

7

DIETRICH BONHOEFFER

Under the Constraint of Grace

HERE I AM SITTING IN THE PARK in front of the University. Barth lectures this morning. I had a short talk with him [a while ago]. This evening there is a discussion in his house with [monks] from Maria Laach. I'm looking forward to it immensely."[1] Bonhoeffer had traveled to Bonn in great anticipation of his first visit with Karl Barth. Barth had moved the previous year from Münster to take the prestigious chair in Reformed theology. Bonhoeffer's parents hoped he would join them for a short holiday at their country house. He had returned only a few weeks earlier from an eventful nine months in America—an academic year at Union Theological Seminary that included a four thousand mile cross country road trip, another fourteen hundred miles on Mexican trains, Cuba for Christmas, and one overnight stay in the hamlet of Elmhurst, Illinois—and his parents wanted a little time with their globetrotting twenty-five-year-old son. But Bonhoeffer was on a pilgrimage of sorts, and as much as he adored his parents and the house in the eastern Harz Mountains, nothing was more important to him now than a rendezvous with Herr Professor Barth.

There was much that surprised Bonhoeffer when the two finally

---

[1]Dietrich Bonhoeffer, *No Rusty Swords: Letters, Lectures and Notes 1928-1936*, ed. Edwin Robertson, trans. Edwin Robertson and John Bowden (New York: Harper & Row, 1965), p. 119.

met. In photographs, Barth struck a handsome pose—a man of refined features with a slender and elegant face. But when Barth entered the lecture hall for the first class, "he looked dreadful," Bonhoeffer said. Barth paid little attention to his dress. He coughed and smoked constantly. He appeared disheveled and sickly. "Does Barth always look so bad?" Bonhoeffer asked his friend Erwin Sutz.[2] There were good reasons for the professor's disheveled look. Barth was still recovering from a bout of diphtheria, and the seminar began at 7:00 a.m. More important, Barth had recently begun work on the first volume of his *Church Dogmatics,* and he was beginning to grasp the enormity of all that lay ahead: rebuilding the crumbling edifice of Christian orthodoxy as a life's work. Barth had celebrated his forty-ninth birthday earlier in the year.

Barth's summer course had been announced as "Prolegomena to the Study of Dogmatics."[3] At 7:00 a.m. sharp, five days a week, after a short reading from the Losungen and a hymn, the man went straight to the doctrines themselves; although getting to the point in Barth's case rarely involved brevity. He lectured three hours every morning from manuscripts over which he had labored meticulously, often well after midnight. Once after his move to Basel, Barth agonized all night over the doctrine of divine sovereignty only to cancel class that day because he had not been able to state the matter to his satisfaction. He lectured on Christology, Trinity, incarnation, resurrection, the divine attributes. His intention was to stand inside "the strange new world of the Bible" and let its "wild and crooked tree" grow freely, without constraint.[4]

Bonhoeffer had been eager to hear Barth, and even at this early hour (Bonhoeffer being a late riser), and with Barth slightly off his game, he found the lectures riveting. "He really is all there. I have never seen anything like it before." But his early exchanges with Barth and the other students were another matter. The students seemed territorial and uncommonly deferential to the master.[5] And Bonhoeffer—despite his two

---

[2]Ibid.
[3]Some disagreement exists on the title of the summer seminar: Introduction to Schleiermacher's *Glaubenslehre* (Doctrine of Faith) has also been given as the subject.
[4]Ibid., p. 40.
[5]Ibid., p. 120.

doctoral dissertations to Barth's none—worried suddenly that he might be a "theological bastard."

In the Berlin theology faculty, Bonhoeffer's eclectic views were benignly tolerated. Bonhoeffer was the scion of the Berlin intellectual elite that encouraged its youth to traverse inviting and unfamiliar landscapes. This was essential to humane learning. In America, where Christians fashioned their theology like a man orders his car from the factory, all ideas were on the table if they served a useful end. Bonhoeffer encountered the New World as a blank canvas of possibility. Bonn was different. "No Negro passes 'for white,'" Bonhoeffer said. Images of his road trip through Mississippi and Alabama returned to him as an apt description of life among the Barth epigones.[6] In Bonn no less than in Birmingham the keepers of the gate will "examine your finger nails and the soles of your feet," he said. The Barth circle kept vigilant guard over its property. "Up till now they still haven't shown me hospitality as the unknown stranger."[7] And for the first week, after the seminar concluded at 10:00 a.m. and the other students hurried off together, Bonhoeffer found himself with a lot of free time in a city he found uninspiring. (10:00 a.m. was usually around the time Bonhoeffer, a late sleeper, started waking up.) He looked over class notes, read "some really interesting and lucid books"—studies in economics he may have brought home from New York—checked the proofs of his book *Act and Being,* read sections from Barth's *Ethics II,* took walks and wrote letters.[8] "I am all alone here," he said.[9]

A disagreement between Bonhoeffer and Barth arose one day after class.[10] Bonhoeffer was having tea in the professor's office, and the two were discussing the proper relationship between theology and ethics. The disagreement turned on the issues similar to the ones that sparked Bonhoeffer's lively exchanges with Reinhold Niebuhr the previous year in New York—but in a way that offered further evidence of Bonhoeffer's theological transformations during the American year. Barth was explaining to Bonhoeffer his understanding of the peculiar place of the-

---

[6]Bonhoeffer, *No Rusty Swords*, p. 120.
[7]Ibid.
[8]Ibid., p. 122.
[9]Ibid., p. 119.
[10]Ibid., p. 121.

ology among the disciplines—theology is the science that ventures a word about God, the second-order reflection on the church's distinctive speech and practice, the writing that seeks to capture the bird in flight, to speak the impossible—when Bonhoeffer asked what this had to do with reality. Bonhoeffer agreed with Barth on most of the basics. He agreed that the theologian must be a servant of the church. But Bonhoeffer moved now with the conviction that theologians must be willing to speak clearly and pay up personally. He found Barth impervious to the ethical—and social—dimension of doctrine, and aggravatingly so.

Barth responded with equal candor: Christian theology bore no responsibility for changing society. Theology makes nothing happen in the ordinary sense; indeed, as he would soon write in his essay *Theological Existence Today,* theology ought to be *practiced* "as if nothing else had taken place." He accused Bonhoeffer of "turning grace into a principle" and "thereby beating everything else to death."[11] In New York, Reinhold Niebuhr had criticized Bonhoeffer's exposition of the doctrine, which he submitted in a term paper and seemed to traditional Niebuhr rather lifeless. "Your conception of grace is overly transcendent," Niebuhr said.[12] There was no ethics there. But now in Bonn, Barth feared that Bonhoeffer was too eager to apply the doctrine of grace to ethics, to make the social connection. His view was not transcendent enough!

Bonhoeffer was surprised by Barth's reaction. In America, in the company of radical Christians, social gospel reformers, and African American churchmen, Bonhoeffer had experienced, for the first time in his life, the vitality of doing theology closer to the ground. The preeminence of the one great light, he now believed, must further inspire hope-driven interventions in a broken world. Bonhoeffer bit his tongue and said nothing further but later that evening he wondered—as he told Sutz—"just why everything else ought *not* to be bludgeoned to death."[13]

Bonhoeffer was relieved to learn from another student that Barth had thoroughly enjoyed the exchange. The professor himself welcomed the

---

[11]Bonhoeffer, cited in Ilse Todt et al., "Editors' Afterword to the German Edition," in *Ethics,* DBWE 6:411.

[12]Dietrich Bonhoeffer, *Barcelona, Berlin, New York: 1928-1931,* DBWE 10:451n13.

[13]Bonhoeffer, cited in Todt et al., "Editors' Afterword to the German Edition," DBWE 6:411n7.

contrarian voice. When the seminar resumed the next day, he asked Bonhoeffer to introduce himself to the other students. And an invitation soon arrived for a meal at the professor's home. "Barth [is much] better than his books," Bonhoeffer wrote afterward. "There is with him an openness, a readiness for any objection which should hit the mark."

Bonhoeffer left Bonn pleased to have heard Barth develop his position in more detail and also opine on a variety of other subjects. The three weeks had included "many real *bons mots*" and Bonhoeffer confessed that his initial impressions of the Barth circle had probably been too harsh. His students were after all people really interested in Jesus Christ, who tried to conceal their "pride of knowledge." They also turned out to be less restrained than first appearances; at a party celebrating the end of the semester, they performed a play Barth had written at the age of fifteen in the style of Schiller. Still, it was "time to go back home."[14]

Bonhoeffer's plan, such as it was, was to complete the process of his ordination to the ministry and work two part time jobs: as a chaplain at the Technical University in Berlin, and as an unpaid lecturer in the theology department at Berlin University, where he had earlier completed his doctorate. Two dissertations and a full slate of comprehensive examinations and his only options were an unpaid teaching post and an uninspiring chaplaincy—neither of which came with an office. There was some good news in the arrangements however: he had two months before the fall semester began. Two free months usually meant a leisurely stay at the eastern Harz mountains, or on the Baltic Sea, combined with interesting travels. Sutz asked Bonhoeffer to join him in Zurich for a few days, followed by a hiking expedition in the Alps. Sutz liked the thought of the two former Union classmates having time to read and talk in more tranquil environs than the corner of Broadway and 121st Street in New York. But Bonhoeffer passed on the kind offer. "Please go ahead and enjoy your mountains and solitude," he said.[15]

Instead, Bonhoeffer landed an invitation to an ecumenical conference in Cambridge, England, called (in the optimistic fashion of the early ecumenical movement) the World Alliance for Promoting International

---

[14]Bonhoeffer, *Ethics*, DBWE 6:121-22.
[15]Ibid., p. 122.

Friendship Through the Churches. This alliance had been founded in 1914 with the mission of working through the churches and across denominational divisions to promote world peace. Already, in 1931, two years before Hitler's rise to power, the World Alliance, as all ecumenical organizations, was held in suspicion by many church and political leaders in Germany. Yet Bonhoeffer was eager to attend, as the burgeoning ecumenical scene appealed to his cosmopolitan sensibility, and after persuading his parents to cover the fees, he caught a plane for the United Kingdom. "My sojourn in America," he said later, "made one thing clear to me: the absolutely necessity of co-operation [among the churches of the nations]."[16]

Bonhoeffer distinguished himself as a brilliant young ecumenist in Cambridge. His initial contribution was insisting that the movement strengthen its mission with firmer theological foundations. He made the point in response to certain Anglo-American delegates who seemed more interested in results than convictions, and rather too syncretistic as well. Bonhoeffer listened, debated and negotiated as one possessing that most rare of theological virtues—the ability to lay aside doctrinal objections for the sake of a higher good, the good being in this case the affirmation of the global, ecumenical church. Legitimate points of dispute had surfaced, many of which could have easily brought the proceedings to an end. But Bonhoeffer recognized that beyond doctrinal and creedal disputes lay the urgent mandates of peace and with it the work creating initiatives for local congregations—in other words, finding common ground on which Christians across the ecumenical spectrum might craft clear and concrete ways of proclaiming Christ as peace. These proposals formed the concrete mission of the church in nations of the West.[17] "The real key to Bonhoeffer's message," Visser 't Hooft recalled, was his "hunger and thirst for reality, for living the Christian life and not merely talking about it."[18]

[16]Bonhoeffer, cited in Mary Bosanquet, *The Life and Death of Dietrich Bonheoffer* (New York: Harper & Row, 1968), p. 98.
[17]Ernst-Albert Scharffenorth, "Editor's Afterword to the German Edition," in *Berlin, 1932-1933*, DBWE 12:490-94.
[18]Willem Adolf Visser 't Hooft, foreword to *The Steps of Bonhoeffer: A Pictorial Album* by J. Martin Bailey and Douglas Gilbert (New York: Pilgrim, 1969), pp. v-vi.

The week in Cambridge made a profound impression on Bonhoeffer. It was a decisive moment in Bonhoeffer's "turning from the phraseological to the real." The twenty-five-year-old academic theologian who had once intoned the glories of the Prussian army and lamented the "shame of Versailles" in the tradition of German Protestant liberalism now wholeheartedly affirmed the "unanimous message to the churches of the world." Equipped with his new bludgeon of the spirit, he called for a substantial reduction of armaments in all forms right down to the lowest degree; for a reasonable and just relationship between the nations under arms; and for the security of all nations against military aggression.[19]

After the conference, Bonhoeffer said he felt as if he had taken a leap into the unknown. Indeed on the home front, at least for anyone paying attention, Bonhoeffer's remarks in England were met with a hostile reception. Professors Paul Althaus of Erlangen and Emmanuel Hirsch of Göttingen coauthored a critical response in the *Hamburger Nachrichten*, which presaged the closing of the German Protestant mind. The two distinguished scholars, holders of prestigious chairs at two of the nation's finest universities, declared in no uncertain terms that in the current world situation there could "be no understanding between us Germans and the nations that were victorious in World War." In the view of Althaus and Hirsch, who could not yet be counted as extremists, any German who believed otherwise disowned their "destiny and their birthright."[20]

Otherwise, Bonhoeffer's hymns for a worldwide Christian fellowship played to an empty audience, and he was left searching for direction. His Cambridge address and leap into the global ecumenical communion put Bonhoeffer on a collision course with the German church, for whom

---

[19]Bonhoeffer, *No Rusty Swords*, p. 136; Bonhoeffer sought to frame the language of peace in the context of the dynamic God-human encounter. In contrast to the Anglo-Saxon view (represented at the World Alliance) that international peace was an ideal, an absolute, a "final order of perfection, valid in itself," an inevitable "part of the Kingdom of God on earth"—a view based on nineteenth-century doctrine of historical optimism—Bonhoeffer argued now that "the forgiveness of sins . . . remains the sole ground of all peace!" (pp. 168-69). Forgiveness of sins is therefore the "ultimate ground on which all ecumenical work rests" precisely because the "broken character of the order of peace" results from human rebellion against God.

[20]Paul Althaus and Emanuel Hirsch, cited in Larry L. Rasmussen, "Editor's Introduction to the English Edition," in *Berlin, 1932-1933*, DBWE 12:20n69. Also see Renate Bethge, *Dietrich Bonhoeffer: A Life in Pictures*, Centenary ed. (Minneapolis: Fortress Press, 2006), p. 54.

the internationalist turn posed a threat to the homeland.[21] "I just cannot
see how to get things right . . . in the unprecedented situation of our
public life," he said. "The cheap consolation that I am doing the best I
can, and that there are people who would in fact do much worse, unfortunately is just not sufficient."[22]

On a clear autumn day in 1931, Bonhoeffer finally returned to Berlin.
It was time to start the new semester. Arriving at the Anhalter Bahnhof,
the yellow brick train station on a busy corner of Wilhelmstrasse, his
father's chauffeur waited in the black Mercedes. Bonhoeffer was exhila-
rated by the week in Cambridge and equally by the hope of leaving
Germany again very soon—before the end of the month as it turned out.
The ecumenical movement toward which he had remained indifferent
in his student years now satisfied his desire to live with a greater openness
to the world. In the next year he would join his brothers and sisters to
travel to gatherings in Amsterdam, London, Prague, Chamonix, Ceirno-
horské, Kúpele, Gland and multiple visits to Geneva.[23]

But there were some inescapable realities to face upon his homecoming, the less than exhilarating details of the part-time jobs and uncertain prospects for future employment. While Dietrich was still in
America, his brother Klaus had sent him a grim report on recent developments in Germany. "People are flirting with fascism," Klaus said. If
the "radical wave" of right wing sentiment pulled the educated classes
into its momentum, then Klaus feared that it would be all over "for this
nation of poets and thinkers."[24] Bonhoeffer's friend, Helmut Rössler,
had warned of a "purified, glowing national pride" linking arms with "a
new paganism."[25]

Bonhoeffer had accepted the offer of *Privatdozent* in the theology de-

[21]The ecumenical sphere in contemporary usage includes cooperation between the two major
    Western churches, the Roman Catholic and the Protestant. The ecumenical movement of the
    1930s was intra-Protestant: Roman Catholic doctrine regarded Protestantism as an [inau-
    thentic] representation. See Ferdinand Schlingensiepen, *Dietrich Bonhoeffer, 1906-1945:
    Martyr, Thinker, Man of Resistance* (New York: T & T Clark, 2010), p. 81.
[22]Bonhoeffer, *No Rusty Swords*, pp. 123-24.
[23]Eberhard Bethge, *Bonhoeffer: An Illustrated Introduction in Documents and Photographs*,
    trans. Rosaleen Ockenden (London: Collins, 1979), p. 44.
[24]Klaus Bonhoeffer, cited in Rasmussen, "Editor's Introduction," in Bonhoeffer, *Berlin*, DBWE
    12:4.
[25]Rössler, cited in Bonhoeffer, *No Rusty Swords*, p. 73.

partment at Berlin University. He would keep the position, despite numerous interruptions, until being removed from the post in 1936 by the Nazi minister of education.[26] Still when Bonhoeffer moved back into his old room in Berlin-Grunewald, the awareness of the new realities hit first on a personal level. His assignment at the Berlin Technical University proved singularly frustrating. This Hochschule for the applied sciences was housed in a neo-Renaissance edifice occupying a forlorn urban trace on the easternmost edge of Charlottenburg. Bonhoeffer's offer to lead discussion groups on stimulating theological topics found exactly zero interest among the future engineers of Germany. He told his brother Karl-Friedrich he felt like a housewife who puts a lot of effort in her cooking "only to see it gobbled up like all the rest."[27]

In the first week of the fall semester, one disgruntled student twice tore down the fliers from the campus kiosks that announced the new programs of the term, fliers Bonhoeffer had taken pains to produce and post. Even after Bonhoeffer posted a "letter of concern" and new fliers on the same kiosks, the culprit struck again. This prompted in turn another round of fliers and another, less pastoral, letter. "To the fellow student who has now felt compelled to remove this notice for the third time!" Bonhoeffer wrote. "Why so secretive and why always the same joke, or why so terribly angry?" And then a plaintive, "Why not come round to see me sometime?"[28]

Attempts to host lectures, prayer services, and study groups ran aground, along with high-minded summons to "really concentrate on the Gospel and not get sidetracked." All remaining hopes were dashed when not a single student attended the first gathering of his study group, "The Crisis of the State and the Gospel" and "Jesus Christ." Morning devotions were canceled for lack of interest. During office hours he sat at a temporary desk waiting in vain for a visitor to arrive.[29] The few who came to see him wanted help with their finances. There was one exception: he seems to have caught the attention of some fraternity men

---

[26]See Eberhard Bethge, *Dietrich Bonhoeffer: A Biography*, trans. Victoria Barnett, rev. ed. (Minneapolis: Fortress Press, 2000), p. 173.
[27]Bonhoeffer, *Berlin*, DBWE 12:89.
[28]Ibid., p. 69.
[29]Ibid., pp. 118-20.

who agreed to a discussion on ecclesiology—so long as they met in a beer hall near the Alexanderplatz and Bonhoeffer picked up the tab.

Bonhoeffer was not one to easily discourage. He appeared, if anything, more insulted than demoralized by the philistines at the Technical University, and he turned his attention to his leadership in theology at Berlin University, his alma mater. The position of *Privatdozent* at Berlin University resembled the post—one might say plight—of an academic lecturer in a medieval university. Whatever income he received depended wholly on the good graces of his students, whose attendance was voluntary.[30] A barrage of new duties "placed a strain upon even" his capacious energies, as he struggled to find projects and relationships that brought him into contact with people outside the academy. He offered university lectures and doctoral seminars; he preached sermons and gave public talks, prepared candidates for confirmation and graded papers.[31]

For years Bonhoeffer had moved at an exhilarating pace: university studies in Tübingen of Berlin, Rome, Barcelona, New York, Cuba, England and Mexico. But now he was back in a city that felt to him increasingly spectral—and in his mid-twenties. He felt the shock that comes when one reckons for the first time with the costs of dissent. He was joining a faculty whose political orientation he no longer shared, and a church whose preaching he found stultifying and dull—and loneliness overtook him.[32] He told Sutz he felt "dreadfully [alone] even sitting in a whole crowd of people."[33]

The situation led Bonhoeffer into an unfamiliar season of self-examination. At one point in that unsettled autumn of 1931, Bonhoeffer decided he would rather be called a Christian than a theologian. His interest in the Lutheran doctrine of justification continued to shift and make uncomfortable demands. He asked how the Christian should act

---

[30]Bosanquet, *Life and Death*, p. 101.

[31]Eberhard Bethge, *Costly Grace: An Illustrated Introduction to Dietrich Bonhoeffer* (New York: Harper & Row, 1979), p. 44.

[32]Bethge, *Dietrich Bonhoeffer*, p. 173. Also see Bonhoeffer's citations on the same page.

[33]Dietrich Bonhoeffer to Erwin Sutz, *Berlin*, DBWE 12:102. In a letter to Paul Lehmann six months earlier, Bonhoeffer commented on the state of affairs in the universities: "A prelude to what can be expected from the National Socialists at the university is taking place right now in Halle, where the students (and not only the theology students) refuse to continue studying if a recently called pacifist professor of theology, who is an extraordinarily capable man, is not fired immediately [a reference to Dehn]. The intellectual level now entering the universities is simply dreadful" (letter of November 5, 1931, to Paul Lehmann, DBWE 11:61-63).

"under the constraint of grace" in obedience to Jesus. In September Bon-hoeffer's second book *Act and Being* was published by the Berlin-based Trowitz and Sons to scattered but favorable reviews—reviews he promptly dismissed as "far too scanty a recompense."[34] Holding the volume in his hands, Bonhoeffer called it an altogether disagreeable product.[35] His article "The Christian Idea of God," which appeared in the *Journal of Religion,* one of the premier North American theological quarterlies, left him "disgusted and ashamed."[36] In fact, heavy editorial changes in the English translation produced fairly mediocre results. The heavy scaffolding of academic God-speak produced an effect as claustrophobic as the midday trams. "Some-times I wish that I could go somewhere into the country to get out of the way of everything that is wanted and expected of me. It is not that I am afraid of disappointing—or at least I hope not that primarily—but that sometimes I simply cannot see how I am going to get things right."[37] In the company of the Barthians, he had felt "an illegitimate among thorough-breds," but among the Berlin professoriate, he struggled to breathe. "My theological origin is becoming suspect and they obviously feel to have nourished a snake on their breast," he said. "There is nobody there who could teach us theology."[38]

In an Ascension Day sermon, he described authentic faith as an orphan-like existence. He asked how a person "torn by homesickness" can rejoice in life; how a dissident Christian can bear the rejection he must inevitably face? Bonhoeffer hoped, in this period, that the church would carry the weight of outcasts, and it may have been only the memory of the black churches of America that enabled such an auda-

---

[34]Bonhoeffer, *No Rusty Swords,* p. 123.

[35]Dietrich Bonhoeffer, "To Erwin Sutz, Berlin, February 28, 1932," in *Ecumenical, Academic, and Pastoral Work: 1931-1932,* DBWE 11:96.

[36]Clifford Green, "Editor's Introduction to the English Edition," in *Barcelona, Berlin, New York: 1928-1931,* DBWE 10:36.

[37]Bonhoeffer, *No Rusty Swords,* pp. 123-24.

[38]Dorothea Wendebourg puts Bonhoeffer's perception in a wider context: "This assumption came out of a feeling of alienation. Probably it was not completely true because there are several wit-nesses of respect for the young lecturer from his colleagues. In summer 1933, when he was al-ready on leave and on his way to England, the faculty even thought about calling him to succeed to Titius' chair that was free. They were aware that Bonhoeffer was 'our best hope of the faculty.'" Dorothea Wendebourg, "Dietrich Bonhoeffer und die Berliner Universität," trans. Ingrid Muel-ler and Charles Marsh, *Berliner Theologische Zeitschrift* 23 (2006): 285-312.

cious hope: the church, or a remnant thereof, bearing witness to truth in an era of propaganda, and mediocrity, and doing so joyfully.

Desperate for fresh air, Bonhoeffer lobbied the senior faculty to bring Karl Barth to Berlin as the successor to Arthur Titius. "Now Barth is really someone from whom poor, desolate Berlin could learn a thing or two about God."[39] But an assistant lecturer's endorsements carried little weight and his efforts were unsuccessful. Bonhoeffer wrote in an essay that Christ means freedom—freedom from "the lie that I am the only one there, that I am the center of the world."[40] But around the theology department it often felt like he was the only faculty member there. "I hardly ever see [any] of the professors," he said. "But I'm not incredibly sorry about that." The massive gray-stone edifice on Unter den Linden had all the charm of a mausoleum. The affable liberal men who had once filled the ranks of the faculty—like Bonhoeffer's beloved teacher Adolf von Harnack—had been replaced by scholars bunkered down in their offices. "Luckily I have my practical work," he said.[41]

On the fifteenth of November 1931, Bonhoeffer was ordained to the ministry at the Saint Matthias Church near the Potdamer Platz. It was not an especially memorable day. But he was now eligible to preach and administer the sacraments. In sermons of the period, he spoke of the Psalmist whose felicitous piety had been rudely unsettled in his encounter with the living God.[42] He said that the church must exist under the constraint that its first order of business was to proclaim "the words of Christ that there should be peace."[43] He admonished hearers to live without hesitation on the truthfulness of God's promises. To have faith was to live "totally" and unreservedly in the company of Jesus.[44] He was drawn into an intimate reading of the Sermon the Mount, Jesus' most

[39]Dietrich Bonhoeffer, "To Erwin Sutz, Bonn, July 24, 1931," in *Ökumen, Universität, Pfarramt: 1931-1932*, DBW 11:20, my translation.
[40]Dietrich Bonhoeffer, "Sermon on John 8:32: Berlin, Ninth Sunday After Trinity (Worship Service at the End of the Semester), July 24, 1932," in *Ecumenical, Academic, and Pastoral Work: 1931-1932*, DBWE 11:465-71.
[41]Bonhoeffer, *No Rusty Swords*, p. 140.
[42]Ibid., pp. 125-32.
[43]Dietrich Bonhoeffer, "Sermon on Matthew 24:6-14: Berlin, Reminiscere (Memorial Day), February 21, 1932," in *Ecumenical, Academic, and Pastoral Work*, DBWE 11:419-28.
[44]Dietrich Bonhoeffer, "Devotions on John 8:31-32: Berlin, Technical College, Beginning of Summer Semester 1932," in *Ecumenical, Academic, and Pastoral Work*, DBWE 11:465-71.

radical teachings on the extremes to which he calls his followers in their witness to peace. "Blessed are those who hunger and thirst for right-eousness, for they will be filled. . . . Blessed are those who are persecuted because of righteousness, for theirs is the kingdom of heaven" (Matthew 5:6, 10 NIV). These words were to be acted on in trust and singleness of mind.[45] The strange, new world of the Bible (as Karl Barth had called the counter-cultural impulse of the gospel) stirred his thoughts with cathedral-glory and he saw his life from a new perspective.

In February 1932 Bonhoeffer rented a second floor room from a master baker named Heide at 61 Oderberger Strasse, and moved from his parent's house in Grunewald to the working class neighborhood of Wedding. He had been placed as a pastoral assistant at Zionskirche around the corner. The assignment could not have pleased him more. "It's about the worst part of Berlin," he said to Sutz, "with the most dif-ficult social and political conditions." After his immersion in Harlem, the move to an urban parish felt like a homecoming of sorts. Except that the fifty teenage boys who fell under his supervision, sons of unem-ployed factory workers, proved more unruly than any child he had taught at the relatively silk-stocking Abyssinian Baptist. "The young men behaved like mad things," Bonhoeffer said of the youth group.[46]

But he discovered soon enough that boys could be brought to attention by the telling of Bible stories, the more dramatic the better. Bonhoeffer obliged happily, applying a theatrical flourish to his recitation of the "simple Biblical stuff with emphasis [on] the eschatological passages." The result usually produced "absolute quiet," he said. He was pleased with his success, and even more relieved. He told Sutz he no longer feared the fate of his unfortunate predecessor who dropped dead on the job.

Moving into a neighborhood hit hard by factory closings to be near his fifty new confirmands, visiting the boys and their families in massive public housing blocks, praying for the unemployed and destitute as they struggled amidst "indescribable poverty, disorder, and immorality," of-fering "soul care" to teenagers in crisis—this was at last the "real work."[47]

---

[45]Bethge, *Dietrich Bonhoeffer*, p. 204.
[46]Bonhoeffer, *No Rusty Swords*, p. 140.
[47]Ibid.

The prospects for the winter ahead were "perfectly horrible," with as many as seven million Germans likely to lose their jobs. "The misery is frightful," Bonhoeffer said, "and the most terrible thing of all is the hopelessness of this situation." The nation was on the verge of a complete breakdown. "We know how much we would need the church, especially during the next winter, but what is its message and who will listen to it?"[48]

Bonhoeffer devoted most of the second semester to his confirmands. He invited them in groups of twos and threes to Herr Heide's boarding house, served them supper, played recordings of classical music and Negro spirituals, taught them to play chess, read Scripture and told Bible stories. Sometimes he shared an account from his travels, and concluded the evening with "a short spell of catechizing." He marveled at the power of the spoken word of Scripture—with the benefits of his own rhetorical flourishes—to render the young ruffians spellbound, sitting before him with their mouths wide open.[49] No dramatic conversions or revival took place; the boys were simply paying full attention to the gospel, but that was miracle enough. "Perhaps the foundation has been laid for a faith that will grow."[50] Their ardor seemed evidence of divine protection; the refusal to collapse under duress, their "great—and I think also moral—power of resistance."[51]

Bonhoeffer found himself drawn to these people on the margins, "far away from the masquerade of the "Christian world"—the "little people" who lived "more under grace than under wrath."[52] His youth work in inner-city Berlin made Bonhoeffer acutely aware of the limitations of his training. Home visits left him feeling that he would have been better prepared for such situations had he studied chemistry instead of theology. "It sometimes seems to me that all our work comes to grief on the care of souls."[53] He struggled to say the right thing.

During his three months in Wedding, Bonhoeffer received a copy of Karl Barth's new book, *Fides Quaerens Intellectum*. In this slim but ex-

---

[48]Dietrich Bonhoeffer, "To Paul Lehmann, Berlin, August 23, 1931," in *Ecumenical, Academic, and Pastoral Work*, DBWE 11:43.
[49]Ibid., p. 150.
[50]Ibid., p. 151.
[51]Ibid., p. 140.
[52]Ibid., p. 37.
[53]Ibid., p. 151.

plosive volume, Barth plumbed St. Anselm's well-traveled ontological argument for the existence of God and reached new insights on the nature of faith. Barth showed that the argument depended on a prayer; and this discovery further signaled Barth's robust commitment to academic theology at precisely the time Bonhoeffer had begun gravitating toward a theology of Christian practices—although Bonhoeffer found Barth's book a splendid read.[54] Church life became the joyful counterpart to Bonhoeffer's work at the university. "Christ existing as community"—the eloquent but finally empty concept of his second doctoral dissertation—he found now in life together with the working class parishioners of Zionskirche. "What a liberation!" he said.

As an early Easter present for his confirmation class, he took the confirmands hiking on trails in Friedrichsbrunn. "Except for one broken window pane everything is still intact," he said to his parents. On the happy occasion of the boys memorizing the catechism, he threw a party to celebrate their success, complete with "sausages, cake and cigarettes."[55] Bonhoeffer had been confirmed as a child in the well-heeled parish church of leafy Berlin-Grunewald, though he rarely darkened its doors. Even during the year of his ordination exams, he attended services only sporadically. "I came to the Bible for the first time," he later said, and a "new and unexpected meaning" broke through its ancient words and phrases.[56] The Moravian Prayer Book his governess had given him as a child became the wellspring of his daily readings. He fell in love with the disciplines of devotional life. He organized spiritual retreats for the youth group, which he often held at his hut on four rolling acres near Biesenthal, which his parents had given him. He encouraged his confirmands to read Scripture with prayerful concern for the church and an attention to God's will. He spoke of a communal life of "obedience and prayer." Observing Bonhoeffer's new fervor, some family members and friends grew worried. Colleagues at the university joked of the monkish disciplines appearing in their ranks. Above all, the Sermon on the Mount moved into the center of his

---

[54]Ibid., pp. 140-41.
[55]Bonhoeffer, *Berlin*, DBWE 12:76.
[56]This phrasing comes from Inge Scholl's beautiful memoir, *The White Rose: Munich, 1942-1943* (Middletown, CT: Wesleyan University Press, 1983), p. 16.

thinking. He was haunted by the simplicity and directness of Jesus' teachings, the concreteness of their demands, "their objectivity."[57] The themes of Bonhoeffer's church talks clustered around a profound consideration: What kind of theologian and pastor—*what kind of Christian*—must we encourage for the uncertain years ahead?

Despite feeling alienated from the faculty, Bonhoeffer's question, as well as the manner in which he explored answers in his classes, was received by some students as a welcome break from business as usual. Bonhoeffer was not entirely alone in his discontent. Wolf-Dieter Zimmermann arrived at the university a cynical minister's son. He stopped by Bonhoeffer's lecture after hearing a fellow student describe the young *Privatdozent* as something different. Coming to the department in the footsteps of his father, Zimmermann's initial forays into the theology department had, he said, bored him "infinitely." There was "the pedantic juggling [of] Greek words," Professor Sellin's "formalistic" dealings with the book of Isaiah, rote translation of medieval texts (never to ask "what they meant, how they were related to God's actions") and "theological concepts [that] seemed meaningless . . . and gave me no guidance." Zimmermann decided to give Bonhoeffer a try. He attended first the course, "The Nature of the Church."[58] The "disheartening sight" of the sparsely attended class, only a smattering of students in large room, gave Zimmermann pause. He wondered whether he should not retreat, but "stayed out of curiosity," and was glad he did. "A young scholar stepped to the rostrum with a light, quick step, a man with very fair, rather thin hair, a broad face, rimless glasses with a golden bridge. After a few words of welcome he explained the meaning and structure of the lecture, in a firm, slightly throaty way of speaking. Then he opened his manuscript and began." Bonhoeffer explained that in these late times it was not unusual to hear people ask whether the church still had any relevance, whether they still need God. But this question, he said, was wrongly put. The paramount concern is "whether we are willing to offer our lives to

---

[57]Bethge, *Dietrich Bonhoeffer*, pp. 203-6.

[58]Wolf-Dieter Zimmermann, "Years in Berlin," in *I Knew Dietrich Bonhoeffer*, ed. Ronald Gregor Smith, Wolf-Dieter Zimmermann and Käthe Gregor Smith (New York: Fontana, 1973), pp. 58-59.

the church and the world, for this is what God desires."[59] Every sentence hit the mark, Zimmermann said. Bonhoeffer spoke directly to the issue that most deeply troubled him.[60]

It was not that Bonhoeffer turned ideas into easy formulas. His appeal was not as a popularizer. He lectured from meticulously written notes. He covered the fields of ecclesiology, systematic theology, biblical exegesis and church history. But the intellectual scaffolding, as Bonhoeffer constructed it, created a space where existential questions of faith and life, largely ignored by academic theologians, became inescapable. "Where is God? How does God meet us and what does God expect from us?" He spoke in a different voice. Bonhoeffer taught that an answer to these questions must begin with the more basic answer, "Who is this Jesus Christ, the one who encounters us in the Word of God?"[61]

As the youth group thrived in Wedding under his direction, barely a half mile away in Berlin-Mitte but a world apart, a small circle of university students formed around the young assistant professor, attracted to his subject and his style—a ponderous, pastoral theologian who soared into the heights but returned always to the origins. He spoke of God, Jesus Christ and the church in ways that sounded countercultural.[62] At the end of the fall semester 1932, when Bonhoeffer proposed that the class find a more suitable location than a sparsely-filled lecture hall at the university, Zimmermann offered his modest rooms in the attic floor of his father's parsonage at the Königstor near Alexanderplatz. Twelve students and the teacher met there for discussion, "sitting on every possible piece of furniture." The seminar usually ran for three hours. The air was thick with tobacco smoke. Topics ranged from the sacraments to salvation to ethics, but it was not so much the subject matter that made the evenings unforgettable. "What was far more important for us," a student recalled, "was working together to find clear ways of thinking," practicing single-mindedness, "learning not to slink off into side-issues, or to be satisfied with premature cheap answers."[63]

---

[59]Ibid., p. 61.
[60]Ibid., pp. 61-62.
[61]Ibid., p. 61.
[62]Ibid.
[63]Ibid., pp. 61-62.

Bonhoeffer applied his full powers to his lectures. Educating theologians and pastors in a nation on the eve of enormous and catastrophic changes placed great demands on teacher and student alike. Bonhoeffer had no intention of offering intellectual shortcuts. Seeing the world anew through the peace of Christ summoned every available resource. If "pure, abstract theorizing" illuminated the concrete situation, his habit was to gently rub his fingertips over his brow and do the hard work.[64] A question which student Albert Schönherr later confessed, the gesture always drew his attention to the professor's "big, Kant-like forehead." Seminars closed with a gentle *Danke,* and the invitation to reconvene in a nearby café to take up other subjects—which might range from the hot political topics to reminiscences of the Spanish bullfights.[65]

As Bonhoeffer welcomed newcomers and visitors each week, the class grew to a size that could no longer fit comfortably into Zimmermann's rooms. So he made the decision that the seminar should return to the university and meet once again in the lecture hall. This time the desks were filled, and it was not uncommon to find more than two hundred students sitting in rapt fascination.[66] More than fifty joined him for his "open evenings," when discussion of the week's lectures ran free, untethered to the syllabus or assigned topics.[67] Some of the students, having heard of his intensity at the podium, were at first surprised by the sound of his voice, high and slightly tremulous, "like a choirboy."[68] "In old papers I have noted down about him," Zimmermann recalled. "Near and far away at the same time, keeping a distinguished distance and yet ready and open." He has immense powers which are also immensely disciplined. Conflicts were experienced and borne by him in an almost "holy" way.

Bonhoeffer did not look like a man burdened by study, and he was, in fact, strongly-built, broad shouldered with an athletic frame, six-feet-one and ruddy complexioned, resembling more a skier than a scholar. "We followed his words with such attention that one could hear the flies

---

[64]Ibid., p. 62.
[65]Ibid.
[66]Bethge, *Dietrich Bonhoeffer*, p. 207.
[67]Zimmermann, "Years in Berlin," p. 62.
[68]Ibid.

humming," another student recounted. "Sometimes, when we laid our pens down after a lecture, we were literally perspiring."[69] No doubt his lack of sentimentality was a large part of his appeal, along with his deft and well-furnished mind, and his arousing "table talk" after the work was done. But students were also drawn to a more personal and perhaps more intimate quality. Bonhoeffer lived each day as a *bon vivant,* as if wanting to show that the pursuit of God inspired a rich and multi-layered worldliness. He would later discuss the musical aspect of po-lyphony as an apt metaphor for a humanism grounded in the incar-nation. Living in the fullness of the risen Christ enabled the capacity to see clearly. The technical concerns and philosophical terminology that distinguished his earlier academic writings, continued to animate his vocabulary, but as building blocks of a more vivid and expressive lan-guage. Bonhoeffer was interested in the whole person. And more than anything else the uncommon concern of a professor for the well-being of his students left the deepest impression. "In my days at a German university," wrote Paul F. W. Busing, "no one took any responsibility for nurturing the spiritual life."[70] Unless someone went on his own ini-tiative to visit a student chaplain or pastor, he was dependent on his own resources.

A photograph taken during a retreat in the village of Prebelow cap-tured Bonhoeffer and some of his university students in a perfect whim-sical moment. But the photograph is not an ordinary portrait. Only Bonhoeffer looks directly into the camera. He appears younger than most of the others; although attired in a beige tweed vest, white dress shirt and a tie—and sporting knee-high hiking boots—he is the best dressed. His demeanor is gentle and confident. His blonde hair, swept casually to the right, has begun to show signs of thinning. He seems completely at ease in his body as the men and women around him are captured into a spirit of good cheer. On the front row a man raises his

---

[69]Ferenc Lehel, "Seen with the Eyes of a Pupil," in Smith et al., *I Knew Dietrich Bonhoeffer,* p. 68. The scholar Ilse Tödt edited Lehel's class notes for the splendid little volume, *Dietrich Bonhoeffers Hegel-Seminar 1933: Nach Den Aufzeichnungen von Ferenc Lehel* (Munich: Christian Kaiser Verlag, 1988).

[70]Paul F. W. Busing, "Reminiscences of Finkenwalde," *Christian Century* 78, no. 38 (Spring 1961), p. 1108.

eyebrows and merrily plays a flute. Two women lean gently into each other, their arms draped casually around their shoulders. One man crouches alongside Bonhoeffer with a stick clutched comically in his teeth—it is an inside joke, perhaps, as others look on and smile broadly.[71] The scene evokes play and simple joy.

Bonhoeffer remained an outsider to the tenured professoriate throughout the years 1931-1933 and indeed until he was finally removed from his unpaid adjunct post in 1937. This distance—guarded in both directions—defined his habitation in the academy. Nevertheless, during this singular period between his return from America in 1931 and the deluge of 1933, Bonhoeffer became an unlikely, albeit minor, celebrity in the Berlin avant-garde. He gave voice to a spiritual restlessness that connected with students and pastors as well as artists and intellectuals. Ernst Barlach, the artist and playwright, heard about Bonhoeffer in a conversation with friends at a coffee house. Barlach invited Bonhoeffer to the salon he convened out of his Prenzlauer Berg apartment.[72] Every Tuesday night Barlach opened his rooms, with their famous black-papered walls, to a coterie of artists and writers—and now a theologian. Barlach's reputation had soared in these Weimar years with his wood carvings of the weak and infirm, and his gnarled bronze sculptures. His play about a hedonistic squire who contemplates suicide had recently premiered at the Staatstheater. While Bonhoeffer's own aesthetic tastes reflected the forthright and conservative standards of his family—he mostly ignored Hesse, Beckmann, Zweig, Schönberg, Honegger—his new theological style, observed in his lectures, sermons and writings, merged familiar images and ancient convictions with bold shapes and slashes, creating a subversive effect. "It is difficult to characterize the Bonhoeffer of those Berlin years," Wolf-Dieter Zimmermann recalled. "My memory has retained some moments of that time, whereas others have hardened into concepts, unconsciously. With astonishment I learned that he was a committed socialist and a pacifist." This revelation came as a shock to the German pastor's son, who had been raised on a diet of Luther's doctrine of the two kingdoms; it seemed to Zimmermann

---

[71]Bethge, *Dietrich Bonhoeffer: A Life in Pictures*, p. 53.
[72]Although he kept the apartment in Berlin, he lived in the town of Güstow/Inselsee.

so extreme that for a while he altogether mistrusted Bonhoeffer's views on Christian ethics.[73]

Creation and Fall brings one into the *Grossesaal on Unter den Linden* to hear the twenty-six-year-old Dietrich Bonhoeffer's lecture on the first book of the Bible.[74] Bonhoeffer's lectures on Genesis began Tuesday, November 8, 1932, and ended Tuesday, February 21, 1933, spanning the fateful winter of rancor and discontent as mass revolts by Nazi loyalists brought a violent end to the Weimar Republic, and Adolf Hitler was installed as chancellor of the German Reich on January 30, three weeks before the final class period.[75] The subject of the lectures was the holiness of God, God the giver of all good gifts, the origin and the end of creation's story. Free of theoretical scaffolding and scholarly throat-clearing, the lectures remained nonetheless the most ponderous of all Bonhoeffer's writings. The style introduces a concentration altogether different from the earlier academic writings. *Creation and Fall* is expressionistic and poetic, meditative and devotional, a luminous theology of dissent. It is the work of a Christian dissident awakening to his strange habitation in "the anxious middle."[76]

Creation and Fall resembled no other course in the curriculum. Only indirect attention went to debates in the guild; the published volume lacks footnotes. None of Bonhoeffer's contemporaries is mentioned by name. *Creation and Fall* is a dazzling, high-energy word event: it is not intended to be a systematic or historical subject. Delivered in five-hundred-word bursts of densely textured prose, the narrative flow and structure create a space of contemplative awe for the purpose of remembering the righteousness and transcendent mystery of the Creator. In the beginning God created. In the beginning there is only God. In the beginning God created the heavens and the earth. "Not that first God was and then God created, but that in the beginning God created." The beginning defines the basic distinction that only God is God; that God creates out of freedom rather than necessity; that the creature exists in

---

[73]Zimmermann, "Years in Berlin," p. 67.
[74]John W. de Gruchy, "Editor's Introduction," in *Creation and Fall,* DBWE 3:1.
[75]Ibid.
[76]Bonhoeffer, *Creation and Fall,* DBWE 3:30.

proper relation to the beginning by accepting its unsurpassable limit. This distinction must guide our thoughts and actions in all that follows, for it is only out of the anxious middle that we can learn the truth about the beginning.[77] The beginning marks humankind's mortal habitation and inescapable condition. "We do not know of this beginning by stepping out of the middle and becoming a beginning ourselves." The boast that we are masters of new beginnings is "accomplished only by means of a lie," although there are deceptions far graver than this. Humankind would love to turn back to its origins, to a "land of magnificent rivers and trees full of fruit."[78] But we cannot, and the realization that we are finally powerless against the absolute beginning, that despite the cunning of warriors and demigods we cannot master the origin—that is the great humiliation. That is terror's exile, the thought that cannot be tolerated in silence.

The students in the lecture hall could not have easily missed the political resonances and defiant notes in these brooding meditations on sin. He had opened the Bible to unleash the living Word against a church and nation on the threshold of catastrophic heresy.[79] The joyful and unscripted sojourns of people cleaving to Christ in an idolatrous age—this theme was the one remedy to egotism and delusion. Bonhoeffer said that in addition to reading the Bible as God's Word to us, the time had come for learning to read the Bible "against ourselves as well."[80] Bonhoeffer never discussed his spiritual life from the pulpit or podium. He regarded self-revealing talk in sermons as a vanity. But he had undergone a profound change in the past two years. "I no longer believe in the university," he said on the eve of the horrible year 1933. "In fact I never really have believed in it."[81]

[77]Ibid., pp. 30-31.
[78]Ibid., p. 81.
[79]de Gruchy, "Editor's Introduction," p. 3.
[80]Bonhoeffer, cited in Schlingensiepen, Dietrich Bonhoeffer, p. 93.
[81]Dietrich Bonhoeffer, London, 1933-1935, DBWE 13:217.

8

BONHOEFFER AND THE END
OF THE CHRISTIAN ACADEMY

KEITH L. JOHNSON

DIETRICH BONHOEFFER'S *VISION* MAKES HIM an especially interesting conversation partner. He just seems to see things differently than
the rest of us, as if he instinctively knows something about God that most
of us spend our lives seeking, but can never quite find. This unique vision
can make reading his work both an enriching and unsettling experience.
My task in this chapter is to bring Bonhoeffer's vision of Christ, reality
and history into conversation with the Christian academy to see if it
might equally enrich and unsettle us. I am using the phrase "Christian
academy" here in a particular sense to identify the network of professors,
students and staff gathered at schools dedicated to Christian higher education in the liberal arts and the sciences, particularly at the under-
graduate level. I have chosen the term "academy" rather than "college" or
"institution" because my focus is more on the *people* than the places. And
for the purposes of this chapter, I also am distinguishing the "Christian
academy" from those scholars and students one might find at a seminary
and from Christians serving faithfully in non-affiliated institutions, such
as state schools. By definition, the Christian academy seeks to be both
Christian *and* academic: its scholars and students aim to be faithful to
Jesus Christ while also seriously engaging truth claims offered by the
wider world of scholarship within the liberal arts and sciences. At many

Christian liberal arts institutions, this engagement is described as the "integration of faith and learning," which is defined as the attempt to show how the truth claims of academic learning correspond to the truth claims that arise from Scripture. The question working behind this essay concerns the character and purpose of this endeavor. *Why* do we integrate faith and learning? What is the end, or goal, of the Christian academy?

While Bonhoeffer himself never participated in the Christian academy as defined here, he makes an interesting conversation partner for it, because he spent his professional life living within the tensions that define it. He was trained to be a theologian in a state university by teachers who instructed him in the highest tradition of critical scholarship. He later taught at and led a seminary designed to train pastors for the church, and there the instruction focused as much on worship and prayer as it did on critical inquiry. So, over the course of his life, he lived and worked as a student and professor between the worlds of the academy and the church. And interestingly, Bonhoeffer seems to have become *more* rather than less faithful as a result of living within this tension. By his own recollection, he began his career as an ambitious, somewhat self-centered scholar from a family of scholars; however, by nearly all recollections, he became a scholar whose life and death were shaped determinatively by Christ, Scripture and the church.[1]

What might we learn from him? What might Bonhoeffer have to say to those of us who live and work in the Christian academy today? What would he say is the proper goal or purpose of our efforts? Bonhoeffer himself never asked or answered these questions directly, so my task in this essay is to work constructively to articulate what he might say were he to address the question. The goal is to stay faithful to his claims in their original context while translating and appropriating them into our own time and place. Of course, translating someone's thought to address

---

[1]Bonhoeffer himself remarked on this transition in a 1936 letter to Elizabeth Zinn, a distant relative: "I plunged into my work in a very unchristian way, quite lacking in humility. I was terribly ambitious, as many people noticed. . . . Then something happened which has tossed about and changed my life to this day. For the first time I discovered the Bible. . . . I had often preached, I had seen a great deal of the church, spoken and written about it—but I had not yet become a Christian. Instead, I had been my own master, wild and undisciplined." Cited in Ferdinand Schlingensiepen, *Dietrich Bonhoeffer 1906-1945: Martyr, Thinker, Man of Resistance*, trans. Isabel Best (London: T & T Clark, 2010), p. 95.

questions he himself never considered is by its very nature a risky and somewhat speculative endeavor, but it also, I would argue, is a very Bonhoeffer-like thing to do. To this end, I have summarized what Bonhoeffer might say to the Christian academy in the form of three positive claims. These claims work cumulatively, with the first two operating at a more theoretical level to provide the foundation for the third, which presents what I would take to be his vision for the purpose of the Christian academy. After working through these claims, I will offer reflections about what we might learn from them and how we might apply them concretely.

CHRIST THE CENTER

First, the Christian academy must begin from the presupposition that the person and work of Jesus Christ intrinsically defines all created reality and human history. This may sound like a fairly straightforward and uncontroversial claim, but that is only if it is misunderstood. In Bonhoeffer's hands, this claim entails the death and resurrection of all forms of human knowledge in light of the crucified and risen Jesus Christ. For him, to think about the world in a Christ-centered way is a very particular endeavor: it involves making Christ's justifying work on the cross the absolute basis and criterion of disciplined knowledge in all its forms.

Working behind Bonhoeffer's approach is his conviction that humanity does not inhabit nature, but *creation*—and creation is ordered from start to finish by God's plan for it in Jesus Christ. "When God in Jesus Christ claims space in the world," he says, "even space in a stable because 'there was no other place in the inn'—God embraces the whole reality of the world in this narrow space and reveals its ultimate foundation."[2] Created reality and human history should not be understood as the context into which Christ enters, therefore, as much as they should be seen as the space and the place *contextualized* by God's plan in Christ, a plan that extends beyond the horizon of the natural world and the limits of human knowing. The "whole reality of the world has al-

---

[2]Dietrich Bonhoeffer, *Ethics*, DBWE 6:63.

ready been drawn into and is held together in Christ. History moves only from this center and toward this center."[3] Christ is not auxiliary but basic to reality and history, and anything that is real and knowable has its meaning only in and through its relationship to him and his particular work of salvation.

This way of seeing reality and history challenges views that would define them in distinction from the particularities of the biblical narrative about Christ's life, death and resurrection. For example, Bonhoeffer would not embrace the approach that takes truth claims derived from the "book of nature," combines them with truth claims derived from the book of Scripture, and then tries to explain how the two books fit together. From his perspective, this approach starts from the mistaken assumption that there is a "preexisting historical space"—the book of nature—that can be defined first in distinction from the person and work of Jesus Christ.[4] This assumption is problematic because creaturely reflections on nature and human being—reflections that Bonhoeffer thinks adhere to the "temporally conditioned presuppositions of metaphysics"—have already defined what is true about reality and history *before* Christ himself enters the scene.[5] This preexisting definition thus restricts what Christ can reveal from the outset, and it often does so in ways that blunt the depth of human sin and God's judgment against it. For similar reasons, Bonhoeffer rejects the idea that natural and theological knowledge can exist as two distinct yet complementary ways of knowing the truth about God and God's relationship with the world, as if there were two avenues by which we can know one and the same subject matter.[6] Bonhoeffer calls this approach a retreat to "a general theory of being," and he argues that it blocks "the road to the genuinely theological concept of sin and grace."[7] Bonhoeffer's Lutheran approach to justification is driving his argument here. As Bonhoeffer sees it, Jesus

---

[3]Ibid., p. 58.
[4]Dietrich Bonhoeffer, "Lectures on Christology," in *Berlin: 1932-1933*, DBWE 12:325.
[5]Dietrich Bonhoeffer, *Letters and Papers from Prison*, DBWE 8:364.
[6]For this view, see John Henry Newman's remarks that "all knowledge forms one whole, because its subject-matter is one," in *The Idea of a University*, ed. Frank M. Turner (New Haven: Yale University Press, 1996), p. 45.
[7]Dietrich Bonhoeffer, *Act and Being*, DBWE 2:75.

Christ's death on the cross is definitive for the whole of reality and history, and there is no way to think about human being apart from this event and the fact that it reveals to us both that we are sinners under God's judgment and that Christ's grace and righteousness are our only hope. Any approach that brings what humans can know by creation together with what humans know by grace without accounting for Christ falls into abstraction, because it proceeds as if it were possible to talk about human being in distinction from the story of human sin, God's judgment against it and Christ's justifying death for it.[8] Bonhoeffer draws a stark line on this point: "There is no ontological specification of that which is created that is independent of God being reconciler and redeemer, and human beings being sinners and forgiven."[9] In other words, there is no way to talk about creation, humanity or history apart from the biblical story that finds its center in Jesus, the crucified one. "In the Christian doctrine of being," he insists, "all metaphysical ideas of eternity and time, being and becoming, living and dying, essence and appearance must be measured against the concepts of the being of sin and the being of grace or else must be developed anew in light of them."[10]

In concrete terms, Bonhoeffer's approach means that the Christian academy must see the world through a holistic lens of creation, sin, judgment and grace, so that no truth claim about reality or history stands apart from them. "Theological thought goes from God to reality, not from reality to God."[11] The Christian academy has to see reality and history through a biblical lens rather than reading the Bible through the lens of their preexisting assumptions about reality and history. To fail to do so is to proceed with an idealistic rather than truly realistic view of the world. Or, as Bonhoeffer puts it: "Apart from Christ as the origin, essence, and goal of life . . . and apart from the fact that we are

---

[8]Ibid., p. 74: "We must ask, in other words, where there is in fact a being of human beings in general that is not already determined in every instance as their 'being-in-Adam' or 'being-in-Christ,' as their being-guilty or being-pardoned, and only as such could lead to an understanding of the being of human beings. But then, a priori, the possibility of a guarantee of the divine continuity of being loses any basis."

[9]Ibid., p. 151. "Only in Christ do human beings know themselves as God's creatures."

[10]Ibid.

[11]Ibid., p. 89. He continues: "Human beings must be placed by God into reality if there is to be room for reality in their thought" (p. 90).

creatures who are reconciled and redeemed, we can only arrive at bio-
logical or ideological abstractions."[12] This means, he says, that Christology "is the invisible, unrecognized, hidden center of [all] scholarship," because human knowing proceeds rightly only when it is
ordered in and through Christ himself, the one "in whom are hidden
all the treasures of wisdom and knowledge" (Colossians 2:3).[13] On a
practical level, Bonhoeffer would say that this means that the Christian
academy must immerse itself in a Christ-centered study of Scripture,
reading and speaking the text to one another again and again so that it
becomes the foundational story for their lives. Our primary task, he
insists, is to be "attentive listeners and participants in God's action in
the sacred story, the story of Christ on earth. God is with us today only
as long as we are there."[14] When Christians begin to see themselves and
the world in this way, they will see that they live and work in the time
"between promise and fulfillment," a time between the ages.[15] They also
will recognize that the unity of Christian thinking about God and the
world—the very unity that exists as the presupposition of the integration of the claims of the faith with the claims of academic learning—
is strictly "an eschatological possibility," because this unity lies in God
himself.[16] The goal of the academic life lived in a world defined by Jesus
is not to figure out how everything fits together, but to seek after God,
and this occurs by grace through the power of the Spirit as we think
and live faithfully as Christ's disciples.

THE ACADEMY AND THE CHURCH

Second, *the Christian academy must see its own life and work as intrinsically connected to the life and work of the church.* For Bonhoeffer, this
second claim would follow as a corollary to the first. If reality and

---

[12]Bonhoeffer, *Ethics*, DBWE 6:251.
[13]Dietrich Bonhoeffer, *Berlin*, DBWE 12:301.
[14]Dietrich Bonhoeffer, *Life Together and Prayerbook of the Bible*, DBWE 5:62.
[15]Bonhoeffer, *Berlin*, DBWE 12:325. See also his earlier remarks: "We can never comprehend
our existence as a whole, because it is entirely founded on God's word—and God's word demands faith. Only to faith, in revelation, do we have access to knowledge that we are sinners
in the wholeness of our being, since it is only then, by God's word, that the wholeness of our
being can be placed into the truth" (Bonhoeffer, *Act and Being*, DBWE 2:137).
[16]Bonhoeffer, *Act and Being*, DBWE 2:89.

history find their center and meaning in the person and work of Jesus Christ, then to understand and participate in reality and history rightly, we must be aligned with what Christ has done, is doing, and will do in them. Bonhoeffer argues that this alignment happens in and through the church, which is the community defined by Christ's work in all three of its tenses. Christ judged humanity and justified the church on the cross, he lives in and for the church in the present through the church's practices, and he leads the church toward its promised future through the church's life in the power of his Spirit. The church is the community shaped by Christ's costly grace who lives in the pattern of the cross for the sake of the world in the hope of the resurrection. By living in this way, Bonhoeffer thinks, the church testifies to God's plan for history, fulfilling Paul's claim in Ephesians that God will make his divine wisdom known to the rulers and authorities "through the church" (Ephesians 3:10).

For Bonhoeffer, the question would not be *whether* or *if* the Christian academy should be connected to the church, as if that connection were optional or severable. Independence from the church—at least in terms of the Christian academy's distinct identity and mission—is not optional for the academy if it claims to be *Christian*. Rather, the question is *how* it should be connected to the church. What concrete shape should the relationship between the Christian academy and church take? Bonhoeffer's answer would correspond to his account of how we come to know and follow Jesus Christ. If Christ himself is the center of reality and history, then knowledge of reality and history must begin with the particular and concrete way Christ reveals himself to us. And one of Bonhoeffer's central convictions is that there is no neutral standpoint from which we can begin to ask about or have access to Christ without being confronted *by* him and called to live in responsibility *to* him. We cannot know and follow Christ on our own terms, as if there were a way to be Christian other than the specific path of discipleship to him. Christ comes to us and personally demands a response of obedience—and both his call and our obedience take place in the church.

This account of how we know and follow Christ distinguishes Bonhoeffer's approach from both the presuppositions of the academy in which he was trained and the most prominent theological trends of his day. Bonhoeffer's teachers, which included Adolf Schlatter and Adolf von Harnack, taught him to view Christ through the lens of historical-critical methods and to consider him objectively as a historical figure in distinction from the church's faith and practice. Despite his respect for them, Bonhoeffer never sat easy with his teachers' instruction, and this was partly due to his attraction to Karl Barth's critique of their method. Barth argued that the historical-critical approach left Christ as little more than an object under human scrutiny and control. Bonhoeffer shared these worries, arguing that to approach Christ primarily as a figure from the past is to treat him more as a power than a person, as if he could be assessed in terms of the "influence he has had in history."[17] This approach, he insists, "leads in the direction of trying again to get behind Christ's claim, and to ground it in our own."[18] It assumes the distinctively modern conviction that God has been "pushed out of the world" and must be reinserted into it by our efforts.[19] Yet the fact that Bonhoeffer would adopt these Barthian critiques of his teachers does mean that he was satisfied with Barth's alternative to their view. Barth had developed a theology of revelation that focused on the transcendent God's breaking into history through his Word, which is Christ himself. Christ remains "wholly other" from the world, always beyond history even as he enters into history to judge and justify it. Bonhoeffer worried that this approach so strongly emphasizes Christ's *distinction* from the world that his revelation *in* the world never takes on concrete historical form. Among other things, Bonhoeffer thought that Barth undermined the relevance and the efficacy of the church's practices. If Christ always remains distinct from the world, how could the church truly be his body *in* it?

Facing these two unsatisfactory alternatives, Bonhoeffer sublated them into a higher synthesis. Along the trajectory of his teachers, he argues that Christ must be approached in historical terms; yet with Barth, he insists that Christ is not "the object of religion, but something

[17]Bonhoeffer, *Berlin,* DBWE 12:310.
[18]Ibid., p. 304.
[19]Bonhoeffer, *Letters and Papers,* DBWE 8:455.

else entirely, truly Lord of the world."[20] So Bonhoeffer views Christ historically, yet not merely as a figure of the past, but also as the resurrected, ascended and living Lord of the present. "Christ's ascension," he argues, "means that, with Christ's distancing, his presence everywhere becomes possible."[21] He does not come to us "as timeless truth, but rather as truth breaking into a concrete moment, as God's speaking to us . . . God's Word personally addressed to the human being, calling him to responsibility."[22] Jesus is present to humans here and now precisely as "the Crucified and Risen One."[23]

Christ's personal address occurs in and through his church, which exists as the means and the form of his revelation to human beings in present reality and history. This proclamation takes place in both Word and deed through the church's preaching and sacraments. The sermon is "the form of the present Christ" speaking through the proclaimed Word,[24] while the sacraments enact a visible word, as "God hallows the elements of bread and wine by speaking the divine Word" through them.[25] "If we want to hear [Christ's] call to discipleship," Bonhoeffer insists, "we need to hear it where Christ himself is present. It is within the church that Jesus Christ calls through his word and sacrament. The preaching and sacrament of the church is the place where Jesus Christ is present. To hear Jesus' call to discipleship, one needs no personal revelation. Listen to the preaching and receive the sacrament!"[26] Note how Bonhoeffer pushes against the notion of an independent revelation, ruling out the idea that Christian existence is severable from the concrete practices of the church, as if Christians could be free agents who might just as well function independently of the com-

---

[20]Ibid., p. 364.

[21]Bonhoeffer, *Berlin*, DBWE 12:312.

[22]Ibid., p. 317. Or his earlier remark: "There is only one possibility for me to be truly searching for God—that I already know who God is. There is no such thing as blindly setting out to search for God. I can only search for what has already been found" (p. 303).

[23]Ibid., p. 310.

[24]Ibid., p. 318.

[25]Ibid., p. 319. On this point, he argues: "The sacrament, in the form of nature, engages human beings in their nature" (p. 318).

[26]Dietrich Bonhoeffer, *Discipleship*, DBWE 4:202. Also see his earlier remark: "Christianity without the living Jesus Christ remains necessarily a Christianity without discipleship; and a Christianity without discipleship is always a Christianity without Jesus Christ" (p. 59).

munity. As he sees it, the church is central to God's plan for the world,
and if believers are to be true disciples of Jesus Christ, their discipleship must occur in and through Christ's community. The proclaimed and visible Word they receive in this community is none other
than the word of the cross, the word of their justification. This Word
declares God's judgment against their sin, their freedom in Christ's
righteousness, and Christ's call to repent and obey on the path of discipleship. As a result, it "places the church community into a relationship of responsibility for the world."[27]

Indeed, for Bonhoeffer, Christ's presence in the church means that
the church plays a pivotal role in reality and history: "The space of the
church is the place where witness is given to the foundation of all reality
in Jesus Christ."[28] Or, as he puts it elsewhere: "The church should be
understood as the center of history."[29] This means that the church's way
of living and being must take a particular form. Christ speaks and acts
in the church "for me," Bonhoeffer argues, "he stands in my place, where
I should be standing. He stands there because I cannot, that is, he stands
at the boundary of my existence and nevertheless in my place."[30] Christ
binds himself to the people judged and justified by him and forms them
into his community, and this act frees them to follow after him in obedience. This is why "the righteousness of Christ should not just be taught
[in the church], but *done* [by the church]."[31] Jesus Christ saves and forms
a community that lives in his image: "The presence of Christ as Word
and sacrament is related to Christ as church community, just as reality
is related to form."[32] Christ "takes action as the new humanity," and the
church is the concrete and specific "form he takes."[33] And since Christ
himself lived and died for the sake of the world, the community that
bears his image also lives and dies for the world.

---

[27]Bonhoeffer, *Ethics*, DBWE 6:357.
[28]Ibid., p. 63.
[29]Bonhoeffer, *Berlin*, DBWE 12:326. See also his remark in *Letters and Papers from Prison*,
  "The church stands not at the point where human powers fail, at the boundaries, but in the
  center of the village" (DBWE 8:367).
[30]Bonhoeffer, *Berlin*, DBWE 12:324.
[31]Bonhoeffer, *Discipleship*, DBWE 4:120.
[32]Bonhoeffer, *Berlin*, DBWE 12:323.
[33]Ibid.

This insight puts us in position to assess the place and role of the Christian academy in relation to the church. The life and work of the Christian academy is intrinsically related to the life and work of the church because its confession that Christ himself defines reality and history arises in and through Christ's revelation through the church and its practices. The claim to be *Christian* is inseparable from these practices and thus inseparable from the community that confesses Christ and lives in his image for the sake of the world. The key question involves the nature of this connection. From Bonhoeffer's perspective, this connection would have to center on each believer's personal responsibility to obey Christ within the context of the larger church community. This is where our focus on the *Christian academy* rather than *Christian institutions* becomes helpful. Institutions do not receive the Word and the sacrament, but people do. Being a Christian scholar or student does not mean simply being a part of a Christian institution; it means being responsible to Christ within the concrete reality of one's particular life and calling in the academy in connection to the church and its mission. On Bonhoeffer's terms, this would mean living as a researcher, teacher and student through the church for the sake of the world. But what does it actually look like to live in this way? How do the members of the Christian academy, in their intrinsic relationship to the church, live as obedient disciples of Christ for sake of the world within the context of their academic vocation?

ACADEMY FOR THE CHURCH

Third, *the Christian academy exists in and for the church in order to help the church exist in and for the world.* Bonhoeffer's understanding of the Christian academy's relationship to the church would follow from his account of the church's relationship to the world. If the church stands in the center of history because Christ makes himself present in and through it—and if the church is committed to following after Christ through its confession and obedience—then the church will exist for the world by living in obedience to Christ in both word and deed. This way of being for the world is the being of a disciple. Yet this way of being runs counter to the church's "natural instinct for self-preservation," because it calls the church to live for the sake of others rather than for itself.[34] So, the church needs to be both encouraged and held accountable so that it actually will live in this pattern. The Christian academy participates in the life of the church in precisely this way: by encouraging the church and by holding it accountable.

To unpack what this looks like, we can turn to Bonhoeffer's claims about religionless Christianity in a world come of age. The key to understanding these claims is to recognize that they are not about religion as much as they are about Christ. Bonhoeffer insists that the crucified and risen Christ cannot be constrained by a priori assumptions that bind him to particular cultural expressions, because these assumptions place Christ on our terms rather than the other way around. In the modern world, he thinks this happens in one of two ways: either Christ is thought to work strictly in the inner spiritual life of the Christian—"he lives, he lives, he lives within my heart," as the old hymn goes—or he is thought of as a metaphysically transcendent being who acts beyond history rather than in it.[35] "Neither [assumption] is appropriate," Bonhoeffer argues, "either for the biblical message or for people today," because both assumptions relegate Christ to a spiritual plane divorced from reality and history.[36] If Jesus Christ is the center of reality and history, then he lives and works in them *as they are*. Only when we see reality and history in light of him do we see *how* he lives and works in reality and history today.[37]

This is where Bonhoeffer's unique vision comes into play: from his prison cell, he began to realize that several centuries' worth of assumptions about religion had been stripped away, and now the world was finally in position to see Christ as he truly is: "Our coming of age leads us to a true recognition of our situation before God."[38] Bonhoeffer's worry, however, is that while the world may be ready to see Christ anew and afresh, the church is not, because the very changes that make the world ready for the gospel leave the church vulnerable before the world. "The

---

[34]Bonhoeffer, *Ethics*, DBWE 6:359.
[35]See Bonhoeffer, *Berlin*, DBWE 12:313 and *Letters and Papers*, DBWE 8:455.
[36]Bonhoeffer, *Letters and Papers*, DBWE 8:372.
[37]Ibid., p. 362. The meaning of Bonhoeffer's famous question: "Who is Jesus Christ for us today?" becomes more clear from this perspective.
[38]Ibid., p. 478.

foundations are being pulled out from under all that 'Christianity' has previously been for us," and in this situation, the church's instinct is to fight for its survival by claiming God and Christ as the church's possession over against the world.[39] This manifests itself in the church's withdrawal from the world and its act of closing off its intellectual and spiritual life to the world because of the threat it perceives. Yet Bonhoeffer argues that to withdraw from the world in this way is to betray the church's mission. It is a "counsel of despair, a sacrifice made only at the cost of intellectual integrity,"[40] an abandonment of the world "to its own devices."[41] A church that focuses on its own "self-preservation, as if that were an end in itself," is a church failing to live in the pattern of Christ.[42] The faithful church will be one that embraces the world in confidence that Jesus Christ has already gone before it. "In Christ, we are invited to participate in the reality of God and the reality of the world at the same time, the one not without the other."[43] It is in this particular Christ-centered sense that the church exists for the world: "The church is not there in order to fight with the world for a piece of its territory, but precisely to testify to the world that it is still the world, namely, the world that is loved and reconciled by God. . . . The church can only defend its own space by fighting, not for space, but for the salvation of the world."[44] In other words, if the church really is the space and the place where Christ proclaims and visibly demonstrates himself as the center of all reality and history, then the church cannot be an end in itself, but rather it must be a community ordered toward an end *outside* itself. It lives in this way when it follows in line with Christ and adopts the pattern of his life, proclaiming the gospel of the judgment and justification of the cross to the world for the sake of the world's salvation.

---

[39]Ibid., p. 363. Also see p. 426.

[40]Ibid., p. 478.

[41]Ibid., p. 373. This is the mirror image of the same mistake Protestant liberals made in the nineteenth and twentieth centuries, as Bonhoeffer notes: "The weakness of liberal theology was that it allowed the world the right to assign to Christ his place within it; that it accepted, in the dispute between the church and the world, the—relatively mild—peace terms dictated by the world" (p. 428).

[42]Ibid., p. 389.

[43]Bonhoeffer, *Ethics*, DBWE 6:55.

[44]Ibid., pp. 63-64.

This account of the church and its mission puts us in position to see how Bonhoeffer would understand the role of the Christian academy. Like the church, the Christian academy is ordered beyond itself, because its scholars and students' primary task is to engage the ideas, claims and arguments of the wider world of the liberal arts and sciences in the name of Jesus Christ. This task requires discernment: sometimes it means standing over against the world by proclaiming judgment against ways of thinking that run contrary to the gospel; at other times, it involves seeing God's hand at work in the world in new and unexpected ways. From Bonhoeffer's perspective, this task lines up perfectly with the church's mission. The church can live for the world only when it sees the world as it truly is, because only then can it engage the world honestly and faithfully. The Christian academy is uniquely positioned to equip the church for this task by modeling what it looks like to discerningly yet honestly embrace the world in its concrete particularity. This is what the integration of faith and learning is all about: it is the task of figuring out how to engage the world *as it is* from the perspective of the gospel of Jesus Christ. This task is not an act divorced from the life of the church or an act in tension with the church's mission; rather, it is a concrete and living act of witness *to* the church, a testimony about *how* Christ is working in the world and how the church can join him there faithfully.[45] Through the integration of faith and learning, the Christian academy thus bears witness both to the world and to the church: it testifies to the world about the gospel and to the church about what the world is really like.

Bearing dual witness in this way is no easy task. How might the Christian academy go about it faithfully? Although Bonhoeffer himself does not look in this direction, perhaps we can take the events of Acts 15 as reflective of his line of thinking. Paul and Barnabas have been working as missionaries on the far reaches of the empire, and Gentiles are being converted in great numbers. Controversy soon arises over whether

---

[45]Bonhoeffer, *Letters and Papers*, DBWE 8:406: "We should find God in what we know, not in what we don't know; God wants to be grasped by us not in unsolved questions but in those that have been solved." The church's task is to *unveil* to the world how God in Christ is working by proclaiming Christ's work in the world through its preaching and sacramental life.

Gentile converts should be circumcised. So Paul and Barnabas travel to Jerusalem to report to the church there about the conversion of the Gentiles and to ask about the question of circumcision. The church in Jerusalem debates the issue thoroughly, and it is not an easy debate: this question cuts to the heart of what the church believes about Christ and the gospel. As the text presents it, their eventual decision to accept uncircumcised Gentiles does not signify the church's capitulation to cultural pressures, but rather, it marks the church's movement more deeply into the gospel, because it leads the church into a fuller understanding and proclamation of the true nature of Christ's justifying grace.

Bonhoeffer sees the church's engagement with a world come of age through an Acts 15-style lens. From his perspective, the church knows that it is living out its mission faithfully when it is being confronted with the same types of questions and decisions the church in Jerusalem faced. If the church is to embrace a world come of age, he argues, "all Christian thinking, talking, and organizing must be born anew."[46] The Christian academy, by its very nature, exists on the frontier of this renewal, and so it is uniquely positioned to participate in the process. It functions in the role of a contemporary Paul and Barnabas: as those sent from the church out into the world, who then are called to report back to the church about what God is doing in the world. As Bonhoeffer would see it, the goal of this back-and-forth exchange is to equip the church for its mission, and this may involve enriching and unsettling the church in equal measure. Often the church might be encouraged in its thinking and better able to engage the world through what it learns from the integration that goes on in the Christian academy. Sometimes, however, the church might be challenged by the academy's insights, and it may have to consider reforming its ways of thinking, speaking and acting in light of what God is doing in the world. The Christian academy may call the church to act against its self-preserving instincts, to test its speech and thought in light of new developments, and to raise questions about its methods and practices in light of the world around it.

---

[46]Ibid., p. 389. In a later letter, Bonhoeffer remarks that this means that the church's preaching and action "must now be interpreted in a way that does not make religion the condition for faith" (p. 430).

From Bonhoeffer's perspective, the chief benefit of this kind of exchange would be that it checks any desire either the Christian academy
or the church might have to be self-sufficient in its relation to Christ. To
engage the world as it is, the church must empty itself and pattern its
mind after the mind of Christ who did not consider his own status as
something to be held onto but took the form of a servant, humbling
himself in obedience even to the point of death (Philippians 2:5-8). The
church that embraces a world come of age is a church who adopts this
cross-shaped pattern of life.[47] It is a church that lives a life of continual
repentance, Bonhoeffer says, of "not thinking first of [its] own needs,
questions, sins, and fear but allowing [itself] to be pulled into walking
the path that Jesus walks" in the world.[48] The Christian academy exists
in this same way, not only because it has to model what it looks like to
be faithful to the gospel within the liberal arts and sciences, but also
because it does so from *within* the church. That is, the members of the
Christian academy are also members of the body of Christ, and so they
are held accountable by the body as a whole. The Christian academy
proceeds in their integrative task as people who, together with their
brothers and sisters outside the academy, hear the judging and justifying
Word, receive the sacrament, and are called to participate in the church's
mission in faith and obedience. So, at one and the same time, the church
holds the academy accountable by helping its members hear and adhere
to the gospel, which helps the academy's members know when and how
to exercise their discernment in relation to their disciplines; and the
academy, in turn, equips and challenges the church about when and
where to embrace the world in confidence that the living and active
Christ already has gone ahead of it. "The renewal of the West," Bonhoeffer says, "lies completely in God's renewal of the church, which leads

---

[47]On this point, Bonhoeffer argues that the church gains a hearing in the world, not by "dominating, but helping and serving," which means that it must confront "first within itself and
then without the world, the vices of hubris, the worship of power, envy, and illusionism as
the roots of all evil," so that it might gain "power not through concepts, but by example." See
ibid., pp. 503-4. In an earlier letter, Bonhoeffer had remarked: "That is the opposite of everything a religious person expects from God. The human being is called upon to share in God's
suffering at the hands of a godless world. Thus we must really live in that godless world and
not try to cover up or transfigure its godlessness somehow into religion" (p. 480).
[48]Ibid., p. 480.

[the world] into community with the resurrected and living Jesus Christ."[49] The Christian academy exists precisely to go out into the world in order to use the insights it gains there to fuel the renewal of the church for the sake of the church's mission, so that the world might know Jesus through the church.

ASSESSMENT AND CONCLUSION

So goes Bonhoeffer's vision for the Christian academy, at least according to this analysis. How might we assess and apply it? I will offer five observations. First, working behind Bonhoeffer's approach is a particular account of nature and grace. Debates about the relationship between nature and grace concern the connection between the being and capacities humans have by virtue of their creation and those they have as a result of God's grace in Jesus Christ. Bonhoeffer's approach to this relationship is distinct, because in his view, there is no way to understand created human being and capacities rightly apart from the fact that humans are totally rather than partially sinful in their being and that God has judged and justified their sin at the cross. This means that knowledge of the crucified and risen Christ is determinative for *any* claim we might offer about human being and capacities. We cannot talk about human being in *ideal* terms, as if it could be considered in light of its creation alone; rather the only human being we can talk about is the concrete, fallen human being who actually exists, the one who stands under judgment and in need of grace. A strength of this approach is that it prevents us from abstracting human being and life from the story of Scripture. It also challenges the sometimes unreflective embrace of certain types of natural theology within the Christian academy and rules out the instinctive deism that governs much of the wider academy's and sometimes even the church's account of God's relationship to creation. These things help make our thinking about God and the world less self-referential by prompting us to look to Christ and Scripture rather than ourselves in order to speak rightly about God and God's relationship with humanity. The question this approach leaves us with,

---

[49]Bonhoeffer, *Ethics*, DBWE 6:142.

however, involves how it might relate to other approaches to the relationship between nature and grace, particularly Roman Catholic accounts, if it can relate to them at all.

Second, does Bonhoeffer's account—and especially the idea of the back-and-forth exchange between the academy and the church—place the Christian academy in some kind of elevated position within the church? Not really. In fact, the translation and application offered here—where I applied Bonhoeffer's theology to the context of the Christian academy—could be made, with some adjustments, to nearly every area of the church's life. Bonhoeffer would argue that every single member of the body of Christ has a responsibility to see the world through the lens of the crucifixion and resurrection, to live in intrinsic connection to church's being and mission, and to go out into the world and then return to the church to equip and challenge it to see the world as it is. The Christian academy is just one member doing what the *entire body* should be doing. We might even make the case that Bonhoeffer's approach gives us an idea of what the teaching office of the church looks like within the context of the priesthood of all believers. From the very beginning, Christians have believed that the Holy Spirit works to keep the church accountable as it reads Scripture, worships and follows Christ in the world. But there has been room to say that the Spirit works by gifting particular people within the church both to speak for the church and to call the church to reform if need be. Bonhoeffer's approach gives every Christian a way to participate in this process, because every Christian has the responsibility of calling the church to account, at least with respect to the church's mission in the world. Not everyone is in a position to instruct the church about its interpretation of Scripture or its worship, but every single believer, if he or she is obeying Christ's command to go out in the world, has the responsibility of keeping the church accountable to the reality of the world so it can truly live for the sake of the world. So, while everyone does not participate in the same way, every Christian has a role in teaching the church and calling it to account. The Christian academy certainly has a unique place in this process. The diversity of disciplines represented within it—as well as the fact that it is designed to train students to bring together their faith with their academic learning—

puts it at the forefront of the intersection of Christ and culture. But it does not stand at this intersection alone.

This connects to the third point. If Bonhoeffer is right, there is no way to for the church to be the church without seeking to know the world as it truly is, and the Christian academy is one way—although certainly not the only way—that the church gains this knowledge. This means that the Christian academy's work is valuable and important for the life and mission of the church. At the same time, if Bonhoeffer is right, then the Christian academy cannot do what it does faithfully apart from its intrinsic connection to the church and its mission. Serious academic learning goes hand in hand with a life of obedience to Christ *within* the church, and the aim of this life of obedience is to build up the church for the sake of the church's mission in the world. This conception of the relationship between the Christian academy and the church challenges the way that the academy thinks about its task. The academy's goal cannot be merely to offer a Christian perspective or worldview on higher education; rather, the goal has to be to form disciples who think and live faithfully *in* the church for the sake of the world. This means that academic instruction has to go hand in hand with concrete Christian practices such as worship, prayer, Bible study and service that take place on campus. But these practices on campus should be aimed toward prompting students to connect with and enrich the same practices off campus in their churches rather than serving as a replacement for the practices of their churches.

This brings us to the question of the fourth point: What church are we talking about here? Who is "the church" in Bonhoeffer's account? Bonhoeffer's answer would be: it is *Christ's* church, the church in which he proclaims himself in Word and sacrament. So, "the church" in his account conceivably could be any church in which believers hear Christ's Word and receive his sacrament. There is room for some flexibility here, given the fact that we are translating Bonhoeffer's thought to our own time and place. For example, one could talk about ordinances rather than sacraments and still fit Bonhoeffer's vision as outlined here, as long as one could talk with Paul about proclaiming the Lord's death every time one eats the bread and drinks the cup (1 Corinthians 11:26). In fact, having a Christian academy whose members have differences within a larger gospel unity could enrich Bonhoeffer's vision, since this diversity would feed into exactly the kind of honest exchange that marks the academy's mission more generally. No one church is going to fit Bonhoeffer's vision of "the church" perfectly, and in many ways, that is the point: it is the ideal toward which we strive, and every member of the universal body is responsible for moving their local body in this direction in some way or another.

Fifth, and finally, what might Bonhoeffer's vision for the Christian academy actually look like in practice? Here goes an attempt: Imagine a student studying the natural sciences at a Christian liberal arts college. She approaches the content of her discipline fearlessly, refusing to shut herself off from any theory, idea or fact in it. She is confident that this world is *God's* world, and that whatever she finds there will be consistent with who he is and what he has revealed. And yet figuring out *how* it is consistent is not immediately obvious; it takes disciplined effort and a long-term commitment. She has to proceed in the process with discernment, honesty and courage. She does so in community with her fellow students, faculty and staff, and also in community with her local church. She worships, reads Scripture, prays and obeys within both of these communities, with the life of each community enriching her experience of the other. Her academic studies do not pull her away from Scripture, but rather, they prompt her to go more deeply into it, searching it to see whether or not what she is learning in her discipline corresponds to it. Perhaps at times she lives in tension, unable to find immediate answers. Sometimes she has to challenge her discipline, rejecting its claims and explanations in light of the claims of Scripture; other times, she brings what she has learned from her discipline back to her church, asking questions and challenging her church to think anew and afresh about what it is doing in light of what she has learned. This does not detract from her faith in Christ or her commitment to her church; rather, it prompts her to hold more tightly to them, because she sees the very task of working through these questions as an act of obedience to Christ and his mission. Now imagine a business student doing the same thing in the same church. An anthropology professor. An artist. A psychologist.

Now imagine people from outside the academy doing the same thing in that church: a foster care case worker, a local businesswoman, a nurse, a retiree, a politician, a server at a restaurant, an recent immigrant, the list goes on. Imagine all of them living in the pattern of bringing the questions and experiences of their lives in the world back to the church to ask questions of the church. Now imagine the church listening to these testimonies, accepting the challenges these questions pose instead of closing its ears to them; turning to Scripture and prayer for discernment; working together to figure out what Christ is calling them to do as a church; and then going out to meet the world that it now understands more clearly as it *really* is, and doing so in the name of Jesus Christ. *This* is Bonhoeffer's concrete picture of how those inside the Christian academy live with those outside it within one church. It is a picture of a community with one hand firmly grasped onto the world, refusing to let it go, while its other hand is firmly grasped by Christ himself, sitting at the right hand of the Father. In this position the church stands between two worlds, its arms stretched out across history, its very life bearing witness to the crucified one for the sake of the world's salvation.

9

BONHOEFFER'S CHRISTOLOGICAL TAKE ON VOCATION

LORI BRANDT HALE

Vocation is responsibility, and responsibility is the whole response of the whole person to reality as a whole.

DIETRICH BONHOEFFER, 1940[1]

DIETRICH BONHOEFFER LIVED HIS LIFE and faced his death by hanging—at the hands of the Nazis—driven by a powerful understanding of vocation as responsibility. Inherent in Bonhoeffer's conception of responsibility is his deep and thoroughgoing Christology. Moreover, embedded in both vocation and responsibility is the whole of his theology, including his ideas about costly grace, discipleship, *Stellvertretung* (vicarious representative action), ethics as formation and this-worldly Christianity. In short, Bonhoeffer posits vocation, christologically understood, as responsibility—that is, as a response to the call and claim of Jesus Christ on one's life. Today, above the ever-growing cacophony of competing claims about vocation, meaningful work, and "purpose-driven" lives, Bonhoeffer's idea sounds a chal-

---

[1]Dietrich Bonhoeffer, *Ethics*, DBWE 6:293.

lenging but substantive note. Above all, it provides a way to understand vocation as a hermeneutic or interpretive lens that shapes and orients one's way of living in the world and in relationship to that world, to God and to others.

THE THEOLOGICAL EXPLORATION OF VOCATION

In 2002 Augsburg College, where I teach, redesigned its general education curriculum to better reflect the mission and vision of the place. At the same time, the college was a new recipient of a Lilly Endowment funded grant for the theological exploration of vocation, an idea that fit very well with the college's commitments to faith and service, among other things. The result, in part, was the creation of two core courses, housed in the Religion Department, called Christian Vocation and the Search for Meaning I and II. A senior keystone experience revisiting vocation was also developed.

In the Search for Meaning courses we introduce Christian theology as well as the basic tenets of other major world religions—Judaism, Islam, Hinduism and Buddhism—and explore, with levels of complexity that increase from the first course to the second, the rich concept of vocation. But it is no easy task. We start with a basic understanding of the term, looking to the Latin *vocare*, which means "to call." *Vocation* is a call or calling; it connotes a sense of being called. This basic definition is the starting point for our classroom discussions. It helps dispel a variety of false preconceived notions about the term, especially when most students have heard the word vocation primarily associated with a trade or skill, as in vo-tech or vocational schools. The Latin root of the term also facilitates an introduction to the idea that a call comes from a caller, perhaps God. Thus, we can posit our exploration of vocation as a theological one. However, a survey of the various theological takes on vocation—from a traditional Catholic perspective to ideas developed in the Protestant Reformation to contemporary Christian views—serves only to remind students that it is a very complicated matter with no clear-cut answers.

A traditional Catholic understanding of vocation certainly emphasizes this idea that a vocation is a calling—particularly a calling from

God—but it also relegates that call to one of religious life: to priesthood, the diaconate or life in a religious order. Many contemporary Catholic communities regularly pray the "Prayer for Vocations":

> God, we earnestly ask You to bless this archdiocese with many priests, Brothers, and Sisters who will love You with their whole strength and gladly spend their entire lives to make you known and loved. Bless our families, bless our children. Choose from our homes those needed for your work. Mary, Queen of the Clergy, pray for us, pray for our priests, Religious, and deacons. Obtain for us many more.[2]

The Catholic view of vocation is a very limited one.

The Protestant Reformation ushered in many theological and ecclesiological changes, including a redefinition of vocation. Martin Luther guides our understanding of vocation out of the cloister, as it were, and into the world. He asserts that all have a calling from God to service in the world and famously gives the example that Christian cobblers are not called to put little crosses on the shoes they make but to craft good and reliable footwear. At the same time, Luther's work makes it clear that vocation is about our core identity, shaped by grace and faith alone, and not about what we do or achieve in the world. Yet how we live in the world, and how we live in relation to others, still matters.[3] Another way to say that human identity is shaped by grace and faith is to say that humans are saved from the constant pursuit of righteousness and salvation by the saving act of Christ on the cross. Men and women are thereby freed to live in service to the neighbor and the world.[4]

For students, we have translated this Lutheran understanding of vocation into a visual: a triangle with God (the caller) at one point, the self (with particular interests and skills) at the second point, and the neighbor or world (with challenges and needs) at the third point. In the intersection of God, self and world, one's vocation comes into view. This is a great place to start the conversation about vocation, but it is not a great

---

[2]From a bulletin of the Cathedral of St. Paul, Archdiocese of St. Paul and Minneapolis, May 2012.

[3]Martin Luther, *Treatise on Good Works,* Luther study edition, trans. and ed. Scott H. Hendrix (Minneapolis: Fortress Press, 2012).

[4]Martin Luther, *Freedom of a Christian,* trans. Mark D. Tranvik (Minneapolis: Fortress Press, 2008).

place to end the conversation. *Is vocation something I do and have and need to find?* The formulaic nature of the triangle certainly makes it seem that way. *What if I don't find it? Or don't hear the call? Will my life be vocation-less?* These questions are common student questions. They are coupled with a strong sense that vocation is something they need to find and identify, and that it is a definite field of activity that will come to be known with certainty. Vocation is something you do (act). Ironically, Luther was trying to move away from a "good works" theological model in which doing particular things had salvific efficacy. I think Luther got it right, because in a fundamental way, he was suggesting a view of vocation rooted in a theology of the cross that is about a way of being in the world (being). But the message for students, especially at the introductory level, is, at best, mixed. *Is God calling me to a particular activity in the world or way of being in the world or both? Does the "vocation triangle" clarify or confuse the matter?*

Other voices in our classroom conversations about vocation have offered a range of ways for students to consider the concept but either do not address the challenges proffered by the model described above or introduce new complications or both. Frederick Buechner maintains that vocation, that place God calls you to, is where one's deep gladness meets the world's deep need.[5] It is an attractive idea, but one riddled with a host of problems. Similar student questions persist: *Is vocation some thing, some job, some limited activity? My vocation lies in the intersection of the world's need and my own deep gladness; what if I do not find it? Is there only one vocation for me?* A sense akin to panic overwhelms students who conclude that there is a particular calling for them which they may or may not be able to identify. But this is not what is most troubling about Buechner's account. Rather, what is profoundly problematic lies in these questions: What if the world's deep need requires me, bids me, to act against my own best interest? What if I am called, say, to participate in a conspiracy to take down a tyrant? My own deep gladness seems a problematic criterion for serving the world.

Parker Palmer, conversely, moves us away from the potential stasis of

---

[5]Frederick Buechner, *Wishful Thinking: A Seeker's ABC* (New York: Harper & Row, 1973).

the models that emerge from Luther and Buechner, or pseudo-Luther and Buechner. Palmer sees vocation as reclamation of one's true and authentic self. In fact, he says that the deepest vocational question is not, "what ought I to do with my life?" but "who am I?" and "what is my nature?"[6] He captures the possibility that vocation is not something I have or need to find, but a way of being in the world, a hermeneutic for everything I do. To me this view—in the midst of life that is messy and dynamic, joyful and sometimes tragic—provides a fruitful way of thinking about vocation. But the answer to what constitutes the ground of this self, or authentic selfhood, is largely absent in Palmer. Moreover, the sense that vocation is a call or calling is also largely absent. And that is concerning.

Interestingly, Palmer hints at that grounding while vindicating, as it were, Buechner's emphasis on deep gladness. He writes, "Buechner's definition starts with the self and moves toward the needs of the world: it begins, wisely, where vocation begins—not in what the world needs (which is everything), but in the nature of the human self, in what brings the self joy, the deep joy of knowing that we are here on earth to be the gifts that God created."[7] Palmer goes on to say that Buechner's attention to gladness is not selfish. "The Quaker teacher Douglas Steere was fond of saying that the ancient human question 'Who am I?' leads inevitably to the equally important question 'Whose am I?'—for there is no selfhood outside relationship. We must ask the question of selfhood and answer it as honestly as we can, no matter where it takes us. Only as we do so can we discover the community of our lives."[8] I like the question, "Whose am I?" And I agree with the premise that there is no selfhood outside relationship. But I am not satisfied. What does it mean to "ask the question of selfhood and answer it as honestly as we can, no matter where it takes us?"

In general, several questions emerging from the theological exploration of vocation persist. Most important is this one: does the theo-

---

[6]Parker Palmer, *Let Your Life Speak: Listening to the Voice of Vocation* (San Francisco: John Wiley & Sons, Jossey-Bass, 1999), p. 15.
[7]Ibid., pp. 16-17.
[8]Ibid., p. 17.

logical exploration of vocation proffer a view of vocation that rescues the idea of vocation from extremes in either direction? That is, does this exploration save vocation from being understood as a predetermined path or role (perhaps religious) that must be identified correctly (on one hand)? Does this exploration prevent reducing vocation to ethics in some traditional understanding of that term (on the other)? Does it do both? Including Bonhoeffer's work in the discussion allows affirmative answers to both questions. By contrast, Bonhoeffer's view of vocation claims it as a hermeneutic, that is, a way of orienting oneself in and to the world as well as in relationship to God and to others. In the end, Dietrich Bonhoeffer's way of thinking about vocation is meaningful, challenging and deserving of a much broader reading.

BONHOEFFER'S VIEW OF VOCATION

Bonhoeffer's view of vocation is a powerful alternative to the ones described above, although it could be said that it is not a departure from Luther's view but an expansion of it. Bonhoeffer posits vocation as responsibility; more specifically, he claims vocation is a response to the call and claim of Jesus Christ on my life. As suggested above, embedded within this understanding of vocation is the whole of Bonhoeffer's theology. Neither is easily unpacked nor easily dismissed. Vocation as responsibility is about both act and being, about self and other; vocation as responsibility depends on the self-revelation of God in Jesus Christ and on those who will conform themselves to him. Vocation as responsibility takes seriously Martin Luther's call to live with the constant knowledge of death and resurrection. Vocation as responsibility offers a valuable and perhaps surprising perspective vis-à-vis persistent questions about the relationship between Christ or Christianity and culture.

In his classic book *Christ and Culture*, H. Richard Niebuhr notes five prevalent ways that Christianity has interacted with culture: Christ against culture, Christ of culture, Christ above culture, Christ and culture in paradox, and Christ transforming culture.[9] Dietrich Bonhoeffer's rich understanding of vocation serves to synthesize his own work and life,

---

[9]H. Richard Niebuhr, *Christ and Culture* (New York: Harper & Row, 1951).

and proffers an understanding of the relation between Christ and culture that deems H. Richard Niehbur's classic categories on the subject (virtually) beside the point. "Because in Jesus Christ God and humanity became one," writes Bonhoeffer in *Ethics*, "so through Christ what is 'Christian' and what is 'worldly' become one in the action of the Christian. They are not opposed to each other like two eternally hostile principles. Instead, the action of the Christian springs from the unity between God and the world, and the unity of life that have been created in Christ."[10] This understanding of the unity of reality is the foundation for Bonhoeffer's claim that "vocation is responsibility, and responsibility is the whole response of the whole person to reality as a whole."[11]

ETHICS AND THE GOOD

Bonhoeffer writes explicitly about vocation and responsibility in a section of his *Ethics* titled "History and Good."[12] More precisely, we find this work in a second manuscript called by this title. Bonhoeffer's work on *Ethics* was in progress at the time of his death and was pieced together and published posthumously. The second manuscript revisits themes introduced in the brief first draft, but adds considerable substance and includes sections that are important for a deep understanding of his claims about vocation. Of particular note are the sections claiming "Christ as our life" and defining responsibility in christological terms. They provide the foundation for understanding Bonhoeffer's christological take on vocation. Moreover, it is important to have a general working understanding of his approach to ethics because it is a departure from traditional ways of understanding the field, and is critical to his claims about vocation and responsibility.

"The question about the good always finds us in an irreversible situation: we are living." These are the loaded opening words of this "History and Good" section. Vocation for Bonhoeffer has both theological and ethical characteristics and implications, so he starts here with this idea of the good—and based on reading other parts of Bonhoeffer's *Ethics*—

---

[10]Bonhoeffer, *Ethics*, DBWE 6:253.
[11]Ibid., p. 293.
[12]Bonhoeffer, *Ethics*, DBWE 6:246-98.

it is clear that this question about the good points to this "irreversible situation," this "we are living," because the question about the good is the wrong ethical question. For Bonhoeffer, the ethical question is not "what does it mean to do good?" but "what is the will of God?" If you are like me and have seen the Bonhoeffer documentary by Martin Doblmeier and Journey Films a thousand times, or maybe fifteen or twenty, you can picture South African theologian John de Gruchy, in his bright blue shirt, talking about this question. With almost a chuckle, he remarks that this question—what is the will of God?—sounds anachronistic in our ears.[13] But he helps us understand that Bonhoeffer is overturning the history of ethics. That is, he is challenging traditional ethical systems based on abstract or universal principles.

"Ethical thought," Bonhoeffer writes, "is still largely dominated by the abstract notion of an isolated individual who, wielding an absolute criterion of what is good in and of itself, chooses continually and exclusively between this clearly recognized good and an evil recognized with equal clarity."[14] But Bonhoeffer is incredulous. No such person exists. No such criterion exists. And good and evil do not appear in anything like a pure form in history. The familiar "Who Stands Fast?" section of his well-known essay "After Ten Years," sent as a letter of support to his coconspirators and marking ten years of Hitler's rule, begins: "The huge masquerade of evil has thrown all ethical concepts into confusion. That evil should appear in the form of light, good deeds, historical necessity, social justice is absolutely bewildering for one coming from the world of ethical concepts that we have received."[15] One of the challenges of Bonhoeffer's own National Socialist context was that no facile way to identify what was good and what was evil existed. It was just not that simple. But Bonhoeffer's point is that simple: people do not live in an abstraction; they live in real historical situations that call for real actions and ethical agency.

Put another way, ethics in the abstract are not ethics at all; they miss the point. In Bonhoeffer's view, ethics in the abstract remove ethical

---

[13]Martin Doblmeier, *Bonhoeffer*, Journey Films, 2003.
[14]Bonhoeffer, *Ethics*, DBWE 6:247.
[15]Dietrich Bonhoeffer, *Letters and Papers from Prison*, DBWE 8:38-39.

problems from real life to a static formula without relation to life as lived and experienced in a particular time and place. Those who try to live this way—depending on abstract ethical principles—define the "good" only in relation to those principles. So, the "good" remains an abstraction. Moreover, their so-called ethical decisions take no account of the other and require either a privatization of life, a retreat from existence altogether (Bonhoeffer does have monastic life in mind here), or alternately, create a religious fanaticism that is equally not grounded on real life or genuine encounter with actual human beings. Bonhoeffer's ethics and his understanding of vocation depend on both: real life and genuine encounter.

Bonhoeffer's Sociality of Theology and Other Key Theological Themes

It is important to note that genuine encounter with and between human beings is a theme in the framework of Bonhoeffer's ethical and theological thinking from the beginning of his work. In *Sanctorum Communio,* he claims "the social intention of all the basic Christian concepts."[16] In other words, he posits the sociality of theology and asserts that "human beings exist only in relationship to, and responsibility for, other human beings."[17] More explicitly, he says that in this encounter with another, that other makes an ethical claim on me, and I am called to respond. In other words, Bonhoeffer's ontology is relational. For him, a person *is* only in relationship (encounter and response) with another person. But it is not a direct relationship, it is a mediated relationship. It is mediated by the divine you, God; and by that he actually means that it is mediated by the incarnate God, Jesus Christ. From the beginning in 1927, Bonhoeffer's ontology is also christological.

Bonhoeffer's claims about the social intention of all Christian concepts and his understanding of ethics distanced from principles and abstractions are familiar to students of Bonhoeffer. They also are underscored by other foundational themes in his corpus, including his famous

---

[16]Dietrich Bonhoeffer, *Sanctorum Communio*, DBWE 1:21.
[17]Stephen R. Haynes and Lori Brandt Hale, *Bonhoeffer for Armchair Theologians* (Louisville: Westminster John Knox Press, 2009), p. 79.

call to costly grace and discipleship. In light of my work—and my campus conversations in particular—on vocation, a brief rehearsal of Bonhoeffer's ethical, theological and christological foundations is nothing short of exciting. Bonhoeffer's contributions are critical in addressing a number of challenges and frustrations in exploring vocation with students (suggested above) in part because he does not reduce vocation to one category—ethics or theology, for example. His understanding of the essential, social nature of humanity is a key to a more complex view of vocation. Moreover, the continuity between his dissertation work *Sanctorum Communio* in 1927 and the drafts of *Ethics* in the early 1940s on this essential sociality, with its identification with Jesus Christ, is remarkable. In his dissertation he writes, "The Christian person achieves his or her essential nature only when God does not encounter the person as a You, but 'enters into' the person as I."[18] The self-revelation of God in Christ makes this "entering" possible. Essential human nature is linked inextricably with the vicarious act—the vicarious death—of Christ on behalf of humanity. As Clifford Green notes,

> Bonhoeffer builds up his argument to the position where humanity as a whole is the "I" standing before God as the "You." Adam "represents" and "personifies" created and fallen humanity before God; Christ represents and personifies God before humanity and the "new humanity" before God. In other words, Christ reveals God to humanity and at the same time stands as the "new I" in whom all humanity participates. So the self, or I, is reconfigured christologically. Christ is the center of one's being or coming into being.[19]

In this view, there is a difference between ethical being and essential humanity. The former, ethical being, comes about in a concrete situation, in a particular time and place. Essential humanity, with its Christological restructuring, is not tied to historical circumstances.

The profound interconnections of Bonhoeffer's theological themes and the deep roots they provide for his understanding of vocation are striking. In *Discipleship*, Bonhoeffer affirms the unmerited and merciful

---

[18]Bonhoeffer, *Sanctorum Communio*, DBWE 1:56.
[19]Haynes and Hale, *Bonhoeffer for Armchair Theologians*, pp. 87-88.

gift of grace and justification, but he famously ties it to repentance, discipleship and transformation. Hence, grace in Bonhoeffer's estimation is costly, but it also is freeing. Costly grace frees the Christian to act on behalf of others and to take responsible and vicarious action, even if that action comes at great personal cost and requires one to accept guilt. Bonhoeffer works these ideas out most fully in his use of the idea of *Stellvertretung* and the notion of ethics as formation to Christ. Suffice it to say that both embrace the christological restructuring of humanity (essential humanity) that reconfigures the way one is called to live in the whole of concrete reality.

THE CHRISTOLOGICAL PARADOX: THE YES AND THE NO

It is no surprise, then, that in *Ethics* the christological reconfiguration of humanity encompasses the whole of life. Jesus says, "I am the Life," (John 11:25) and this claim about reality is one we cannot ignore. This revelation and proclamation of Jesus Christ is the proclamation that our lives are outside ourselves and in Jesus Christ. We do not come to this understanding on our own. It comes to us from outside. It encounters us and when we are struck by it, "we recognize that we have fallen from life, from our life. We recognize that we live in contradiction . . . to our life. In this word of Jesus Christ we thus hear the No spoken over our life . . . [rather] we still live from the life called Jesus Christ, the life that is the origin, essence, and goal of all life and of our life. The No spoken over our fallen life . . . becomes a hidden Yes to new life."[20] The "new I," in which all participate, is Bonhoeffer's earlier formulation. We see hints of grace in this articulation as well, for Christ as life is the life we cannot give ourselves; it comes from outside. It is a gift. "Nevertheless, it is not a distant and strange life unrelated to us, but our own real daily life."[21] In Bonhoeffer's words, "it is the Yes of creation, reconciliation, and redemption, and the No of judgment and death over life that has fallen away from its origin, essence, and goal."[22] We live in a dialectical unity of the Yes and the No. We live "now stretched between

---

[20]Bonhoeffer, *Ethics,* DBWE 6:250.
[21]Ibid., p. 251.
[22]Ibid.

the No and the Yes" in the "contradictory unity" marked by the already accomplished reconciliation of the world to God in Christ's saving act, responsive to the call of God and neighbor and world.[23] This dynamic response, christological in its origin and ethical in its outcome, is a powerful way to frame the idea and call of vocation. What it means to "live" starts to become synonymous with a profound sense of vocation as an orientation to the world (as life) that shapes the whole of one's life. "We 'live' means that in our encounter with other human beings and with God, the Yes and the No are bound together in a unity of contra-diction, in selfless self-assertion, in a self-assertion that is a surrender of myself to God and to other human beings."[24] Moreover, the unity of life in Christ, the interplay of the Yes and No, happens over and over again in concrete reality, in real life.

The emphasis on concrete reality slams us up against Bonhoeffer's own incredibly difficult historical reality. It is no wonder that he said sometimes the responsible action requires a person to choose between right and wrong or good and evil, but more often it asks for a choice between two rights or two wrongs. Regardless, to be responsible is to live one's life as an "answer to the life of Jesus Christ (as the Yes and No of our life)."[25] In "After Ten Years," Bonhoeffer asserts that "The ultimate responsible question is not how I extricate myself heroically from the situation but [how] a coming generation is to go on living."[26]

This kind of responsible life, a life responsive to the call of Christ and the call of neighbor, is made possible by Christ's vicarious representative act *(Stellvertretung)*. Christ acted vicariously on behalf of all humanity, taking on the sin and guilt of the world. In so doing, he freed us; he freed us to do the same. He freed us to act vicariously on behalf of others and to take on guilt in that responsible act. Only months before he is sent to Tegel prison, Bonhoeffer writes, "Only today are Germans beginning to discover what free responsibility means. It is founded in a God who calls for the free venture of faith to responsible action and who promises for-

---

[23]Ibid.
[24]Ibid., p. 254.
[25]Ibid.
[26]Bonhoeffer, *Letters and Papers*, DBWE 8:42.

giveness and consolation to the one who on account of such action becomes a sinner."[27] He echoes the sentiment in *Ethics:* "Those who act responsibly place their action into the hands of God and live by God's grace and judgment."[28] The implications for vocation are striking. Vocation understood as responsibility replete with freedom from sin and death and, thereby, willingness to take on sin and death opens the door to acting on behalf of others in significant ways. But not every concrete reality and need will require service unto death. "The attention of the responsible people is directed to concrete neighbors in their concrete reality. Their behavior is not fixed in advance and for all by a principle."[29] This attention to the real needs of real people is an effective summary of Bonhoeffer's notion of ethics as formation. He writes,

> Christ did not, like an ethicist, love a theory about the good; he loved real people. Christ was not interested, like a philosopher, in what is "generally valid," but in that which serves real concrete human beings. Christ was not concerned with whether the "maxim of an action" could become a "principle of universal law," but whether my action now helps my neighbor to be a human being before God.[30]

Ethics, responsible action, even—maybe especially—vocation, "should not be about what the good is, can be, or should be for each and every time, but about how Christ may take form among us today and here."[31]

AN UNLIKELY STORY OF VOCATION

Reading Bonhoeffer on vocation and responsible action, even on living in the contradiction or tension between the Yes and the No to one's own life, is a challenge because we know that in his context and life, in his response to the call and claim of Christ on his life, he gave up his life. Maybe it is hard to imagine ourselves following after Bonhoeffer's example. But he would be the first to say that every concrete situation, every real person we encounter, calls us to consider anew what constitutes responsible

---

[27]Ibid., p. 41.
[28]Bonhoeffer, *Ethics*, DBWE 6:268-69.
[29]Ibid., p. 261.
[30]Ibid., pp. 98-99.
[31]Ibid., p. 99.

action and how "Christ may take form among us today and here." In closing, I would like to share a true story of vocation as responsibility as Dietrich Bonhoeffer understands it. In it, the three key characters respond ethically, responsibly, and I argue, christologically to one another.[32]

She was talking about forgiveness, about the human inability to forgive absolutely. She was supposed to be talking about this theme. I had assigned it. Together we had been reading two texts on the themes of forgiveness and reconciliation: one by a theologian at Yale, a Croatian national, and the other by a South African theologian thinking through post-apartheid realities and possibilities. Each student had chosen an individual topic for a research paper, but all had to incorporate one or the other (or both) of these themes. So my fifty-plus-year-old student began to tell of her project and her doubts about the possibilities of forgiveness. A young student, nineteen or twenty years old, sitting to her left, joined the conversation. He was much more hopeful, optimistic even, that forgiveness is real and present, certainly possible with God's help. I locked eyes with my older student. I knew her. She had been in two previous classes with me. She didn't disagree with his last point, but she had lost sight of God's promises. He kept talking. He recognized his own youth and began speculating about whether he'd had enough life experience, really, to test his views on this matter. I lost track of everything he said; I was still holding the gaze of Margaret, pleading with my eyes for her to share the story that had left her with so many doubts. She couldn't. We both knew her silence let Tommy's words echo emptily in the room, but no one else noticed our moment.

Two weeks passed. A small group from the class had gathered to workshop their papers. Margaret went last. She began to review the basic claims of her paper, then stopped. She took a deep breath and said, "I have to tell you a story." Slowly and carefully she began to tell the story of the loss of her son: How he'd been coming home from work. How they'd had a funny conversation at her kitchen table the

---

[32]The names of the students in this story have been changed.

day before. How he'd been killed instantly. How the stoned juvenile driver had been given community service and probation. How she couldn't find it in her heart to forgive that irresponsible kid. How she'd been struggling with her faith. How she thought that God might be able to forgive, but had come to believe that humans do not have the capacity to forgive.

Everyone was quiet for a moment. Then, quietly and respectfully, Stephan said, "Seven years ago someone, a person, forgave me for something I did even though I didn't deserve it and it changed my life; it transformed me. That forgiveness has a positive impact on my life every single day." He didn't say what he did or who forgave him. He didn't need to. But he did open the door for Tamara to speak. She was sitting next to Margaret. She turned to her and began. "When I was 16 years old, I hit and killed a six-year-old child with my car." Words are inadequate to express the weight and import of her words. A profound silence surrounded us. I think it was prayerful silence. Tamara didn't cry, but the tears began to flow down Margaret's cheeks. She asked Tamara if she would share what happened. It was a split-second misjudgment and a young girl trying to follow her sister across a country road. No drugs. No alcohol. We fell silent again.

This story is a story about vocation as responsibility. It is a story of three students who, in turn, respond—who risk a response—to the ethical demand of the other(s) and who allow themselves to be stretched, even called, across the deep contradiction of the Yes and the No, and who give form to Christ in that moment. Margaret asserted herself (Yes) by surrendering her doubts and her fears, that is, by surrendering her very self (No) to her classmates; by risking judgment and guilt for her inability to forgive the young driver who killed her son, she embraced the reconciling promises of Christ and through Christ the very forgiveness that eluded her. Her decision to speak was an ethical decision.

Margaret's decision, her action, made a claim on Stephan, who embraced the same contradiction, the Yes and No, giving form to Christ then and there. Stephan's response was a christological one. Moreover, his response called Tamara to surrender herself before God and her classmates, to live that encounter in such a way that the No of self-disclosure became a Yes to the already accomplished reconciliation to God through Christ's saving act and incarnate presence in that encounter. Each student's contribution, understood as responsible action, makes this story a profound example of vocation in which vocation is christological and hermeneutical at its core and offers a way of being in the world and in relationship to others. Put bluntly and in light of classroom conversations about vocation, to talk about vocation as a predetermined activity or path or as a fixed ethical principle makes no sense.

FAITH AS THIS-WORLDLY

In July 1944, one day after the conspiracy's failed assassination attempt on Hitler's life (but unbeknownst to Bonhoeffer), Dietrich wrote an important letter to his friend and confidant Eberhard Bethge:

> Later on I discovered, and am still discovering to this day; that one only learns to have faith by living in the full this-worldliness of life. . . . [T]his is what I call this-worldliness: living fully in the midst of life's tasks, questions, successes and failures, experiences, and perplexities—then one takes seriously no longer one's own sufferings but rather the suffering of God in the world. Then one stays awake with Christ in Gethsemane. And I think this is faith: this is metanoia. And this is how one becomes a human being, a Christian.[33]

And this is how one embraces vocation as a hermeneutic that calls us to responsible action and faith simultaneously in the world, in relationship to God through Christ and in relationship to others. In short, this perspective may be the one from which we live; it is the beginning of what me might call a "vocation-driven life."[34]

---

[33]Bonhoeffer, *Letters and Papers*, DBWE 8:486.
[34]Thanks to my colleagues, students, friends, and family who contributed to this work. A special thanks to Paul Lutter, Russell Kleckley, Matthew Maruggi, Mark Tranvik, Ann Leahy and Joe Hale.

10

THE SECRET OF FINKENWALDE

Liturgical Treason

JIM BELCHER

ON THE MORNING OF JULY 21, 1944, Dietrich Bonhoeffer, along with other prisoners in the Tegel Prison sick bay, was listening to the radio when he heard that the plot to assassinate Adolf Hitler (code name Operation Valkyrie) had failed the previous day.[1] Although the briefcase bomb had exploded near Hitler's feet in the secret Wolf's Lair in East Prussia, killing a number of high ranking officials, amazingly Hitler survived, spared by the strange design of the thick wooden table that blocked most of the blast. Hitler was stunned but ecstatic that he survived, crediting divine providence. No sooner was he done celebrating than he began rounding up, torturing for information and executing those involved. Colonel von Stauffenberg, the man who planted the bomb, a devout Catholic, shouted just before he was executed, "Long live sacred Germany!"

While Bonhoeffer was not involved in this plot, he knew about it and waited anxiously for its success. Its failure was bad news, not only for Germany, but also for his sixteen-month-old case that was awaiting trial. Now everyone who had given him cover in prison was either in prison or dead. But it got worse. In September the Gestapo discovered the secret

---

[1]The following historical account is based on Eberhard Bethge, *Dietrich Bonhoeffer: A Biography,* trans. Victoria Barnett, rev. ed. (Minneapolis : Fortress, 2000), pp. 827-28.

"Chronicles of Shame" (the Zossen Files), kept by his brother-in-law Hans von Dohnanyi, detailing the history of Nazi atrocities and the two failed assassination plots in March 1943. The files contained Bonhoeffer's name, proving for the first time his direct involvement in the plots. He could no longer deny his role. The discovery dashed any hope of a release from prison. "Grim impressions" and his deep fear of torture must have returned. He may have even considered suicide.

But instead, he decided to escape. Corporal Knoblauch, his favorite guard, agreed to help. The plan was for Dietrich to dress in a mechanic's suit and simply walk out of the prison with Knoblauch at the end of the day. From there he would go into hiding and then would leave the country as soon as possible. On September 24, Bonhoeffer's sister Ursula and her husband delivered to Knoblauch's home a package with the mechanic's suit and some money. A false passport and a flight to Switzerland were arranged. The plan was now in motion. But then something unexpected happened, an event that would force him deeper into the moral crucible than he had ever been before.

◆   ◆   ◆

On a drizzly and cold morning in early April 2011, we arrived at Marienburger Allee 43, located in the leafy Charlottenburg section of Berlin, an upper middle class neighborhood of two-story, well-manicured homes. The house, built by Karl and Paula Bonhoeffer in 1935 for their retirement, contained an attic room, built for Dietrich whenever he was in Berlin. Knut Hämmerling, a graduate student living at the house, greeted us at the door. Small in stature, with thinning brown hair, dressed in jeans and a plaid button-down shirt he wore wire-rimmed glasses. "Welcome to the Bonhoeffer House," he said warmly in fluent English with a strong German accent.

With my wife, Michelle, and our four children, I had scheduled an appointment to see the house, in part to relive the moments in the movie *Bonhoeffer: Agent of Grace* that the kids had seen a few days before. We were in Berlin as part of an eleven-month tour of England and Europe. A year of pilgrimage, a year of homeschooling abroad. Berlin was one of our stops.

Pointing out each room on the ground floor, Knut began telling us about that fateful day of April 5, 1943. Bonhoeffer had returned home around noon. With the two failed assassination attempts from the previous month on his mind, Bonhoeffer must have been anxious for word. Had the plots been discovered? Would he be implicated? He needed to talk with his brother-in-law Hans von Dohnanyi to get an update.

Knut explained that Dohnanyi, who was married to Dietrich's sister Christine, was well connected to the anti-Hitler elements in the military intelligence and had kept the Bonhoeffer family informed of Nazi atrocities from the early 1930s. For many years Bonhoeffer did not get involved, acting only as a sounding board and conscience for those in the resistance. But by the time of the "Night of Broken Glass" in 1938 where Jews were tortured, close to a hundred murdered and thirty thousand deported to concentration camps, he had thrown his lot in with the conspirators. In early 1940 von Dohnanyi informed him that war with Europe was imminent. In August of 1940 when he was looking for a way to avoid the draft, he met at the house with Hans and a few key men in the conspiracy. They suggested he join the military intelligence (as a double agent) and become a more active part of the resistance. This would keep him out of the war but at the same time give him the chance to put his strong convictions about stopping Hitler into practice. He took their offer.

Returning to the afternoon of the arrest, Knut said, "Dietrich called the von Dohnanyi residence. A strange voice answered. Right away he knew that von Dohnanyi had been arrested and they were searching his home." They would come for him next. Not wanting to wake his elderly parents from their afternoon nap, Bonhoeffer went next door to his sister Ursula Schleicher to explain what had happened. While she began preparing him a large meal, he returned to his attic room to destroy key papers and planted a letter, back dated to provide plausible deniability.

"Let me show you Bonhoeffer's room," said Knut, as he moved toward the stairs. We climbed to the top. The attic room contained a bed, a striped rug, and some bookcases—spartan like a monk's cell. My son Jonathan sat down at the desk. "Dietrich wrote parts of his *Ethics* at that desk," said Knut, as well as his essay, "After Ten Years," which provided the theological justification for his involvement in the conspiracy. After finishing it, he gave it to a few key friends and then hid a copy in the rafters to keep it from the Nazis.

Motioning to the area in front of the bookcases, Knut said, "Right there a cot was set up for his best friend, Eberhard Bethge, who was a frequent guest at the house." Dietrich and Eberhard would spend hours each day reading and talking about theology, the church and what needed to be done to rid Germany of Hitler. Years later, Bethge, who would become Dietrich's official biographer, summarized what he and Dietrich were thinking just before they joined the resistance. "We were approaching the borderline between confession and resistance; and if we did not cross this border, our confession was going to be no better than cooperation with the criminals. And so it became clear where the problem lay. . . . We were resisting by way of confession, but we were not confessing by way of resisting."[2] They realized that if they wanted to avoid "cheap grace," that is, a counterfeit faith that does not produce discipleship, they needed to act. It was now time for "confessing by way of resisting."

I sat down in his chair. I looked out the window and saw Ursula's house next door. "There used to be a garden path connecting the two homes," said Knut. "The owners of number 42 put up a fence years ago." After he had gotten his papers in order, Bonhoeffer walked across the garden path to his sister's to eat his last big meal and to wait. Over those few hours they must have discussed all the possibilities—where he would be taken, what charges would be brought against him, and whether the Gestapo would discover the conspiracy. Around 4 p.m., his father came over to tell him that two men were here to see him. He returned to his attic room. The Gestapo found the paper he had planted. Then they searched his room.

As I got up from his desk and walked around the attic, I wondered if Dietrich worried about them finding his essay in the rafters. "Who stands fast?" he asked in the essay. Only the man "who is ready to sacrifice all . . . when he is called to obedient and responsible action in faith

---

[2]Eberhard Bethge, *Friendship and Resistance: Essays on Dietrich Bonhoeffer* (Grand Rapids: Eerdmans, 1995), p. 24.

and in exclusive allegiance to God—the responsible man, who tries to make his whole life an answer to the questions and call of God."[3] Providentially, the Gestapo did not find it. They arrested him, cuffed him and took him away.

As we descended the stairs, I realized that he had made his courageous decision to act, to resist the Nazi evil, while surrounded by family and friends in the comfort of his home. Now on his way to prison, with the ever-present threat of torture and execution hanging over him, would he be so courageous?

◆ ◆ ◆

When the black Mercedes arrived at Tegel Prison, located in the northwest section of Berlin, Bonhoeffer was taken to the reception area, processed and then placed in the admission cell for the night.[4] The staff was instructed not to talk to him and the warden called him a "scoundrel." The cell was bitter cold. The blankets smelled so foul he refused to use them, making the first night of sleep restless as he tried to stay warm. He could hear prisoners being tortured, their screams penetrating his cell throughout the night. At dawn a piece of bread was thrown into the cell.

The next day he was moved to another cell on the top floor of the prison where those on death row were held. His door only opened for food. No one spoke to him. Separated from family and friends, he was alone. For years he had struggled with bouts of depression and now he longed for home. He wrote, "a few times in my life I have come to know what homesickness means. There is nothing more painful, and during these months in prison I have sometimes been horribly homesick." He missed his family, his friends and his fiancée, Maria.

Finally, two weeks later, when the prison officials discovered he was the cousin of Berlin's military commander Paul von Hase, his conditions improved. He was moved to a new cell on the first floor, a seven-by-ten room with a plank bed, a bench against the wall, and a chamber pot. His food rations improved slightly. But the isolation continued, long days

---

[3]Cited in Eric Metaxas, *Bonhoeffer: Pastor, Martyr, Prophet, Spy* (Nashville: Thomas Nelson, 2011), p. 446.

[4]The following account comes from Eberhard Bethge, *Dietrich Bonhoeffer: A Biography*, trans. Victoria Barnett, rev. ed. (Minneapolis: Fortress Press, 2000), pp. 799-891.

left alone in his cell to ponder and think about his life.

But he did not just sit around. As soon as the authorities returned his Bible, which they had confiscated on the first day, each day he rose early to pray, to sing the psalms and read Scripture. He meditated on a verse of the Bible for thirty minutes. He interceded for others, lifting up his friends and relatives, his former students, some who were in prison or in concentration camps. He prayed for the Jews, who were suffering so much. He prayed for his new friends, both prisoners and guards, at Tegel. His daily liturgy gave him strength. In spite of the isolation, the dark thoughts at night, the constant homesickness, and the fear of torture and execution, Bonhoeffer began to build a life in prison. For hours each day he studied, wrote letters and continued his scholarship.

His strong, optimistic outlook began to win over many guards. Impressed by his strength through trial, his good cheer to all, the guards started to bring their own problems to him, looking for advice or wisdom from this famous prisoner. In return for his counsel, they, at great danger to themselves, smuggled out his letters to Bethge, which years later would bring him great fame. Prisoners also sought his counsel, knowing that he was someone they could talk to, a person who would understand them. Since he was one of the few people that truly cared for others, and not just for himself, fellow prisoners wanted to be close to him.

He was not only surviving in prison but he was also thriving. What was his secret? According to Paul Busing, one of Bonhoeffer's former seminary students, the secret was Finkenwalde.

◆   ◆   ◆

I first read *Life Together* while teaching English in China two decades ago.[5] Our sending organization gave it to us to help us learn to live in community. From the start, no other book so challenged, inspired and directed me into the reality of Christian community. It transformed the way I thought about others. Over the years, I have read it dozens of times, quoted it from the pulpit, and used it for reading groups.

In fact, we were in Germany in part to find Finkenwalde, the place of his illegal seminary that inspired him to write *Life Together*. I wanted to

---

[5]Dietrich Bonhoeffer, *Life Together* (San Francisco: HarperSanFrancisco, 1956).

see the location of the community whose vision had guided me as a pastor for years. But I was not under the illusion that my kids, at their ages, would have much interest in the book or the location. So we planned a trip to his house and the four places he was incarcerated, stuff they would find interesting. Of course I too was interested in these places. But at the time I planned our itinerary six months earlier, I did not see much connection between the stages of his life in Finkenwalde and his life as a spy. But I was soon proved wrong.

As gale force winds attempted to knock us off the road and dust and dirt pelted the side of our RV, we passed through a dense forest of pine trees—piles of freshly cut logs stacked on the side of the road. An hour outside of Berlin, the forest opened up, revealing miles of wide-open countryside, the horizon broken only by an occasional outcropping of trees, a barn and the ever-present post and beam fences. It was the day after our visit to the Bonhoeffer House and we were in search of Finken-walde, a small town 135 kilometers northeast of Berlin, where the illegal seminary was located from 1935 to 1937.[6]

But before we could go to Finkenwalde, we needed to travel to Stettin, located eight kilometers north of the seminary, to visit the Bonhoeffer Study Center. For the past six months I had been trying to track down the address of the seminary, demolished long ago after the war. No one, not even the director of the Bonhoeffer House in Berlin, could tell me the exact location. This was not a good sign. And not speaking a word of Polish or German, I was not anxious to wander around Poland looking for it. I had emailed the study center numerous times asking for the seminary address but never got a response. I thought maybe if I went in person I could get it. It was my last shot. Also, I wanted to visit the study center to talk with them about some new thoughts I had about Finkenwalde and its relationship to Bonhoeffer's later years.

---

[6]In April 1935 the seminary began in a temporary location on the Baltic Sea at Zingst. Two months later, they found a large, country estate near the Baltic seaport of Stettin in a town called Finkenwalde. The main house on the estate had recently been a boarding school. The gymnasium was quickly turned into a beautiful chapel. Local Christians, fiercely opposed to Hitler, hearing of the need, donated furniture for the mostly empty manor house. They were glad to adopt this illegal seminary as their own. They helped whenever they could. Someone even donated a pig. The seminary was off to a good start.

With my kids homeschooling in the back of the RV and nothing but acres of countryside to look at, I began to rehearse what I was going to discuss at the study center. My mind drifted back to China, living in community with two other teachers, studying *Life Together* and trying to make our little community thrive. Bonhoeffer's vision, though hard to attain, inspired us. We were motivated by the fact that every morning he led his students in a forty-five-minute prayer service. First they read a psalm, and then sang a hymn. They read more Scripture, and then Bonhoeffer gave a long pastoral prayer, followed by the Lord's Prayer and concluded by another verse from a hymn. After breakfast they individually meditated on a passage of Scripture for thirty minutes. Following meditation, the rest of the day was filled with lectures, study time, sermon preparation and time for work. During the day there was time for soccer, chess and conversation. Around 10:00 p.m. he led another forty-five-minute service, like a bookend. God had the first and last word of the day.

I had read somewhere that in the first few months, many of the ordinands chafed under this new discipline. They did not see why it was valuable, thinking it was a waste of time. Even the great Karl Barth, when he got word of it, accused Bonhoeffer, his young friend, of creating a seminary with an "odour of a monastic eros and pathos."[7] Bonhoeffer disagreed. He responded to Barth, saying, "The charge of legalism does not seem to me to fit at all. What is there legalistic in a Christian setting to work to learn what prayer is and in his spending a good deal of his time in this learning?"[8] Part of what Barth objected to was what he perceived as an unhealthy individualism, students spending an inordinate amount of time alone in silent prayer and meditation. But as Bonhoeffer tried to make clear, this was just part of the new training, and was anything but individualistic. Each new discipline was done within the context of the new community, shaping the individual to love God and others more.

---

[7]Dietrich Bonhoeffer, *The Way to Freedom: Letters, Lectures and Notes 1935-1939 from the Collected Works, Vol. 2*, ed. Edwin H. Robertson (London: Collins, 1972), p. 121.
[8]Dietrich Bonhoeffer, *A Testament to Freedom: The Essential Writings of Dietrich Bonhoeffer* (San Francisco: HarperOne, 1995), p. 431.

In his *Life Together,* written as a summary of the Finkenwalde experiment, he stressed the disciplines of holding one's tongue, meekness, listening, helpfulness, and bearing. One of the hardest disciplines at the seminary was the rule never to speak about a brother in his absence. Gossip was not allowed and talking behind someone's back was prohibited. They were learning to serve one another. "Once a man has experienced the mercy of God in his life he will henceforth aspire only to serve."[9] They were even required to have a prayer partner to whom to confess their sins, further teaching them how to die to themselves.

But as much as Bonhoeffer's vision for a new community inspired me, over the years I began to have some reservations. There was something about the community at Finkenwalde that did not sit right with me. It was not the disciplines of community life that bothered me. I did not share Barth's concern, though there is always a temptation toward legalism. Rather, it was the isolation, the sense of retreat from the world, a new tribalism that bothered me. It appeared too world-fleeing. And I always wondered if he had given up the experiment as a failure and joined the conspiracy out of frustration with the church.

◆ ◆ ◆

I remember where I was when I began to think differently about Finkenwalde. I was sitting at my study desk in the basement of Wycliffe Hall, doing some reading to prepare for our visit to Finkenwalde. I was reading Craig Slane's book *Bonhoeffer as Martyr* when this paragraph jumped out at me:

> Bonhoeffer believed that it was possible for a community gathered on the basis of Jesus' Sermon on the Mount to provide the necessary ground for resistance against tyranny. The practices of dying to one's self in confession, meditation, and intercession produced openness to others and forged the kind of solidarity required for moral risk-taking. . . . Bonhoeffer's Finkenwalde experiment was anything but a retreat. It was strength training for the moral crucible.[10]

---

[9]Bonhoeffer, *Life Together,* p. 94.
[10]Craig J. Slane, *Bonhoeffer as Martyr: Social Responsibility and Modern Christian Commitment* (Grand Rapids: Brazos, 2004), p. 239.

I had never thought of this before. Is it possible that Finkenwalde was not a retreat from the world, a hiding place from persecution, but a boot camp for engagement with the world? Slane contends that Bonhoeffer, as a strong Lutheran, emphasized the "breach" that takes place in the believer's life at the time of conversion and baptism. Bonhoeffer held strongly to justification and the need for the righteousness of Christ. In fact, he opens *Life Together* by explaining the importance of justification for the believer. The "breach" from the world, argued Bonhoeffer, needed to be continuously reinforced through teaching, theology and the separateness of the community. But this separateness was never the last word or it would lead to tribalism. Along with the narrative of new life, rooted in the transforming power of the gospel, Finkenwalde stressed a ritual that shaped new habits of worship, love for other Christians and the outsider, like the Jew, and the enemy, like the Nazi. It would also provide an antidote to "cheap grace," the illness of faith that does not produce discipleship. Bonhoeffer wrote, "Only he who believes is obedient, and only he who is obedient believes." As Slane adds, "Being immersed in a Christian community—a tradition of seeing whose primary story is the gospel—is ethically formative."[11] Finkenwalde, then, was not a pietistic detour in his life of resistance but a place where daily the students were learning to die to themselves through meditation, confession, the Lord's Supper and intercessory prayers for others. For this reason, "Finkenwalde life was itself ritual."[12]

I will admit I had never seen this before. I had focused on the experience, the oneness and the joy of community in *Life Together*. But I had not realized that this experience of community was shaped in part by ritual, which combined with the narrative of the gospel and empowered by the Spirit have the potential to birth a new community.[13] I had also never seen so clearly the connection between the new liturgy of Finkenwalde and faithful engagement with the world. In the liturgy of community, Bonhoeffer prepared the ordinands for service, to love their

---

[11]Ibid., p. 213.
[12]Ibid., p. 232.
[13]For a helpful explanation of the liturgy of desire see James K. A. Smith, *Desiring the Kingdom: Worship, Worldview, and Cultural Formation* (Grand Rapids: Baker Academic, 2009).

brothers and to love the world. As Slane says, "I submit that Bonhoeffer's plan for a *vita communis* was akin to a laboratory for morality in the midst of a dying church in a dying culture." They were not retreating from the culture; they were learning to engage the world in a whole new way—a way that would not succumb to the power and influence of Nazism. "It became a kind of ritual-liturgical resistance," says Slane, "or perhaps even liturgical treason."[14]

As a church planter and pastor who struggled for ten years to facilitate community in the church, I attempted over and over again to inspire the vision for community by the big narrative of the gospel. This was a key first step. But it often fell on deaf ears. What I did not understand was that it needed to be reinforced with a new ritual, a counter liturgy that encompassed the entire community. In fact, if I had seen the importance of ritual, a daily liturgy of worship and life to go along with the weekly corporate liturgy of the gospel, I might have seen more transformation of individuals and more engagement with the world around us. It was an insight I just missed, though I had read *Life Together* dozens of times. What I needed to have done was find a way to contextualize the ritual of *Life Together* for a working congregation, to train them to participate daily, both individually and corporately, in a liturgy of worship and life that would focus their desire on the kingdom, rather than the liturgies of desire that come from the world around us.

◆ ◆ ◆

After two and half hours of driving, we finally crossed the Polish border deeper into the countryside of Pomerania, far removed from Berlin. My mind was brimming over with thoughts of Finkenwalde and the need for ritual and liturgy to augment the narrative story of the gospel. I kept looking for Stettin. I still had not seen a house in miles. I wondered if anyone lived out here. I guess if you are doing something illegal, in fact, treasonous, this would be a good place to do it—far from the watchful eyes of the S.S.

But being secretive was only one reason for the choice of location. Bonhoeffer was convinced that the church succumbed to Hitler because

---

[14]Slane, *Bonhoeffer as Martyr*, p. 237.

its theology and life did not have the theological and moral resources to stand up to the Nazi ideology, which was a highly ritualized order. The flags, the banners, the music, the uniforms, the parades, the large public gathers of light and sound, the message of Aryan supremacy, all perfectly orchestrated to reshape the desire of the German people, focusing it on the thousand-year reign. Hitler was not just after mindless submission; he wanted to win the minds and the hearts of the German people. He wanted them to worship Germany, to glorify it and most importantly to revere himself, the Führer. To counter this false liturgy, Bonhoeffer knew the church must begin a "new kind of monasticism" that would mold pastors with a new kind of counter-liturgy of worship and desire. But to accomplish this, he needed more than the normal weekly seminary classes or one hour on Sunday. What was required was life in community with his students, shaping and molding them around a new liturgy. That is why not just any location would do. He had been offered a building in Berlin. He turned it down. He wanted to get his students to a remote place for an experiment in community without the distractions of the city. They would be set apart for a time, often six months, and in this time learn how to reengage the world in a different way than before.

About twenty minutes inside the Polish border, we spotted signs for the city of Stettin. As we approached the edge of the city, devoid of trees and greenery, it felt windswept as if it were a dust bowl. People along the street struggled to walk, bent over from the wind, sheltering their eyes from the dust. As we entered the city, once a striking German city, it was rundown, as the buildings had not been renovated since before the war. We stopped at a traffic signal. People looked up from inside their small cars, eyeing our large RV, as conspicuous as a tank driving down a suburban neighborhood.

After winding through city streets for another five minutes, we arrived in front of a large, three-story home—the Bonhoeffer Study Center. As I walked toward the house, it looked freshly painted and rehabbed, in stark contrast to the run down homes around it. Years earlier, a wealthy donor gave the house for the study of Bonhoeffer's work in Finkenwalde. I climbed the front steps to the entrance. I rang the bell. No answer. I rang it again. Nothing. It was Friday afternoon; it must have closed early, and with it my last chance to find the location of the seminary. I kicked myself for this missed opportunity. I was not feeling too capable at this moment. Yet I consoled myself with the knowledge that there was not much to see, the seminary having been destroyed after the war and now only a memorial plaque marked the spot. But I was sad not to have the chance to walk that hallowed ground with my family. And I was doubly disappointed not to be able to talk to these Bonhoeffer scholars about the connection between Finkenwalde and Bonhoeffer's time in prison.

But honestly by then I was all but convinced that this new reading of Finkenwalde was correct. Its life was a ritual, a new liturgy rooted in the gospel of justification that produced people who knew what it was to die to themselves and to love and sacrifice for others, even those outside of the family of God. Unlike what I thought six months earlier, there was a connection between Finkenwalde and Bonhoeffer's time in prison. The secret to his remarkable influence in prison was his experiment in community.

Reluctantly we began our drive back to Berlin. As we headed out of the city, the gale force winds not letting up, I looked south in the direction of Finkenwalde, and saw an outcropping of trees, hiding a farmhouse. I was reminded of that fateful day in October of 1937. With the term over and the students gone home, Bonhoeffer and Bethge went on vacation in the mountains for some much needed rest. Unannounced, the Gestapo arrived at the house and shut down the seminary. The doors were sealed forever. Bonhoeffer's experiment in Christian community and pastoral training was over. But its impact in the midst of the storm would be felt for years, especially in the life of its director.

◆ ◆ ◆

As Bonhoeffer sat in his Tegel cell in July 1944, seven years after the Gestapo closed the seminary, he pondered his escape. The plan was set in motion. But then something unexpected happened. The Gestapo arrested his brother Klaus. If he escaped now, the Nazis would assume Klaus was guilty and they would round up the entire family, including his Maria. The Nazis would have no qualms about enslaving them all in concentration camps. But if he did not escape now, he would be executed. He faced a moral dilemma. But in the end the decision was easy.

He would not put his family into that kind of jeopardy. He knew what he had to do—sacrifice his life for those he loved. His final idol, the fear of torture and death, he had to face. Alone in his cell, he must have thought of the words he wrote years earlier.

> Death is only dreadful for those who live in dread and fear of it. Death is not wild and terrible, if only we can be still and hold fast to God's Word. Death is not bitter, if we have not become bitter ourselves. Death is grace, the greatest gift of grace that God gives people who believe in him. . . . It beckons to us with heavenly power, if only we realize that it is the gateway to our homeland, the tabernacle of joy, the everlasting kingdom of peace.[15]

He wrote those words years earlier in the safety of his pastorate in London. Now those words meant something different. He owned them for real and in the process he experienced a new freedom from the fear of death. Drawing on the resources of Finkenwalde, supported in prayer by his family and friends, his true "homeland, the tabernacle of joy, the everlasting kingdom of peace" would lead him into the future.

Three months after the failed Valkyrie assassination attempt, on Sunday, October 8, 1944, Bonhoeffer's year and a half at Tegel came to an abrupt end. He was moved across town to the Gestapo house prison on Prinz-Albrecht-Strasse. No longer under the watchful eye of his uncle, who had been hanged for his role in the conspiracy, he was now in the grips of the Gestapo.

◆　◆　◆

Looking down into the bombed-out basement of the Gestapo prison, I now saw Dietrich's experience in prison in a different light. I saw it through the eyes of Finkenwalde. It is true, he was here because of his involvement in the conspiracy. That was obvious. But his motivation to resist evil was forged in Finkenwalde. And the way he acted once he was in prison was shaped by a new liturgy of community, rooted in the gospel.

Arriving at Prinz-Albrecht-Strausse, Bonhoeffer discovered that the conditions were much worse than Tegel. He also learned that almost the entire leadership of the conspiracy was in this prison. "It's hell in here,"

---

[15]Quoted in Metaxas, *Bonhoeffer*, p. 531.

said Admiral Canaris, the former head of military intelligence and Bonhoeffer's friend. But Bonhoeffer remained content, drawing strength from his daily routine of Scripture reading, meditation and prayers of adoration, supplication and intercession. Walking around the top perimeter of the cells, I recalled something I had just read that morning in preparation for this visit: "He was always good-tempered," recounts Fabian von Schlabrendorff of his time with Bonhoeffer in the Gestapo prison, "always of the same kindliness and politeness towards everybody, so that to my surprise, within a short time, he had won over his warders, who were not always kindly disposed. . . . He always cheered me up and comforted me, he never tired of repeating that the only fight which is lost is that which we give up. Many little notes he slipped into my hands on which he had written biblical words of comfort and hope."[16] No matter how dark things got inside the basement prison, he always put the concern of others first and "acted as the appointed servant to the Word of Jesus Christ," said Schlabrendorff.

The next morning we left Berlin and drove five hours south to Weimer and the Buchenwald concentration camp, nestled in the tree-covered hills overlooking the city. When we arrived, we went first to the information desk, located in part of the former Gestapo camp headquarters. I asked the man behind the counter where Bonhoeffer's cell was located. He knew right away. Taking out a map, he said, "Right here, in the basement of the Gestapo barracks." It took us a few minutes to walk there, but just outside the camp, we located the Gestapo barracks. All that remained was the basement. For seven weeks this was Bonheoffer's home. Seventeen high-ranking members of the conspiracy—who had been moved here when Prinz-Albrecht-Strasse was destroyed by the air raids—shared twelve cells in the dank basement which formerly housed disobedient S.S. guards.

Starting down the steps, we immediately saw at the bottom a silver plaque on the wall, testimony that Bonhoeffer and others in the conspiracy had been here. After reading the inscription, we turned right and walked down the narrow hallway. It could not have been more than

---

[16] Wolf-Dieter Zimmermann and Ronald Gregor Smith, eds. *I Knew Dietrich Bonhoeffer: Reminiscences by His Friends* (New York: Harper & Row, Publishers, 1966), p. 228.

thirty feet long. On each side were six cells. When they were let out of their cells each day for exercise, the hallway was the only place the prisoners were allowed to go. Six at a time could pace up and down the corridor to stretch their legs. During this time, they were able to talk and share information. Sigismund Payne Best, an Englishman who shared a cell close to Bonhoeffer, later wrote that he was "all humanity and sweetness; he always seemed to me to diffuse an atmosphere of happiness, of joy in every smallest event in life, and of a deep gratitude for the mere fact that he was alive. . . . He was one of the very few men that I have ever met to whom God was real and ever close to him."[17] Best continues, "[His] soul really shone in the dark desperation of our prison. . . . [He] had always been afraid that he would not be strong enough to stand such a test but now he knew there was nothing in life of which one need ever be afraid."[18] Bonhoeffer had accepted death. He had learned at Finkenwalde to focus on the kingdom. His daily habits of devotion helped to keep his desire directed to the eternal. Knowing his destination, he overcame daily suffering and despair and was able to comfort others.

It was now late afternoon and time to leave. We still had a three-hour drive ahead of us, needing to get to the Flossenbürg concentration camp before it got dark. As we drove south into the Bavarian Mountains, the late afternoon sun streamed into the driver's compartment, keeping me warm and putting me in a reflective mood. I began thinking about Bonhoeffer's last six days of life, after he left Buchenwald. His true *telos*, his destination, his true homeland was calling him. Just then, coming through my German radio station, I heard Guns N' Roses singing Bob Dylan's "Knockin' on Heaven's Door."

◆ ◆ ◆

By the end of March 1945, the end of the war seemed near. American guns were heard in the distance. It was only a matter of time before Germany surrendered. Food in Buchenwald was scarce. Bonhoeffer and the other sixteen prisoners fought off hunger and cold. On April 3, the

---

[17]Ibid., p. 514.
[18]Ibid., p. 515.

chief guard informed the prisoners that it was time to go. The Gestapo wanted to move the prisoners further south, out of the liberating reach of the Americans.

After thirteen hours of travel, around noon they reached Weiden, a small town in Bavaria, just ten miles from Flossenbürg. Just outside of town, a police car pulled them over. Two policemen opened the doors of the van. The policemen called two prisoners; Bonhoeffer's name was one of them. One prisoner jumped out. Bonhoeffer leaned back as not to be seen. At that moment another prisoner, who was friends with the one called first, jumped out of the van. The doors were shut and they continued south. Bonhoeffer must have thought he might survive. But it was not to be.

It took four days for the Gestapo and Hitler's judge to realize the mistake. They sent two guards back to find Bonhoeffer. By now the prisoners from Buchenwald were in Shönberg. It was Sunday morning, a week after Easter. Another prisoner asked Bonhoeffer to lead a service. He opened in prayer, read the Scripture for the day: Isaiah 53:5 ("With his stripes we are healed" KJV) and 1 Peter 1:3 ("Blessed be the God and Father of our Lord Jesus Christ! By his great mercy we have been born anew to a living hope through the resurrection of Jesus Christ from the dead" RSV). He then gave a short homily on these verses. Bonhoeffer, recalled Best, "spoke to us in a manner which reached the hearts of all, finding just the right words to express the spirit of our imprisonment."[19]

Just as he had finished the last prayer, the door opened and two men came in.

"Prisoner Bonhoeffer. Get ready to come with us." Everyone present knew what this meant—the scaffold. They all said their goodbyes. Bonhoeffer pulled Best aside and said:

"This is the end. For me the beginning of life."

Hours later, it was late Sunday afternoon when they walked through the main gates of Flossenbürg. Spring had not arrived in the mountains of eastern central Germany and a late afternoon chill had descended on the camp. Two guards led Dietrich Bonhoeffer, a prisoner

---

[19]Ibid., p. 528.

of the state, through Roll Call Square. They turned right and walked past three barracks on the right and the sick bay on the left. At the far southern end of the camp, just inside the barbed wire fence, sat a long building called the detention barracks, comprised of a single row of cells. Special prisoners, mostly Russian and Polish officers, were executed here. In the final year of the war, fifteen hundred special prisoners were brutally murdered, their bodies burned on a massive funeral pyre.

As they entered the barracks, Bonhoeffer was escorted down the hall, watching faces appear in the six-by-nine hole in the doors. Among others, he recognized Admiral Wilhelm Canaris and General Hans Oster, who along with Bonhoeffer were part of the failed plots to assassinate Hitler. The guards shoved Bonhoeffer into an open cell and locked the door. He was tired and hungry. He sat down on the edge of the bed and prayed for strength, both for himself and the other prisoners awaiting death. Just then, his train of thought was broken. A door down the hall swung open. The guards removed General Oster. Thirty minutes later they brought him back. Then it was Admiral Canaris's turn. What was going on? Over the course of the evening guards removed each member of the conspirators one by one. Hitler had sent a judge hundreds of miles to quickly set up a summary court to try the conspirators. But it was a mock court, the verdicts already handed down by Hitler, the final arbiter of justice in the Third Reich. Bonhoeffer was tried last. When he got back to his cell around 2:00 a.m. he fell asleep quickly.

He did not sleep long. At 5:00 a.m., a guard unlocked and kicked open his door. "Get up and undress."

"Where am I being taken?" Bonhoeffer asked.

"To hear the verdict," the guard said. The guard walked to the next cell, leaving Bonhoeffer to undress. Before doing so, he kneeled down in front of his bed, bowed his head and began to pray.

◆　◆　◆

We stood near the spot, just outside the barracks, where the judge, on April 9, 1945, would have read the verdicts and pronounced the sentence—death by hanging. Looking down at the ground, pensively, Herbert Soergel, a local pastor and our Flossenbürg guide, turned to look at the plaque on the wall and the newly placed flowers marking the anniversary of his death, just two days before. He himself had led the memorial service. I asked him what Dietrich might have prayed that last time as he kneeled before the place of his execution.

"I can't be sure," he said. Maybe he was thanking God, grateful that he had given him the strength to make it to the end. Herbert's countenance then brightened, as he asked me, "Do you remember his last letter to Maria?" "I do not," I said. "Well," he said, "it contains a clue to how Dietrich managed to survive faithfully to the end. It may also be a clue to what he prayed that last time before he went to his death. In it he says, 'I have not felt lonely or abandoned for one moment. You, your parents, all of you, the friends and students of mine at the front, all are constantly present to me. It is a great invisible sphere in which one lives and in whose reality there is no doubt. It says in the old children's song about angels: Two, to cover me, two, to wake me.'"[20]

"For Bonhoeffer," said Herbert, "the people in his life were angels, who were constantly with him, even at the moment of death." It is they, his family, his Finkenwalde community, rooted in the grace of Christ, who were with him right to the end. That was his secret. And it was a secret he learned at Finkenwalde, forged by a new liturgy of Christian community.

As I turned to look at the spot of the execution, I imagined Bonhoeffer slowly climbing the steps to the gallows. Did he think of his words from his prison poem *Stations on the Road to Freedom?*

Come now, highest feast on the way to the everlasting freedom, death.
Lay waste the burdens of chains and walls which confine our earthly bodies
And blinded souls, that we see at last what here we could not see.[21]

The noose was put around his neck. He died in seconds. He was free, free to see the face of God, and to enter the kingdom of everlasting

---

[20]Bonhoeffer, *Letters and Papers*, p. 419.
[21]Dietrich Bonhoeffer, *Dietrich Bonhoeffer's Prison Poems*, ed. Edwin H. Robinson (Grand Rapids: Zondervan, 2005), p. 74.

peace. "In almost fifty years that I worked as a doctor, said the Flossenbürg camp physician years later, I have hardly ever seen a man die so entirely submissive to the will of God."[22]

---

[22]Cited in Metaxas, *Bonhoeffer,* p. 532.

CONTRIBUTORS

Jim Belcher was the founding church planter and former lead pastor of Redeemer Presbyterian Church in Newport Beach, California. He is the author of *Deep Church: A Third Way Beyond Emerging and Traditional* (InterVarsity Press). He is the chairman of the Practical Theology Department and head of the DMin program at Knox Theological Seminary in Fort Lauderdale, Florida. His second book, *In Search of Deep Faith*, is to be published in 2013 by InterVarsity Press.

Lori Brandt Hale is associate professor of religion and director of general education at Augsburg College in Minneapolis, Minnesota. Hale serves on the steering committee for the Dietrich Bonhoeffer: Theology and Social Analysis Group of the American Academy of Religion, serves as the secretary for the International Bonhoeffer Society (English Language Section) and is the coauthor of *Dietrich Bonhoeffer for Armchair Theologians* (Westminster John Knox).

Keith L. Johnson is assistant professor of theology at Wheaton College. His research focuses on the theology of the Reformers, especially Calvin; the doctrines of the Trinity and Christology; modern theology, particularly in the Reformed tradition; and the relationship between Protestant and Roman Catholic theology. He is the author of *Karl Barth and the Analogia Entis* (T & T Clark) and "The Being and Act of the Church: Karl Barth and the Future of Evangelical Ecclesiology," in *Karl Barth and American Evangelicalism*. His book, *Thinking After God: The Method and Practice of Theology*, is forthcoming with InterVarsity Press.

Timothy Larsen is McManis Professor of Christian Thought, Wheaton College. He has been a visiting fellow at Trinity College, Cambridge University, and All Souls College, Oxford University. He is a contributing editor for *Books & Culture* and has edited a number of books, including *The Cambridge Companion to Evangelical Theology* (with Daniel J. Treier). His monographs include *Crisis of Doubt: Honest Faith in Nineteenth-Century England* and, most recently, *A People of One Book: The Bible and the Victorians* (Oxford University Press).

Joel D. Lawrence is associate professor of systematic theology at Bethel Seminary in St. Paul, Minnesota. He is the co-chair of the Dietrich Bonhoeffer: Theology and Social Analysis Group of the American Academy of Religion and serves as the bibliographer for the International Bonhoeffer Society. He has presented papers at various academic conferences, has authored numerous articles on theology and ethics, and is the author of *Bonhoeffer: A Guide for the Perplexed* (T & T Clark).

Charles Marsh is professor of religious studies and director of The Project on Lived Theology at the University of Virginia. He is the author of *Reclaiming Dietrich Bonhoeffer: The Promise of His Theology; God's Long Summer: Stories of Faith and Civil Rights; Wayward Christian Soldiers: Freeing the Gospel from Political Captivity;* and *Welcoming Justice: God's Movement Toward Beloved Community* (with John M. Perkins). Marsh is currently writing *Strange Glory: A Life of Dietrich Bonhoeffer*, to be published by Knopf (New York) and Ullstein (Berlin).

Stephen J. Plant is dean and Runcie Fellow at Trinity Hall, Cambridge University, and teaches theology and ethics in the Cambridge University Faculty of Divinity. In 2008 he was the International Bonhoeffer Scholar at the Freie Universität, Berlin. He is vice president of the International Bonhoeffer Society Board. His research interests include the theology of international development, Bonhoeffer studies, the thought of Simone Weil, and politics and theology. He is the author of *The SPCK Introduction to Simone Weil* and *Bonhoeffer* (Continuum), and editor of the journal *Theology* (SPCK/SAGE). His next book, *Taking Stock of Bonhoeffer: Studies in his Biblical Hermeneutics and Ethics*, will be published by Ashgate.

Daniel J. Treier is professor of theology at Wheaton College. His scholarly publications have focused on theological interpretation of Scripture. His current research interests involve Christology and cultural engagement, especially regarding technology. He is currently editing a revision of Walter Elwell's *Evangelical Dictionary of Theology*. He is the author of three books, most recently *Proverbs and Ecclesiastes* in the Brazos Theological Commentary on the Bible, and an editor of several others, including the *Dictionary for Theological Interpretation of the Bible* (Baker).

Reggie L. Williams is assistant professor of Christian ethics, McCormick Theological Seminary, Chicago. He was previously a lecturer in the Department of Religion, Baylor University. His research focuses on the intersection of Christology, race and social justice. Williams analyzes the impact of Harlem Renaissance literature and theology on Dietrich Bonhoeffer's theology-informed Nazi resistance. He is the author of "A Better Unity: A Biblical Illustration of Community" in *Christian Ethics Today* (Summer 2011). His forthcoming publications include "The White Christ" in *The Evangelical Post-Colonial Roundtable*. In 2011, he was a keynote speaker at the International Dietrich Bonhoeffer Seminary at Union Theological Seminary, New York City.

Philip G. Ziegler is senior lecturer in systematic theology at the University of Aberdeen, Scotland. He also serves as the head of the School of Divinity, History and Philosophy. He is the author of *Doing Theology When God is Forgotten: The Theological Achievement of Wolf Krötke* (Peter Lang), a study of the trajectory of the theologies of Barth and Bonhoeffer within the aggressively disestablished Protestant churches of East Germany. His interests include the dogmatic bases of theological ethics and politics and the ongoing significance of the theological legacy of the German church struggle, including the work of Bonhoeffer.

Name Index

34, 77, 120, 121n25, 159,
166, 167, 171, 177
Peter, the apostle, 26, 207
Phillips, Timothy R., 12, 13
Pinnock, Clark, 46
Plant, Stephen J., 7, 14,
41n5, 73, 212
Ramm, Bernard, 46
Rasmussen, Larry L.,
106n45, 137n20, 138n24
Robinson, John A. T., 39,
40, 51, 56
Rössler, Helmut, 138
Runia, Klaas, 55, 56
Samuel, 79, 83
Saul, 79
Sayers, Dorothy, 39
Schaeffer, Francis, 46

von Schlabrendorff, Fabian,
205
Schlatter, Adolf, 29n42, 160
Schleicher, Rüdiger, 75
Schleicher, Ursula, 192-94
Schönherr, Albert, 148
Seeberg, Reinhold, 21
Slane, Craig, 199-201
Soergel, Herbert, 209
Solzhenitsyn, Aleksandr, 52
von Stauffenberg, Claus
Graf, 88
Steere, Douglas, 179
Sutz, Edwin, 18, 132,
134-35, 140, 143
Taylor, Charles, 98, 99
Thurman, Howard, 68
Tillich, Paul, 40-42

Titius, Arthur, 141n36, 142
Treier, Daniel J., 7, 14,
41n4, 91, 212, 213
Tutu, Desmond, 49
Van Dyke, Dick, 39
Van Til, Cornelius, 44-46,
53
Washington, Booker T., 65,
66
Wilberforce, William, 48
Willard, Dallas, 47
Williams, Reggie, 7, 14, 59,
213
Wilson, John, 47
Ziegler, Philip G., 7, 13, 17,
32n53, 213
Zimmermann, Wolf-Dieter,
146-48, 150-51